PERFORMING FEMININITY

ETHNOGRAPHIC ALTERNATIVES BOOK SERIES

Series Editors: Carolyn Ellis and Arthur P. Bochner
(both at the University of South Florida)

Ethnographic Alternatives emphasizes experimental forms of qualitative writing that blur the boundaries between social sciences and humanities and experiment with novel forms of expressing lived experience, including literary, poetic, autobiographical, multivoiced, conversational, critical, visual, performative, and coconstructed representations. Emphasis should be on expressing concrete lived experience through narrative modes of writing.

Books in the Series:

Volume 1, *Composing Ethnography: Alternative Forms of Qualitative Writing*, Carolyn Ellis and Arthur P. Bochner, editors

Volume 2, *Opportunity House: Ethnographic Stories of Mental Retardation*, Michael V. Angrosino

Volume 3, *Kaleidoscope Notes: Writing Women's Music and Organizational Culture*, Stacy Holman Jones

Volume 4, *Fiction and Social Research: By Fire or Ice*, Anna Banks and Stephen P. Banks, editors

Volume 5, *Reading Auschwitz*, Mary Lagerwey

Volume 6, *Life Online: Researching Real Experience in Virtual Space*, Annette N. Markham

Volume 7, *Writing the New Ethnography*, H. L. Goodall Jr.

Volume 8, *Between Gay and Straight: Understanding Friendship beyond Sexual Orientation*, Lisa Tillmann-Healy

Volume 9, *Ethnographically Speaking: Autoethnography, Literature, and Aesthetics*, Arthur P. Bochner and Carolyn Ellis, editors

Volume 10, *Karaoke Nights: An Ethnographic Rhapsody*, Rob Drew

Volume 11, *Standing Ovation: Performing Social Science Research about Cancer*, Ross Gray and Christina Sinding

Volume 12, *The Time at Darwin's Reef: Poetic Explorations in Anthropology and History*, Ivan Brady

Volume 13, *The Ethnographic I: A Methodological Novel about Autoethnography*, Carolyn Ellis

Volume 14, *In Search of Naunny's Grave: Age, Class, Gender, and Ethnicity in an American Family*, Nick Trujillo

Volume 15, *Toward a Methodology of the Heart: Daily Life and Higher Education*, Ronald J. Pelias

Volume 16, *Travels with Ernest: Crossing the Literary/Sociological Divide*, Laurel Richardson and Ernest Lockridge

Volume 17, *Performing Femininity: Rewriting Gender Identity*, Lesa Lockford

PERFORMING FEMININITY

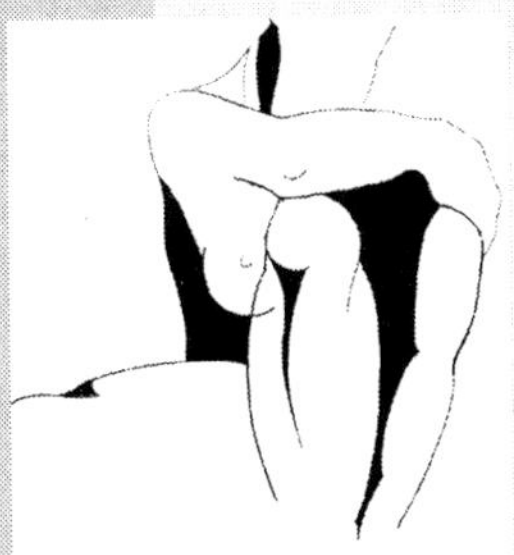

Rewriting Gender Identity

Lesa Lockford

A Division of Rowman and Littlefield Publishers, Inc.
Walnut Creek • Lanham • New York • Toronto • Oxford

ALTAMIRA PRESS
A Division of Rowman & Littlefield Publishers, Inc.
1630 North Main Street, #367
Walnut Creek, CA 94596
www.altamirapress.com

Rowman & Littlefield Publishers, Inc.
A wholly owned subsidiary of the Rowman & Littlefield Publishing Group, Inc.
4501 Forbes Blvd, Suite 200
Lanham, MD 20706

PO Box 317
Oxford
OX2 9RU, United Kingdom

British Library Cataloguing in Publication Information Available

Library of Congress Cataloging-in-Publication Data

Lockford, Lesa, 1958–
Performing femininity : rewriting gender identity / Lesa Lockford
p. cm. — (Ethnographic alternatives book series ; v. 17)
Includes bibliographical references.
ISBN 0-7591-0072-1 (cloth : alk. paper) — ISBN 0-7591-0073-X (pbk. : alk. paper)
1. Body, Human—Social aspects. 2. Feminist theory. 3. Performing arts. I. Title. II. Series
HM636.L63 2004
306.4—dc22 2004004227

Printed in the United States of America

∞™ The paper used in this publication meets the minimum requirements of American National Standard for Information Sciences—Permanence of Paper for Printed Library Materials, ANSI/NISO Z39.48–1992.

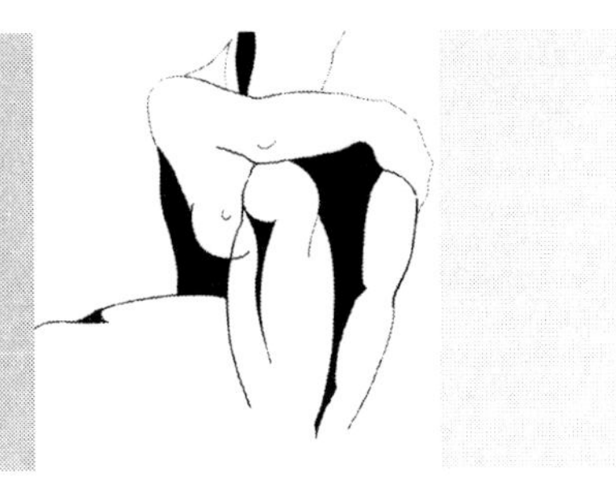

For Ron Pelias

To be labeled the "feminist" writer means one is likely to be excluded from any acknowledgment that you are someone capable of writing about topics that extend beyond this marker. Equally so, to approach feminist publishing with the desire to do work that does not "fit" with the prevailing tone and temper of the movement is to also be excluded.

bell hooks, *Remembered Rapture*

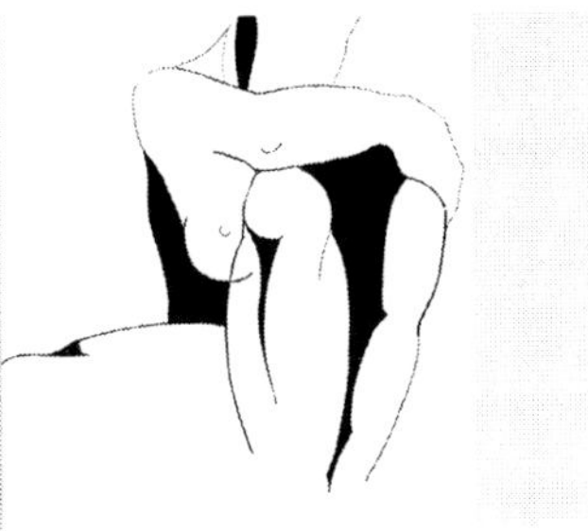

Contents

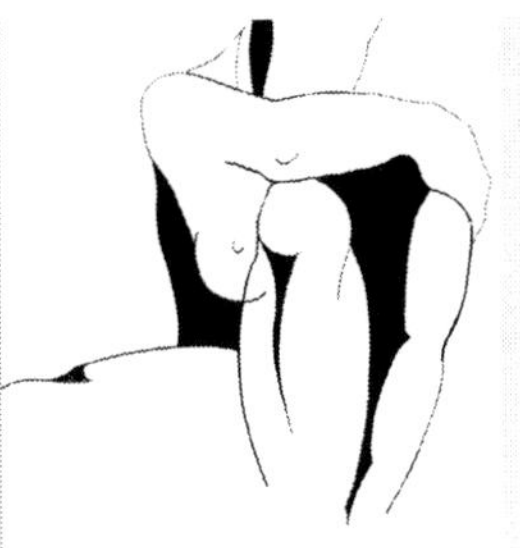

Preface

I began this book from a simple idea. However, the journey I took to get to that idea was not simple. I have long understood that women in general continue to be less socially empowered than their male counterparts. I come to that knowledge based upon my life experience as well as sound scholarship by reputable feminist scholars. No one can reasonably argue that things are not better for women than they once were; and no one can reasonably argue that a gendered system of economic and social iniquity does not continue. In addition to varying degrees of social disempowerment that cut along racial, ethnic, age, sociocultural, and economic lines, women generally continue to be appraised and rewarded for how they do or do not accord with dominant culture's standards of feminine beauty. A systemic and objectifying process of adjudication of women's bodies remains a general condition affecting women; personal and professional standing and advancement depend at least in part on physical "gifts."

The simple idea I began with for this book came as the result of a conversation I had with Ron Pelias, my teacher, mentor, and friend, after I had spouted that fairly well-worn feminist argument about women's objectification. He said, "I bet if you asked women in strip clubs if they felt objectified, they'd say no." Of course they'd say that, I found myself agreeing. Before I could reach for other feminist arguments about how those women have not had their consciousness sufficiently raised, I paused to consider the shift in perspective that his comment urged me toward.

Feminists have long argued that after centuries of women's experience being articulated by others (typically, men in authority), claiming space and giving voice to our perspectives was and is a vital touchstone for the development of empowered being and for revalorizing what traditionally has been considered important in the world. Ron's question made me wonder why it was that some women's voices were allowed to claim space and be heard and others were not. At that time, 1993, published perspectives of sex workers were few. I was struck then by the contradiction between what feminism professed—equality among people—and how the politics of activism can stifle that principle. Sex workers were not being given a place at the feminist table and, although there has been some change during the intervening years since I first came to the topic, sex workers' voices are still sidelined and their concerns dismissed.

One outcome of Ron's comment was that it compelled me to engage in an ethnographic study of strippers. The narratives I co-constituted with the women I met during that year in strip clubs around the United States were then shaped into a one-person show. Those narratives have also appeared in some of my subsequent publications. Some of the insights I gained doing that study appear in this book as well.

But it's not just how Ron's comment urged me to seek out the perspectives of women who work under conditions of pronounced objectification that his comment helps me situate the work in this book. Of more relevance to my work here is how his comment urged me to consider how we women experience our agency and constitute our subjectivity given the pervasiveness of objectification. That is the issue that beats at the heart of this book.

To explore that question, my work here begins with myself, with my negotiation of my agency in gendered performances I have made both in everyday life and upon the stage. Moreover, I consider how femininity is a contested feminist enactment for how it appears to comply with those dominant expectations. Through various methods for textually evoking my performative experiences, I suggest how femininity can be strategically deployed to subvert dominant expectations for women's gendered performances, as well as to further an immanent feminist critique. Through autoethnographic textual representation I seek to engage my readers through visceral connection to the experiences I describe. Autoethnography's governing principle is that evocation leads to more profound understanding than with traditional scholarship where ideas are reported. My hope is that I succeed in doing that.

Although these pages derive from my experiences, they culminate here through significant contributions from a wide range of people. Let me first thank Art Bochner for his persistence and encouragement throughout this process. I am grateful to Mitch Allen of AltaMira for his patience and kindness. I gratefully acknowledge Noreen Barnes-McLain, Lenore Langsdorf, Ron Pelias, Elyse Pineau, Nathan Stucky, and James Van Oosting, my teachers who each mentored and challenged me, and then knew well enough to just get out of my way; though, they were never far when I foundered and needed them. To my colleagues at Bowling Green State University, with particular thanks to Jonathan Chambers, Michael Ellison, and Ron Shields, I am grateful for our intellectual and compassionate community that sustains my heart and mind. I thank C. Turner Steckline and Tracy Stephenson, not only because they supplied the seeds of the idea that eventually culminated in this book, but because they helped nurture me in so many ways over the years. I thank my sister Susanne Lockford for letting me tell the story of her childhood treachery with the bias I give it in these pages. I've never forgiven her for the knee she put through my barricaded bedroom door, but I've forgiven the rest. Karen (Smith) McGrath contributed to my work in incalculable ways. She was ballast when I needed it, loyal in the face of community adversity, and she always possesses a better pair of eyes with which to judge than I. To the women and men who participated in the ethnographic study, I am continually in their debt. Each of them taught me so much. Finally, I thank my mother, Joyce Lockford, because she taught me about persistence and autonomy, because she taught me about the power the intellect can have in shaping material conditions, and because she embodies the model of maternal love; she loves me no matter what I do. So since loving me can sometimes really be a tall order, I'm really grateful to her. Also, I thank her because if I didn't, I'd get in trouble.

CHAPTER ONE

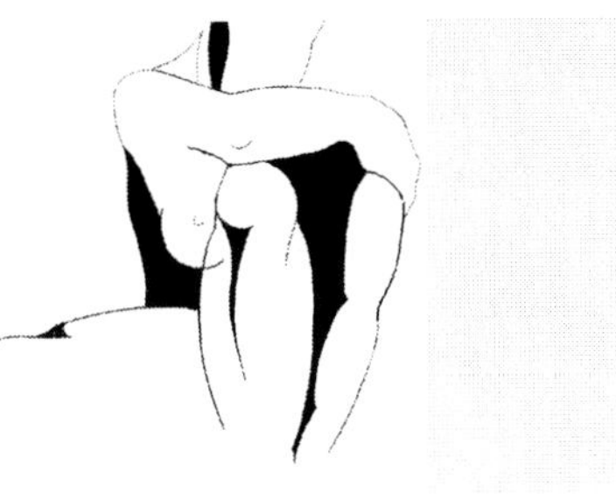

The Abject Body and Subversive Femininity

To perform is to feel vain and vulnerable simultaneously.

—RONALD J. PELIAS

The lived body is thus first and foremost not a located thing but a path of access, a being-in-the-world.

—DREW LEDER

This includes the fact that the text, . . . if it is to be understood properly, i.e., according to the claim it makes, must be understood at every moment, in every particular situation, in a new and different way. Understanding here is always application.

—HANS-GEORG GADAMER

Even in the beginning it always required thinking twice.

The beginning was a June morning in 1958. Seven-and-a-half months into her pregnancy, my mother fell down a flight of stairs after watching *Perry Mason* on television. That night her water broke and I came kicking into the world, literally kicking, for I was born breach. Pulled from my mother's womb six weeks early, I somehow escaped the broken neck or decapitation so possible with breach births. So bruised, I was purple from toe to head. So discolored and misshapen by the violence of my birth, my mother wailed at the first sight of me. Her grief reverberated throughout those sterile, unforgiving hospital halls and her body heaved with a fear that could not be quelled until after the doctor was called. His news that I would survive, that I would survive without a mark, calmed her. Her breathing settled as his authority persuaded her that all traces of my brutal birth would slip away in the days to come, that the marks would eventually remain only as a distant memory, a memory whose only lingering purpose would be as a recurrent story told to me as I grew and told here now as a story with which to begin this book.

To counter my mother's fear and sorrow, the doctor urged her to pick me up again and to cradle me in her arms a second time. He bid her to see beyond the surface of bruises, and to secure her heart in the joyful promise of my healthy future. At the doctor's urging, my mother had to rethink her initial reaction toward me; she had to re-evaluate the emotions that cleft her heart at her initial sight of me; she had to bring me, a hideously bruised lump of purple flesh, close to her bosom, and to re-feel into my being, to open her heart and to welcome me and to reconsider who I was and who I could become.

This book is about performances that, just like the doctor's instructions to my mother, will require *you* to think twice. Specifically, this book is about performances I have given both on the "stage" of the everyday world and within traditional theatrical playing spaces. In order to understand these performances and before you come to judgment about me and about these performances, I ask you, my readers, to think and feel beyond your first impulse, an impulse that may prompt you to close your hearts. As I wrote this book, I too had to reopen my heart and mind as I once again considered these performances. Thus, this book is fueled by a cyclical momentum of interpretive recursivity—that is, a thinking and feeling twice in order to come to understanding—a momentum that not only pulses in my heart and I hope will in yours, but also beats at the heart of the methods of inquiry from which these pages have evolved.

My work originates in my personal experience. Each chapter proceeds from a description of a performance I gave in which I willingly transgressed contextual or cultural expectations and in which I ran the risk of alienating, and often did alienate, the audience. Moreover, my acts of transgression and the audiences' potential or actual alienation meant that I in turn occupied an alienated and sometimes defensive position in relation to the audience. In a word, I became *abject.* I became abject in two ways. First, in some cases I deliberately made myself abject by purposefully transgressing borders of propriety or social norms and thus intentionally engaged in acts of self-abjection. Second,

I became abject when my act of self-abjection prompted the audience's abjectification of me. While my acts may be transgressive, potentially alienating, and abjectifying, I urge you, my audience, not to halt the momentum of your interpretation with that initial reaction. Halting there would be to think only once about what I put before you. If you are willing to forestall reaction, to think twice, and to somatically and affectively engage with me and my performances, you may find how these performances are more than transgressive. Rather, I trust that you will find as I do that they are potentially and positively subversive. By subversive I mean that these acts not only make contextual and/or cultural norms apparent by transgressing them, but through transgression they also endeavor to transform those cultural norms. My aim is clearly liberatory; by subverting these norms I hope to illuminate how ideology is inscribed upon the performing body. Thinking and feeling twice becomes a subversive interpretive practice that I regard as more than an audience member's or reader's act of generosity toward an abject performer or writer. It is a humane acknowledgment and openness toward the continuing bid for social evolution.

The performances I explore here are unified insofar as each may be regarded as a traditionally feminine gender performance. By traditional I mean those performative displays, enactments, or activities that are often called into suspicion by some mainstream feminist scholars and activists because they potentially promote the social expectation that women must be feminine. They are those embodied acts that are considered to contribute to the taken-for-grated cultural assumption that femininity is an abiding part of performing woman and thus, they are enactments that are regarded as potentially complicitous in rendering femininity compulsory for "appropriate" everyday life female gender performances. The performance of such traditionally feminine actions, then, marks a contested space where agency and choice butt against political agendas and ideological constructs. For example, some feminists would argue that actions such as altering one's body size, dancing nude for financial gain, or wearing makeup contribute to the continuance of women's social and cultural oppression by perpetuating the idea that women's value is to be measured through how much they accord to social standards for sexiness or beauty. However, I extend and question this argument by paradoxically exploring how these very same acts may also be subversive and thereby further a feminist agenda. I argue that these traditional acts of femininity may be enacted in ways that subvert socially dominant conceptions of the feminine, further calling into question society's notions for appropriate female gender performance. I am challenging both the socially dominant view and the feminist disavowals of these acts. My aim is to reveal the limits and possibilities of performative choice not only for women in general, but also for those women in particular who consider themselves to be feminists.

My exploration of how both the cultural and the feminist conceptions of femininity condition and constrain women's performative choices, and how these conceptions are constituted in and by the performing body, begins from an autoethnographic impulse. That is to say, I begin with my experience, with my performing body. Autoethnography, as H. L. Goodall Jr. has noted, results in "creative narratives shaped out of a writer's personal experiences within a culture and addressed to academic and public audiences" (*Writing the New Ethnography*, 9). Through the narratives I tell in this book, I endeavor to do just that; these stories are hewn from my personal experience as a performer and as a researcher. Furthermore, the stories that shape each chapter are deliberately told through different writing styles. Doing so provides me with a range of access for both inquiring into and representing my experiences. I begin with a more traditional scholarly writing style in the next chapter as I explore the transformation of body size. In the third chapter, where I examine my changing commitment to feminism during the study I conducted on the work performances of strippers, my narrative voice is foregrounded. I work from a more poetic voice in chapters 4 and 5 to consider how two different theatrical performances influenced my everyday performance as a female academic.[1] Through this range of representation, my goal is to textually evoke my experiences as well as to somatically engage my readers. How much my experience is evoked for you and how much you might be somatically engaged depends at least in part on the style of writing; my anticipation is that your experience depends upon how I represent it. At points these pages may conjure a visceral response; this is deliberate, even when you are prompted to revulsion, rejection, abjection. My aim is that you think and feel. And I ask that you consider a second time.

Thinking and feeling—being open toward interpretive recursivity—is fundamental to apprehending autoethnographic work. Carolyn Ellis notes that when reading an autoethnographic text, she wants the text to summon both her intellect and her emotions. She states, "At the risk of oversimplifying, I want the two sides of my brain to be engaged simultaneously, or for the text to call forth one side and then the other, back and forth, until thinking and feeling merge" ("Creating Criteria," 273). Moreover, Arthur Bochner observes that the most powerful narratives informing autoethnographic work usually entail "structurally complex narratives, stories told in a temporal framework that rotates between past and present reflecting the nonlinear process of memory work" ("Criteria against Ourselves," 270). The self-narratives I have created throughout this book, composed as all narratives are by looking back at the past through the lens of the present, help me to "extract meaning from experience rather than to depict experience exactly as it was lived" (Bochner, "Criteria against Ourselves," 270). Together, through the writing and through reading these narratives, we will extract the meaning of these experiences.

While this book is about my experiences and the evocation of those experiences on the page, this project originates *from* my performing body and is methodologically informed *by* my body. As a performer-centered project, my somatic and kinesthetic engagement is a central focus. Thus the characteristics of recursivity and evocation so fundamental to autoethnography are further nurtured through my attention to my performing body. In doing so, I harvest as well as seed the epistemological ground of performance as a mode of inquiry and way of knowing.

Performing Woman: A Body Marked by Cultural Inscriptions for Femininity

Feminist Cultural Criticism

I situate my argument with and against "feminist cultural criticism." Taking my lead from Susan Bordo, my intention is to identify the cultural critique developed by feminist scholars across a variety of feminist positions who seek to describe the "ideological and institutional parameters governing the construction of *gender* in our culture" ("Whose Body Is This?" 61, original emphasis).[2] I do not assume that all women share an identical cultural experience. Rather, with the feminist cultural critics, I point to how ideology and institutions "press for conformity" to dominant norms (Bordo, "Whose Body Is This?" 62). Contrary to these critics, however, I suggest that some feminist arguments have become so taken for granted that they likewise function ideologically by pressing women toward conformity to performative gender norms.

Femininity as Performance

Feminist theorists have employed the language of performance to describe the condition of being a woman in Western culture. Notably, feminist philosopher Judith Butler urges her readers to consider "gender . . . as a *corporeal style*, an 'act,' as it were, which is both intentional and performative" ("Performative Acts," 272–73, original emphasis). Sandra Lee Bartky summarizes the performative entailments in being a woman thus: "femininity is surely something that is enacted" ("Foucault," 72). The notion of gender as a constitutive act may have originated with Simone de Beauvoir in *The Second Sex*, who pithily identified the concept when she stated "one is not born, but rather *becomes*, a woman" (295, emphasis added). Comments de Beauvoir, "Precisely because the concept of femininity is artificially shaped by custom and fashion, it is imposed upon each woman from without" (*The Second Sex*, 692). On these accounts, gender is a compulsory performance mandated by cultural and social dictates. Not only are gender performances compulsory, they also subject women to reprisals insofar as "performing one's gender wrong initiates a set of punishments both obvious and indirect" (Butler, "Performative Acts," 279).

Insofar as cultural norms for femininity govern women's bodies, they are performative. Acceptable forms of feminine gesture, motility, deportment, adornment, physical embodiment, and activities are dictated by cultural norms. Indeed, so pervasive and specific are the cultural dictates controlling the acts that constitute women's gender performances that a cultural stereotype for feminine qualities is easily recognizable. Germaine Greer depicts the stereotypical patriarchal formula for womanhood as "a doll: weeping, pouting or smiling, running or reclining, she is a doll" (*The Female Eunuch,* 60). She is "dressed, coifed, and painted . . . . [Moreover,] her value is solely attested by the demand she excites in others. . . . [H]er . . . virtue is assumed from her loveliness, and her passivity" (*The Female Eunuch*, 58). While the stereotype has shifted some since Greer penned these words, traces of this feminine archetype linger. They continue to render enactments that support an identifiable constitutive femininity, one that, in the view of many, constrains women's agency.

The feminist cultural critique urges reconsideration of any acts that might perpetuate a female stereotype and that would thereby reinforce cultural imperatives for how women perform gender. Bartky notes the insidiousness of the stereotype's influence, pointing to how so much of this "chauvinized" woman exists in most women and that "her desire reflects the current social norms according to which female desire is, or is supposed to be, constituted. We are supposed to desire as she desires; if we don't, others may punish us; or else, feeling guilty we may punish ourselves" ("Introduction," 8). Thus, the cultural mandate that women perform their gender appropriately may be imposed from without, as de Beauvoir notes, but it is enforced not only by others but also by what women internalize as a moral code of femininity.

That women willingly conform to cultural norms is, according to this view, a result of their internalized oppression. Women experience a "psychological oppression," which is "dehumanizing and depersonalizing" (Bartky, "On Psychological Oppression," 29). Moreover, feminist cultural critics argue that when women embody and perform the cultural stereotype, the status quo is normalized, and in turn, women's autonomy is denied (cf. Bartky, "On Psychological Oppression," 24). Bartky characterizes how women's condition is affected by this systematic dehumanization in the following manner:

> Like the psychologically disturbed, the psychologically oppressed often lack a viable identity. Frequently we are unable to make sense of our own

> impulses or feelings, not only because our drama of fragmentation gets played out on an inner psychic stage, but because we are forced to find our way about in a world which presents itself to us in a masked and deceptive fashion. ("On Psychological Oppression," 31)

Insofar as women experience dependency and lack self-acceptance they are ripe for the development of a "false consciousness," a term Bartky and other feminist cultural critics have borrowed from Marx. Furthermore, by regarding this oppressive condition as "natural," women are induced to perform their womanhood in stereotypically feminine ways (i.e., to strive toward becoming decorative, passive, and petite). While a cultural mandate for women's gender performances exists, the competent performance of this feminine ideal is frustratingly difficult if not impossible. Obviously, not all women have "a pretty smile, good teeth, nice tits, long legs, a cheeky arse, a sexy voice . . . [and] eternal youth" (Greer, *The Female Eunuch,* 61). The elusive ideal not only requires a woman to curb her individual will and subsume her interests and desires to that of men, it also requires massive expenditures on cosmetics, adornments, and—in extreme cases—surgery, as well as rigorous exercise and diet. By calling attention to these aspects of women's experience, feminist cultural critics hope to raise the consciousness of women, alerting them to the oppression that inhibits their self-esteem and introducing psychological tools and strategies with which to free themselves from oppression.

This critique is powerful both for its condemnation of the governing norms and for its visionary call for a female self-performance that would challenge and counter the cultural mandate. Accordingly, in order to counteract the oppressive imposition of culture's performative prescription, a woman can raise her consciousness and stand against the dominant culture's tyranny by refusing to perform traditional femininity. This is precisely what many feminists have done when they choose, for example, not to wear makeup, feminine dresses, or high heels or to enact other traditionally feminine behaviors. Over time, however, the feminist vision has become another standard for female gender performance, a performance that some feminists feel compelled to enact in order to be taken seriously as feminists and as women.

Conflicting Feminisms

As the singular notion of a feminism erupted into multiplicity and difference producing an array of feminisms, multiple ways of performing oneself as a feminist also emerged. Many women recognize that there is no single approved way of performing feminist identity. Despite the advent of multiple feminisms, however, acts of femininity continue to be charged with decidedly unfeminist, if not anti-feminist, attributions. It is within the narrow field of these negatively imbued performative acts that I situate my arguments.

There are perhaps as many feminisms as there are individual women who claim feminist identity, women who adhere to principles they deem feminist, or women who employ a feminist view of the world. Given this plurality of perspectives, it would seem plausible that the establishment of some sort of feminist orthodoxy would fail to take root. However, feminism, broadly construed, is a social movement and the various feminisms constitute a range of critical theories funding the movement's several directions. Within this social and political network, feminist concerns for individual expression and political efficacy sometimes collide with feminist principles. The varying viewpoints fostered by the plurality of feminist positions, far from dismantling rigid ideological constructs, may produce the opposite effect. In short, this plurality has led to what Hirsch and Fox Keller (*Conflicts in Feminism*) have termed "conflicts in feminism." A concern for feminist qualities occasionally overshadows the previously unifying and more traditional feminist concern for women's equality and social justice.

As a social movement, feminism necessitates critique. However, where the critique once may have been directed outwardly toward society, it is now sometimes focused on other feminists. While critical voices may create conflict among feminists, it's also worth noting that these criticisms may also help revitalize and renew feminist political means and goals, further refining and proliferating various feminist perspectives. Critique, therefore, helps to create the conditions that make it possible for feminism(s) to better respond to contemporary women's experience, and to better represent the variety in that experience. As critical of at least one strain of feminism as my argument may be, my aim is nevertheless to further this immanent critical feminist conversation.

Performance as Agency and Ideological Constraint

I begin, as I've noted earlier, with my experience. This is to say that my own performative experiences form the ground from which to make my observations, and as such, they enable me to talk back to theory from the "bottom up." In this book, I place my everyday and aesthetic performances in dialogue with various feminist arguments as a sort of test, if you will, of the salience of these feminist arguments. I also describe and depict how the performing body, in this case, my performing body, struggles with and yields to performance. As Mary Frances HopKins has conceptualized "performance as agency," so too my performances foreground how I negotiate my agency within a site of resistance ("The Performance Turn," 235). The site of resistance includes both the cultural dictates for feminine gender performance and those feminist arguments that shape and chafe me as I endeavor to perform my version of feminism. In short, my descriptions clarify how embodiment is mediated by a complex web of ideological constructs. Each chapter, therefore, charts moments in time in which my performances of subversion are considered as embodied activity, as well as tests of ideological commitment, feminist criticism, and meta-criticism.

Terry Eagleton comments that "Nobody has yet come up with a single adequate definition of ideology" (*Ideology,* 1). He also notes how the various definitions include the notions that ideology helps constitute identity for individual subjects as well as for individuals within social groups, motivate actions, enable sense making, provide structure to social relations, and establish and maintain social regimes of power. Moreover, Eagleton concludes that these numerous and useful meanings of the term are not all compatible with each other (*Ideology,* 1). The confusion that my use of the term may occasion is surely the result of this inherent complexity. Commonly "ideology" is used pejoratively, and as such it connotes false or illusory ideas and partisan thinking. Yet, ideology also connotes an interpretive function; that is, it is the "process of production of meanings, signs and values in social life" (Eagleton, *Ideology,* 1). I cite these two contrasting definitions specifically—one pejorative, the other more neutral—in order to indicate how impossible it would be to achieve meaningful social experience without ideology and also to point out how ideology is also something occasionally to be feared and frequently to be diligently monitored. Loosely construed, ideology derives from two streams of thought. It is either something "preoccupied with ideas of true and false cognition" or something "concerned more with the function of ideas in social life" (Eagleton, *Ideology*, 3). Ideology is thus both suspect and necessary.

In this book, I focus on how ideology, broadly considered, invites as well as invalidates particular performative bodily engagements. I explore how modes of thought that structure social relations and support multiple taken-for-granted assumptions enable sense making as well as encourage or delimit particular types of female performative embodiment. As I explore how I negotiate my agency in each of the performances, I describe the ideological site of my resistance. I note how I understand my body and my self are being made sense of and how I am constrained in my enactment of particular activities. Just as Judith Butler notes that gender is performative, I suggest that ideology is likewise performative. If gender "manifests a set of strategies" for embodiment and these strategies are "never fully self-styled, for living styles have a history, and that history conditions and limits possibilities" (Butler, "Performative Acts," 272), so too does ideology condition and limit the choices for enacting one's being. Performing outside of these established ideological norms—whether those norms are dominant society's or feminists'—potentially renders that transgressive body ripe for abjectification by others. Furthermore, while an innocent transgression of these norms might well invite social punishments, a woman who knowingly transgresses them and willfully seeks abjection as a political tactic may further compound the abjectification that spectators are compelled to unleash toward her transgressive and subversive body. Indeed, from the perspective of those who embrace ideological and social norms, what could be more deserving of abjectification than one who is willfully abject?

The Abject Body

Performing Abjection and Spectator Abjectification

The strategic use of self-abnegation in performance for political or subversive ends has been used by various women in a variety of performances and performative contexts. This strategy is particularly evident in women's performance art. Karen Finley smearing canned yams across her bare buttocks, Annie Sprinkle offering up her cervix for scrutiny by audience members, and Rachel Rosenthal exposing her naked body to the audience while her "bad points" are marked and remarked upon are images that challenge traditional notions of decency, propriety, and standards for appropriate performance content. They also simultaneously level a range of feminist cultural critique. These, and other startling images like them, remain charged with an abiding currency not only as they linger in the minds of viewers, but also as they perpetuate a wealth of contested critical discourse in their aftermath.[3] Performance art resists categorization and therefore exceeds documentation and definition as Jeanie Forte argues ("Women's Performance Art," 217; cf. Phelan, *Unmarked,* 146). Nevertheless, scholars continue to use a variety of terms with which to catalogue transgressive representations in women's performance art: Elinor Fuchs has considered the "obscene body,"[4] Catherine Schuler[5] and Jill Dolan[6] the "pornographic" body, Joanna Frueh the "erotic" body,[7] Shannon Bell the "prostitute body,"[8] Peggy Phelan the "unmarked" body,[9] and Rebecca Schneider[10] the "explicit body."[11] The evocative terminology used by these and other critics and scholars attempts to capture the recurrence in women's performance art of both psychic and physical exposure and the tendency to transgress neat modernist distinctions between public and private spheres. Rather than denoting discrete descriptive categories, these "bodies" mark the meaning of a given performance across a range of overlapping critical foci. Some critics seek to identify performative strategies—often with clearly identifiable performative behaviors deliberately and consciously employed by the performer. Others focus on the emotional and political responses. For art historian and performance artist Joanna Frueh, for example, the erotic informs both her critical work on the page as well as her performance work on the stage.

I am exploring here what I call the abject body. I use the notion of the abject as a lens with which to view the performances I describe in these pages. Like the performance artists I cite above, my performances critique and resist cultural standards and their ideological mandates. Yet, as Marvin Carlson notes, one characteristic common to many performances that are critical and subversive, what he calls "resistant performances," is how such performances play a "dangerous game . . . as a double agent" (*Performance,* 173), for they are both complicitous with and critical of reigning oppressive cultural standards. Performing abjection likewise functions in both these ways and therefore my performances require that you think twice about them. Furthermore, insofar as performing abjection is subversive, it is also, paradoxically, a strategy that potentially produces a refusal of abjection; it subverts by negating the social and cultural sanctions and punishments that audiences in their initial response might feel compelled to impose.

The abject in my performances—those enactments that produce repulsion in my spectators or alienation for me—is the site of critical focus for this project. How the abject can function as a performative strategy or as a spectatorial position reveals the potentially subversive power of the abject body. The abject, through its strategic deployment and visceral response, brings into relief both performer and spectator agency. I mark the differences between these two positions and the agency specific to each by employing the term "abjection" for the general concept, the phrase "performing abjection" for the performative strategy, and the term "abjectification" for what audience members do in response to their exposure to what they consider to be an abject body.

Toward a Definition of the Abject Body

Julia Kristeva explores the experience of abjection in *Powers of Horror: An Essay on Abjection.* Kristeva principally rests her argument upon the notion of abjection as "a composite of judgment and affect" (10). While for Kristeva the abject is clearly a state of being, abjection is the active reaction summoned in the individual in response to abject others and abject objects. Accordingly, Kristeva argues that attaining abject status is not something one would willingly seek (*Powers of Horror,* 209); thus, abjection occurs as a response to the unwitting and/or unalterable abject status of the other. For Kristeva, abjection is the process by which the self delineates itself from the "radically excluded" and therefore abject other (*Powers of Horror,* 2). To render something, or some other, abject is the fitting response to that which is defiled. Yet, beyond being defiled, the abject transgresses. The abject transgresses the boundaries of the clean, the pure, and the proper (*Powers of Horror,* 85); it transgresses the distinctions between the sacred and profane; it "disturbs identity, system, order"

(*Powers of Horror,* 4). Moreover, the abject is "above all ambiguity" (*Powers of Horror,* 9). In short, the abject is that which is both clean and dirty, that which is both sacred and profane, that which breaks borders and is yet held tightly within them. Furthermore, according to Kristeva, "if someone personifies abjection . . . it is a woman, 'any woman,' the 'woman as a whole'" (*Powers of Horror,* 85). For women are, among other things, ambiguous: whether capable of childbearing or not, as embodiments of the maternal they are sacred; whether postmenopausal or not, as beings whose blood is known to flow out over the borders of their bodies, they are profane. The abject breaks the law and women break the Law of the Father simply by being women. Thus, the abject body is radically excluded, a transgressor of borders and law, unclean, unclear, and most aptly personified by women.

It is against this background of women's always already abject status that my performances are engaged. Despite Kristeva's caveat that no person would willingly do so, many feminist performers do deliberately embody abjection as a means of furthering their varied critical feminist agendas. The performances I discuss in the following chapters employ some form of self-abjection enacted as a strategy for cultural or contextual critique. Moreover, each performance transgresses explicit or implicit borders purposefully while generating criticism for the ambiguity of their messages. The various performances I describe throughout this work enable me to distinguish different uses of abjection as a performative strategy, to identify the ways spectators abjectify a performing other, and also to suggest the range of performances for which the concept of the abject body may apply.

Mode of Writing as Access to Bodily Knowing

I have already noted that one central purpose of autoethnographic writing is to textually capture experience in a way that evokes the experience for the readers. It is, as Bochner and Ellis argue, the use of "narrative strategies to transport readers into experiences and make them feel as well as think" ("Introduction," 18). Through using diverse writing styles in the evocation of my performance experiences, I am able to tease out the differences in bodily knowing each mode of writing brings forward. In short, these different modes of writing help me grasp the possibilities for meaning inhering in the experiences (Bochner, "Criteria against Ourselves," 270). So, while this project is on one level an account of how abjection functions across a range of performances, it is also an effort to locate how knowledge is constituted by and through representations of that experience.

Each of the performances I explore are comprised of distinctly different gendered acts; they occur in vastly different contexts from one another, and to the extent that performances can be understood to be accomplished along a continuum from the everyday to the theatrical, they each occupy a distinctly separate location on that continuum. Furthermore, I explore how abjection functions and is negotiated in each performance. How I bodily experience my ideological attachments or how I am constrained by my ideological commitments are revealed through the various ways I've chosen to write and represent the experiences.

The first performance I explore is the transformation of my body size through the performance of weight loss as a member of the Weight Watchers' program. Specifically, I focus upon the everyday performance of stepping onto the scale in front of the Weight Watchers' group leader. I have selected this particular performative moment for how it foregrounds my tensive relationship between my individual desire to alter my body size, the specular economy that conditions female embodiment, and the feminist resistance to cultural control. I argue that in this performance my body is rendered abjectly both by the dominant cultural script that generally presses women to conform to an ideal of feminine body size and by a feminist counterscript that urges feminists not to perform traditional femininity. It is with this performance that I adopt a more traditional scholarly writing style. As such, while my narrative voice is clearly present, it is somewhat subservient to the voices of other scholars contributing to the scholarly conversation on women's weight loss. This writing style will doubtlessly have the effect of representing my performance as more of a report rather than an evocation of it. Consequently, it should be noted that my access to bodily knowledge in this performance is shrouded within the scholarly conversation of other theorists. Yet, by placing my experience in "conversation" with the wealth of scholarly voices critiquing women's concern with weight loss, I am able to contextualize the ideological concerns and sociocultural constraints on women's performativity. This overarching context, as articulated within this first chapter, clarifies the broader milieu that conditions and informs the performances I more artfully and evocatively explore in subsequent chapters.

In the next performance I reveal my experience with Amanda, a twenty-year-old woman I interviewed as part of an ethnographic study I engaged in on women who do exotic dancing for a living. When Amanda pressed me to augment my research by stripping myself, the differences between our roles as researched and researcher became all too palpably evident. In this instance my everyday performance as academic researcher was challenged and informed by my un/willingness to perform the very theatrical/work performance I was studying. I consider the abjectification some women experience as they strip before a paying male public and I also examine how I as a researcher experience abjection because I was engaging in an ethnographic study of sex workers. Through the use of a distinctly narrative voice I gain access to how my understanding and interpretation of this form of labor derives from my embodied experience of feminist and dominant cultural ideological inscriptions.

I then shift my focus to two theatrical performances that I created and performed for differing academic audiences. The first performance I describe, which I called "Spin the Ideological Bottle," demonstrates my deliberate use of self-abjectification in order to make a mainstream feminist statement. In creating this performance I intertwined the generic categories of striptease and game shows to characterize the imbalance of ideological power between male-oriented visions of American history and feminist and/or woman-centered views of American historical relevancy. Through enacting a striptease, a deliberate performance of self-abjectification, I underscore women's experience of ideological and cultural debasement. This performance differs from the other performances I examine in that it articulates the most traditional of feminist arguments; yet, given the content and the context of the performance it is arguably the most transgressive. The second theatrical performance I explore, "Lip Reading," is an examination of consumer culture and the activity of wearing lipstick. I consider my sensuous and tactile experience of applying and wearing lipstick and the resultant experience of abjectification that this problematic self-performance constitutes. Through these two theatrical performances I consider how my everyday performance as woman and as academic was affected and how they effected a culture of abjectification around me. Through my articulation of these two performances I bring focus to the intricacies and intimacies of those experiences and I particularize the difficulties and deliberations I face as I negotiate my agency. I adopt a very personal and poetical voice to access my bodily knowledge within these two theatrical performances.

I conclude the book by drawing together the wide range of experiences I have described and defined in the preceding chapters. I tentatively thematize the experience of abjection and what it means to use the female and feminized body subversively. As I conclude I also survey how the "voices" I employed provided access to my somatic and kinesthetic experience and, concomitantly, what bodily knowledge became present through the diverse ways I represented my experience.

In sum, for the book as a whole, my experience is the ground from which I am able to make evident the tensions between individual desire, principled action, and collective agenda. By centering this work in my performing body, I attempt to provide rich descriptions of particular performances while also elucidating the embodied knowledge generated through these performances. Finally, by employing a variety of modes of writing I endeavor to clarify how differing scholarly representations variously enable access to that embodied knowledge. Thus, with every performance of femininity described in this book, I have had to think and feel, and think and feel again. As you read these pages, I implore you, just as my mother's pediatrician did, to do so as well.

CHAPTER TWO

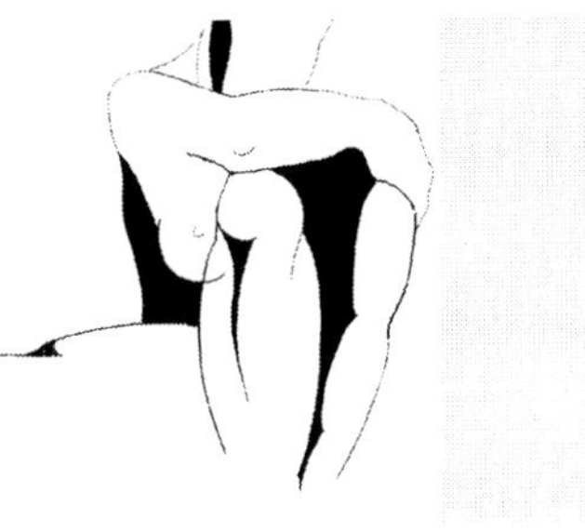

Stepping on the Black Box: Kinesthetic Experience and the Transformation of Body Size

Laugh, and be fat.

—JOHN TAYLOR

The human body is the best picture of the human soul.

—LUDWIG WITTGENSTEIN

Anatomy is destiny.

—AMY COLLINS

A Brief Personal History of the Scale

Shopping trips with my mother to the College Shopping Center in the small Southern California town where I spent most of my childhood were occasions for a heightened awareness of desire. My mother was annoyingly resolute in her refusal to give in to my relentless demands for new pleasures and experiences. Usually I would be sent back defeated, told to replace on the shelves those things that I had attempted to slip into the shopping basket, items I had been sure I could not live without. My persistent questions, tugs at her skirt hem, and pathetic whimpers rarely moved my mother. Yet my insistent pleas to go on the twenty-five-cents-a-ride mechanical horse or the other strategically placed coin-slot children's rides outside the Thrifti-mart would occasionally be granted. Perhaps those times I was on the ride permitted my mother a brief moment of peace of mind.

Just down from the Thrifti-mart, on the pavement between the Drug King and the Woolworth's, standing like a sentry, was an imposing bright red and yellow cast-iron scale. It towered above me. On its enormous, round, glass-covered face black painted numbers circled the dial and a sharp red arrow needle hung ready to spin in the event of a dime being slipped into the slot. Written on the face inside the circle of numbers was the command, "Know Your Weight." This authoritative summons was irresistible to me. I would jump up and down on the scale's steel balance plate pleading with my mother, willing to barter with my soul if need be, for the requisite dime. The desire was fueled all the more as I leaped on and off of the balance plate, feeling it shift around under me. The needle on the dial would jiggle as I jumped, yet remained doggedly at zero teasing me with its potential.

My mother could never understand my desire to be weighed by this machine. Reducing process to product, she argued that I could just as easily (and for free) "know my weight" by standing on the bathroom scale at home.

With time even my mother's will could be whittled away, so finally one day she relented. My mother had to hold me up so that *I* could slip in the dime; I refused to let her do it, for as far as I was concerned, that was part of the enjoyment. After dropping in the coin, lest the "ride" be ruined, I had to wiggle and scream for her not to put me down on the balance plate as she was about to do. Instead, I insisted she let me down on the pavement so that I could then, in my own time, stand on the scale and watch the needle swing on the dial.

I cannot remember the figure on which the needle came to rest. What I do remember is that the event seemed to be over instantaneously: I stood on the scale, the needle moved and came to rest, I leaped off the scale and watched the needle shoot back to zero. Before being tugged down to Woolworth's by an already impatient mother, I leaped back up on the scale testing it in a naive hope for one more go.

My earliest recollection of being publicly weighed occurred when I was nine years old. My mother was an educator and upon earning a sabbatical leave, she chose to take us traveling throughout Western Europe. For the 1966–1967 school year we lived in Paris. I was placed in the *classe des étrangers* (literally translated as the class of strangers), at the École des Filles, Porte St. Cloud. Aside from the fact that my classmates and I were all girls, we had little else in common. Our ages ranged across all the elementary grades. We came from a variety of backgrounds: from the well-to-do, from the middle and lower-middle classes, from different races, and from countries all over the world as diverse as Greece, Kenya, and what was then Yugoslavia. Our families' political affiliations included everything from Liberal Democrat, to Socialist, to Communist, and to Conservative. Despite these differences, our being segregated from the rest of the school's local population created the conditions whereby we became unified in our difference from the locals. We became a small but unified band of diverse foreigners. The school administrators' blatant glorification of French culture, and their obvious efforts to indoctrinate us with it, misfired. Rather than having the intended effect of cultivating our appreciation for all things Gallic, we responded with extreme resistance. The year was punctuated by minor classroom rebellions in which we gleefully set about proving to our French overseers just how uncultured we "strangers" could be. Whenever our teacher left the room, we staged disruptive scenes entailing standing on our desks, screaming, and throwing things across the room.

One bitter midwinter day we were told that on the following day, during our physical education period, we would undergo a series of medical exams. The local health authority was scheduled to test all the children at the school for tuberculosis as part of a national detection campaign. We were told that we would be weighed and undergo a short examination by a doctor. My cohorts and I immediately viewed this as an excellent opportunity to sabotage the system, which we felt unduly attempted to control us. Not all of my associates were willing to participate in this effort; some of them felt sure our intentions would be discovered and were unwilling to take the risk. However, a number of us decided upon a course of action that we believed would affect at least one result of the examinations. The following day, those of us who hadn't chickened out overnight brought in a small assortment of heavy pocket-sized objects: rocks, paper weights, metal scraps, small pieces of construction scaffolding found in the street on the way to school, and the like. It was our intention to secretly carry these objects in our gym shorts' pockets during the weighing-in and thereby spoil the accuracy of our overlords' inquiry. Knowing the truth about something that the authorities did not was the pleasurable sedition we sought. However, when we changed into our gym shorts, we discovered that many of the objects we had brought were either too large to fit into the pockets or so heavy that they pulled our shorts down at odd angles and rendered the ruse obvious. Only the smallest objects could be carried without detection.

We were ordered to line up in the chilly and capacious gymnasium. We stood shivering in the required gym uniform of blue shorts and white short-sleeved shirt. A parade of students had filtered through the hall all day. Our teacher, Mademoiselle Gomme, a towering barrel-chested autocrat, shepherded us along the line until the first student in our class was up next. She then stood next to the scale as we each in turn stepped up to it. She would call out our names and also ensure we did as we were told. The scale was the manual variety in which weights are slid across a horizontal balance beam and equalized to ascertain the weight of the person standing on the scale. There were two lab-coated female medical personnel at the scale as well. One stood behind the scale to maneuver the weights and call out the numbers while the other sat in a chair with a clipboard recording our weight next to our names.

When my time arrived, I stood on the scale duly discomfited by the palpable force of these women's authority and in fear that the small stones in my pockets would be discovered. My name was called by Mademoiselle Gomme, the weights on the scale were efficiently slid into balanced compliance, the woman by the scale called out in French a number determined in kilos, and the seated woman wrote in her ledger. I was then hustled out of the gymnasium into the raw winter air by another faculty member. I was told to line up outside the mobile medical unit that was temporarily occupying a corner of the schoolyard and to await my turn to see the male doctor and be tested for TB. I stood in the drizzle of that grey afternoon wondering if the handful of stones in my pockets had made any difference. While I understood the number in French, I could not translate kilos into pounds. I felt stupid as I shivered in the rain, understanding in that instant how knowledge is power and realizing that I had neither.

As I grew up, I would weigh myself on the blue Sunbeam bathroom scale kept in my mother's bathroom. Over the years, my mother, my sister, and I would consult this simple scale that would, with a swoosh of numbers, reveal the "truth" we sought. When I was a child, my mother would have me stand on the scale every once in a while to measure how fast I was growing. Later I would learn that the scale told more than my weight. As I entered into adolescence I learned, as I had seen my sister do before me, how my identity as a young woman and my sense of social acceptability were enmeshed with how the numbers were to be interpreted. I learned the difference between fat and "baby fat" and by the time I was twelve I knew I could no longer claim to have the latter.

Eventually, after years of bathroom humidity, the swoosh of the dial on the old Sunbeam settled into a creaky squeal. This rusty scale remained the only scale in our house long after it had lost its credibility. I recall how stepping on it would result in one number, then stepping off and then on again would result in an altogether different number. For a time I played a private game in which I simply ignored the largest numbers the scale would provide, even though I knew full well that any number the scale declared could not be trusted to be accurate. This state of misinformation continued in my household for a long time, while we put off purchasing a new scale. We had grown comfortable knowing we did not know the accurate number. I think somehow it seemed that if we did not know the truth about our weight, we couldn't really be held accountable for it. Perhaps I was learning how the silent directive of the red and yellow College Center scale to "Know Your Weight" was less about the salience of being informed of a personal fact and more about a kind of social imperative.

We finally admitted that this resolutely inaccurate scale, although serving to ameliorate any anxiety we may have had over our weight, was not serving the purpose for which it was originally designed. As I became a fully fledged female teenager, stepping on the scale was no longer the child's play at the local grocery store scale it once had been. Rather it was a serious weekly, if not daily, ritual. I repeatedly urged my mother to replace the Sunbeam with a new scale. Eventually she did, and in turn, a series of other scales followed; although none, we felt sure, ever worked as well as the Sunbeam had when it was new.

Weight Watchers and the Publicly Private Adjudication of My Body

In my early thirties I returned to university to work on a Master's degree. By the time I finished the degree, I had gained twenty-five pounds and was the heaviest I had ever been. Many articles of clothing I owned didn't fit; those I could put on felt tight, and I felt awkward in them. Although the contents of my closet belonged to me, they did not belong to the shape I now owned. They hung in my closet, passed over day after day as I searched for something I could wear. Each day that they hung there as my eyes and hands passed over them, they conjured somatic remembrances in me of the slender self I performed in the past and they ignited a desire for a sleek slim self to perform in the envisioned yet intangible future. My body felt as if it were a stranger to these clothes. At that time I experienced a sense of containment and restriction as my desire for change pressed against the kinesthetic reality of my body. This body was not comfortable. Experientially, I was unrecognizable to myself. Maurice Merleau-Ponty uses the terms "habit body" and "the body at this moment" to distinguish the kind of split subjectivity I was now experiencing (*Phenomenology of Perception,* 82). My body, the heavy "body at this moment," created an alien sensory experience of myself as I moved through space. My thighs rubbed together as I walked, a hitherto unknown experience. My body felt rounded, dull-edged, insulated, and guarded. Despite these changes, I nevertheless maintained a sense of my "habit body." This habit body entailed a somatic understanding cultivated over time by sedimented bodily experiences that I "felt" to be slim. Even considering the somatic adjustments made incrementally in the process of aging, my understanding of my bodily engagement with the world accommodated mostly a sense of taut muscle and angled bones. Experiencing changes in my embodiment contradicted my habituated, embodied understandings of myself. In short, my shape had changed and with it my experience of myself changed too. I did not *feel* like myself.

Although the added weight did not appear overnight, the discomfort and alienation I felt toward my overweight body eventually reached a crisis point.[1] I wanted to change this body shape, to rediscover and re-in*habit* the self I understood myself to be. I believed I would have more success achieving this change if I engaged in a program designed to help me lose weight, so I joined Weight Watchers. Joining an organized, commercial weight-loss program, I reasoned, would be beneficial because it would offer a detailed dietary regimen and its weekly membership fee would be an incentive not to stray from the program. The program entailed a weekly weighing-in with the group leader. This publicly private adjudication of my body and my progress in the program was an uncomfortable but nevertheless effective manner of holding me accountable for my weight. Imbued with thirty-three years of struggle and negotiation with bodily and cultural recalcitrance, I thus began a weekly cycle of monitoring the food I consumed, attending Weight Watchers' meetings and standing before my group leader to note the changes on the scale. What follows is a description of a weigh-in offered as a point of access—a weigh-in as a way in, if you will—for understanding my performance of weight loss.

* * *

In the Weight Watchers' meeting room I stand a socially appropriate distance away from the cubicle where members are weighed. In the cubicle with the group leader is another female member, standing on the scale. I stand close enough to signal to the other members in the room that I am next in line, but far enough away that I cannot overhear the discussion going on in the cubicle. When my turn comes I know that the woman who is behind me will stand about where I am now. There are about fifteen women in the room; all but the leader and receptionist are members there for a weigh-in. Some of the members have already been weighed and are sitting in the folding chairs in the meeting area behind me. Other women are lined up behind me awaiting their turn. Although some of the members in the room talk with each other and I occasionally talk with some other members, it feels to me as if we are each alone. I have removed my shoes, jacket, sweater, and belt; they rest on the chair in the meeting area of the room behind me, where I have also left my book bag. Other women lining up to weigh have similarly divested themselves of clothing that they can reasonably remove that might affect the numbers on the scale.

As I stand in my stocking feet, I simultaneously feel how this lining up and semi-disrobing activity is both customary and novel. It is a rehearsed activity done on a weekly basis for the last thirteen weeks since I joined Weight Watchers. Other members in the room also perform the same disrobing ritual, so I am not alone in what might seem to others to be a bizarre practice. Insofar as being semi-disrobed in a public place is not commonplace, the activity is novel. While I feel a little vulnerable removing some of my clothing and revealing my body, which I still experience as overweight, I know that I am surrounded by women who are all engaged in a similar concern. There is comfort in numbers. The woman on the scale steps down. I notice that she is larger than I. I know that I am much closer to the cultural ideal of female embodiment than many of the women in this group. I feel a pang of embarrassment as I acknowledge this to myself. I sometimes wonder if these other members regard me as an invader of a space reserved for "legitimately" overweight women. Do these women, some weighing more than a hundred pounds over their goal weight, resent me? If they had my shape, would they still be here? As I stand here clothed only in a skirt and light blouse, I feel a sense of liberty in my body as I compare myself to these other more overweight women. Should I feel this way?

My group leader, Janice, stands inside the cubicle and next to the scale. She beams her usual smile, which welcomes me as someone she knows. I see her once a week in this relatively private moment and in the more public moments of the meetings. I do not know Janice outside this situation, nor do I want to. We come from different backgrounds. We are different ages. Based upon what I know of her from what she says during the meetings she leads, I see her as a very traditional and conservative person. Our only common interest seems to be her occupational obligation to be interested in my progress in the program. I also know that I like keeping my Weight Watchers' affiliation private and so I am content to keep her at a distance.

Whenever I tell somebody that I go to Weight Watchers, I always feel a pang of embarrassment. This embarrassment stems from three related sources: First, Weight Watchers' public image is of a rather kitschy organization that encourages groups of overweight women (and a few men) to engage in the narcissistic pursuit of losing weight. I believe that by allowing others to know I am a member, that image is potentially reflected onto myself. Second, by acknowledging to others that I am a member, I invite focus to my body by permitting others to know I am concerned about my weight. In that instance, my body shape is theirs to assess. Finally, by informing others that I am a member of a weight-loss organization, my commitments to feminism may be brought under suspicion; my status as an avowed feminist may be compromised; or I risk becoming an example of feminist hypocrisy. Moreover, like Lisa Tillmann-Healy, who has written of her experiences with bulimia, "as a scholar, I'm concerned that fellow academics will dismiss my work as self-absorbed" ("A Secret Life," 86).

Janice is holding a pencil and my record book in her hands. She asks me how my week has been. This is not a phatic greeting. She is referring to how closely I have adhered to the diet program in the preceding week. I respond that I have been "pretty good." I do not know if I have lost weight, although I am hopeful. I wonder how my actions of the last week will affect the numbers on the meter. I wonder about the glass of wine I had on Friday night and if it will hinder my progress. I think about how little I have exercised in the last week. I scan the sensation of my clothes on my body. Is the fit looser this week than last? Over the past thirteen weeks since joining Weight Watchers, the re-emergence of the angularity of my hip bones, a sensation of length in my legs, and sleeker contours along the bones in my face have begun to develop. I have begun to walk differently, with more purpose and dynamism. As I see myself in mirrors, I see a re-emergence of a shape that pleases me. I celebrate myself every time I am able to fit into an article of clothing that has been hanging in my closet in silent mockery during the preceding months. With each week that passes I feel lighter and more agile than the preceding week. With some apprehension, I recall times during these thirteen weeks when I stepped on the scale, thinking I had faithfully adhered to the program, and the meter revealed an increase in weight. I also recall times when I believed I was less faithful to the program and the meter revealed a loss of weight. Even though I feel lighter, I do not trust myself to know if I have lost weight this week. These thoughts pass through me in an instant, but in some sense they have been with me since I woke up this morning. I have taken the following steps to ensure that when I step on the scale the lowest number I can get will appear: I have not eaten lunch even though it is after twelve o'clock; I have intentionally worn a lightweight skirt and blouse despite the slight chill in the autumn air; I have removed some clothes before presenting myself at the scale. Standing before the scale marks a moment of arrest from quotidian life. The step up onto the scale will shatter this moment of liminal uncertainty with technologically accurate revelation. While I know that my weight may fluctuate somewhat during any given day, when I step on the scale the resultant numbers will be permanently etched into my book. The scale's lack of forgiveness makes me slightly apprehensive. The scale makes certain claims; its certainty displaces the trust I have in my ability to feel and assess my weight loss on my own. I feel diminished by the shadow of the scale's authority.

The scale is a modern digital scale. On the carpeted floor is a black metal box that is the part of the scale I am to stand upon. From the back of the black box an electrical cord snakes away, climbing up the wall to a digital display resting on a white wooden shelf. The digital display is placed on the shelf in such a way that when I stand on the scale only Janice and I will be able to see the numbers that appear there. I am aware of the other members standing or sitting near the cubicle in a haphazard line behind me chatting and awaiting their turn.

Janice looks up from my record book, having mentally noted the number from last week. Smiling and gesturing upward with her pencil, she indicates that she is ready for me to step onto the black box. I stand on the black box putting both feet squarely on it. There is no movement in the box as it accepts my weight. My eyes and Janice's eyes immediately look to the meter. Numbers race on the face of the meter, elapsing upward until they begin to slow and come to rest on the numbers one—three—six—point—seven—five. One hundred and thirty-six and three-quarter pounds. As Janice writes the new numbers down in my book, she tells me that I am down three quarters of a pound from last week. I am relieved yet disappointed. I am glad that there has not been an increase but the amount lost is so minimal. Almost seven pounds still to lose to achieve the goal I have set for myself. Janice can see that I am disappointed. She smiles and reminds me that it is better than the one hundred and fifty-five pounds I started out with. I agree, smile politely, though I feel disappointed. Her job is to encourage me and her positive words feel as gratuitous as pickup lines in a bar at closing time. I stand down from the scale and Janice gives me this week's pamphlets. As I walk away I resign myself to the number and resolve to do better next week. The woman in the line behind me is stepping on the scale as I sit on the metal chair where I have left my discarded clothes and book bag. Reaching to put on a shoe, I feel the bones in my behind press against the hardness of the metal seat. I know I would not have felt that a few weeks ago. A hundred and thirty-six, almost a hundred and thirty-seven still seems too heavy to me. How can a quantitative assessment be appropriate for a qualitative experience?

The Feminist Cultural Perspective

Ideology and Performance

This section presents a "perspective" on weight-loss programs for women. I am struck by the inappropriateness of the word perspective. Perhaps it is due to a visualist bias in our language that words summoning our sense of sight so often inflect how we discuss ideology. As I said in the last chapter, ideology has many definitions including as a "process of production of meanings, signs and values in social life" (Eagleton, *Ideology*, 1); but commonly ideology is conceived of as a world*view* or a *lens* to use for understanding the world. Yet ideology is not simply a lens, not merely a perspective. Rather, ideology is a standpoint not only from which I *view* my experience but also from where all my senses are engaged, a place where I enact and feel my being. Regarded in this way, ideology may be understood as something written on, into, and by the body.

The shift from a metaphor of a lens to a metaphor of a performative place helps me apprehend how ideology manifests itself in a stylistics of self. Thus, while what follows may remain a lens *for you, my readers,* with which to view the experience, for me it describes a felt and embodied experience; it describes a way of being and it prescribes a doing of my being, a habituation of gesture, action, and attitude. Ideology, then, is not only a way to make sense of the world, an understanding of the world shaped by ideas (whether those ideas be false or illusory or not), but it generates practical and material expression in the world. By conceiving of ideology in this way I hope to clarify how our ideas not only shape our experience and how our experience shapes our ideas, but I also hope to demonstrate how we understand the world to be more than our conceptual thinking or mentalistic rationality; ideology is also processual, embodied, and experiential. We touch, feel, sense, and enact our ideology. Understanding my experience of the weigh-in, then, requires understanding the feminist ideology that has over time come to shape my experience of the world. Understanding the performativity of my bodily transformation entails understanding the context wherein that performance and that ideology is enacted.

Woman as Body

Several contemporary theorists have explored how the binary oppositions of male/female, mind/body, culture/nature, and subject/object operative within a modernist epistemology function hierarchically and how social power and positive value are linked to the first of these paired terms. For example, in a critique of these reigning modernist hierarchies, Conquergood ("Rethinking Ethnography") appraises the cultural and historical devaluation of the body and the concomitant appreciation of the mind. He states "the body and the flesh are linked with the irrational, unruly, and dangerous—certainly an inferior realm of experience to be controlled by the higher powers of reason and logic" ("Rethinking Ethnography," 180). Other theorists have revealed how these dualisms are fundamentally gendered and how women are culturally defined by their bodies, denied subjectivity, and are associated with the lesser domain of nature.[2] Denaturalizing these dualisms has been an effective feminist strategy for fostering social and philosophical reevaluation of women's social position (cf. Hekman, *Gender and Knowledge,* 5–9). To this end, a number of feminists have directed their critical attention to how women are culturally perceived and understood in terms of their bodies.

The power through which women have been defined in terms of their bodies is palpably experienced by women through the material effects and social practices constraining their agency. John Berger concisely grasps the differences in cultural perceptions of representations of men and women in art and advertising in the following way:

> Women are depicted in quite a different way from men—not because the feminine is different from the masculine—but because the "ideal" spectator is always assumed to be male and the image of the woman is designed to flatter him. If you have any doubt that this is so, make the following experiment. Choose. . . an image of a traditional nude. Transform the woman into a man.. . . . Then notice the violence which that transformation does. Not to the image, but to the assumptions of the likely viewer. (*Ways of Seeing*, 64)

Given that it was 1972 when he wrote these words, the heteronormative assumption operative in his statement can perhaps be forgiven. Nevertheless, Berger insightfully identifies a significant aspect of women's being-in-the-world: It has historically been socially more acceptable for women's bodies to be looked at than men's. Moreover, it has been men who have historically done the looking. This aspect of women's situation was notably and epigrammatically termed by Laura Mulvey as women's "to-be-looked-at-ness," a condition, she argues, that is enforced by the primacy of the "male gaze" ("Visual Pleasure," 11). The male gaze reinforces men's subject position while it simultaneously positions woman as object, specifically as sexual object. In the late 1970s Berger keenly encapsulated the situation in the statement "men act, and women appear" (*Ways of Seeing*, 61). More recently, Susan Bordo suggests that even with the influx of images of men that invite the gaze, the situation for women "has changed very little since Berger came up with his formula" ("Beauty," 141). She adds ruefully, "I never dreamed that 'equality' would move in the direction of men worrying *more* about their looks rather than women worrying less" ("Beauty," 146, original emphasis). While women may not be as alone as they once were in the specular economy, which seemingly objectifies some bodies and not others, cultural perceptions about the differences between women and men in terms of their representations and their collective cultural clout generally continue. For example, Bordo points out how images of men that may invite the gaze are still quite often images of men *doing* some activity whereas women remain the passive object of men's gaze ("Beauty," 139–41). Men act, even while we are invited to watch; women continue to simply appear.

Women's sexual objectification and the social injustice conditioning women's experience has also been considered by feminist theorists who do not work from the psychoanalytic perspective from which Mulvey derived her ideas. Sandra Lee Bartky notes how the process of sexual objectification occurs when a woman's "sexual parts or sexual functions are separated out from the rest of her personality and reduced to the status of mere instruments or else regarded as if they were capable of representing her" ("On Psychological Oppression," 26). Sexual objectification is a process of dehumanization for it "leads to the identification of those who undergo it with what is both human and not quite human—the body" (Bartky, "On Psychological Oppression," 30).

Appropriate female embodiment is mandated by the dominant culture's expectations; simply any body will not do. In order to escape social and cultural stigmatization, women's bodies are generally required to be small, delicate, attractive, and slim. Rosalind Coward observed in 1987 that the ideal feminine form "connotes powerlessness" and as such implicitly supports the imbalance of power between the sexes (*Female Desire,* 41). Since the late 1980s the ideal seems to have expanded somewhat to require that women not only be slim but that they also be fit; increasingly bodily firmness including some muscle, but not so much muscle as to appear mannish and therefore genuinely threatening to men, is the ideal to which women are held. Conversely, Susie Orbach's work with overweight women suggests that a kind of power unavailable to those women who attempt to conform to the slim feminine ideal may attach to large women who remain unapologetic for the space they assume (*Fat Is a Feminist Issue,* 76). Moreover, some of the women in Orbach's study report that being overweight provides them with a kind of "sexual protection" (*Fat Is a Feminist Issue,* 76). They report that they can more easily escape sexual objectification and avoid the fearful task of dealing with their sexual desires (*Fat Is a Feminist Issue,* 76–77). Of course, it is arguable whether or not these tactics of avoidance, escape, or protection through being overweight are indeed strategies for empowerment; nevertheless, both Orbach and Coward seem to suggest that large and/or overweight women somehow reside outside the cultural meanings of femininity and that their status as outsiders in some way has the potential to subvert cultural norms. Similarly, organizations like the National Association to Advance Fat Acceptance (NAAFA)[3] and Overeaters Anonymous endeavor to subvert cultural norms and resist social abjectification by encouraging members to accept themselves and believe that "it's all right to be fat" (Millman, *Such a Pretty Face,* 4). Indeed the NAAFA membership consider themselves to be a "human rights organization" trying to change social and cultural perceptions as well as to promote legislation that will "end discrimination based on body size" (NAAFA's website at www.naafa.org).

While there may be some large women who experience their self-performance as a defiance of cultural standards and who experience this defiance as both empowering and subversive, it is arguable whether or not they can truly escape cultural meanings. Bordo states that

> Even in the second half of the twentieth century, beauty remains a prerequisite for female success. In fact, in an era characterized by some as "post-feminist," beauty seems to count more than it ever did before, and the standards for achieving it have become more stringent, more rigorous, than ever. ("Beauty," 144)

Typically, requirements for appropriate female embodiment are so rigidly dictated and enforced that failure to comply constitutes a breach of social norms. Punishments are often vigorously enacted upon violating women. Even members of NAAFA who find a "comfortable home among their own" at the social gatherings created by the organization, still suffer recrimination in the "outside world" (Millman, *Such a Pretty Face,* 8–9; cf. NAAFA website). Marcia Millman's book *Such a Pretty Face: Being Fat in America* amply illustrates through a collection of personal narratives the negative social and psychological effects that can be experienced by overweight women. One female NAAFA member ends her narrative in which she recounts numerous instances of social censure by saying, "Most of the people in NAAFA are not happy—we would prefer to be thin if we could" (13).

Studies by Berscheid and Walster, by Kaczorowski, and by Patzer, although they only occasionally focus on how gender affects perception, have demonstrated that physical attractiveness positively correlates to social power both in terms of interpersonal prestige and financial reward. Findings, such as those by Kaczorowski, that people who are considered attractive earn incomes 75 percent higher on average than people considered unattractive illustrate the gravity of social penalization endured by the "unattractive."[4] This finding illustrates the material advantage and social privilege granted to those people deemed to accord with accepted standards of beauty. Clearly, the overweight have what Erving Goffman would call a "stigmatized," "spoiled," or "discredited" identity (*Stigma,* 4). Insofar as women are defined by their bodies, the social stakes for social advancement or censure are therefore particularly high for women. The most important and compelling standard for feminine embodiment is being slim. These stakes compel overweight women to engage in strategies of concealment or correction designed to manage how others perceive them. While there may be many reasons for a person's obesity (for example, genetics or pathology), Millman notes that being overweight is generally assumed to be an intentionally incurred condition. Moreover, overweight women are "stereotypically viewed as unfeminine, in flight from sexuality, antisocial, out of control, hostile, aggressive" (Millman, *Such a Pretty Face,* xv; cf.

Spitzack, *Confessing Excess,* 25). While there are, of course, men who are concerned about their weight, it is surely not surprising, given this series of negative attributions for overweight women, that concern with weight loss is primarily a woman's concern (Bayrd, *The Thin Game,* 33, 37; Millman, *Such a Pretty Face,* xiv). Given that "90 percent of those dieting will gain all their weight back, or more, within 2 years" permanent weight loss is something of an elusive ideal (U.S. Congress, House, 2; cf. NAAFA website). As women embark on a cycle of diet and despair in which weight is lost and regained, a "tyranny of slenderness"[5] ensues that exacerbates a woman's desperation with every repeated failure and encourages her to try anything in order to change her shape (Spitzack, *Confessing Excess,* 15). Thus, failure to comply with cultural dictates for female embodiment may produce socially incurred punishments; moreover, the potential severity of these punishments, that is to say, the threat of them alone, virtually ensures that women themselves monitor and discipline their bodies.

Disciplining Women's Bodies

In the weeks before Valentine's day, the sign at a local women-only gym proclaimed, "Give the Best Gift of All—A New Body." Implicitly the gym was touting memberships as gifts to those women deemed to need a place where they could work the "old" body into a "new" one. Of course, while it is impossible to exercise a body into a bona fide "new" body, the benefit promised in the message is obviously not just attained with *any* "new" shape. Through the gift of a membership, the woman is promised the help of experts and technology and a place where she may discipline her body into that which is culturally approved for women. Contemporary trends and media images clarify that besides being small and slim, the ideal female form should have almost no body fat and be contoured with toned muscle. Achieving this "new" body—the culturally approved body—would be the "best" gift to receive because, after all, attaining it would release the overweight woman from the social and personal censure that binds her to that stigmatized status. Of course, the desire for that liberation is precisely what motivates people to sign up for a gym membership, a weight-loss program, or other commercial enterprise designed to capitalize on the transformation of body size. This liberation is bought at the cost of great disciplining. The discourse on inappropriate body size is often accompanied by the taken-for-granted assumption that the body is unruly and in need of disciplining and that we are helpless to control it on our own. For example, in the city where I live a local plastic surgeon's advertisement boldly proclaims that they are in the business of "Restoring Cosmetic Order." They state that they "expertly put your body back where it belongs after it has wandered off."

Aside from invasive surgical procedures, the two most common activities suggested for "successfully" altering one's body shape are diet and exercise. How these practices of diet and exercise are culturally mandated through discursive power and real or anticipated punishments for failure to comply, as well as how women's bodies are disciplined—often by women themselves—form the focus of the work of a number of feminist cultural critics.

Gaining their inspiration from Michel Foucault, these feminists consider how "discipline produces subjected and practised bodies, 'docile' bodies" (*Discipline and Punish,* 138). In sympathy with Foucault's metaphoric invocation of Jeremy Bentham's panopticon, feminist cultural critics likewise locate the mechanism of women's oppression "not chiefly through physical restraint and coercion, . . . but through individual self-surveillance and self-correction to norms" (Bordo, "Introduction," 27). The argument follows that like inmates under the gaze of a panopticon who monitor their behavior on the belief rather than the certainty they are being watched, women objectify and police themselves by internalizing the gaze of an abiding male judge. Bartky clarifies the process in the following:

> Knowing that she is to be subjected to the cold appraisal of the male connoisseur and that her life prospects may depend on how she is seen, a woman learns to appraise herself first. The sexual objectification of women produces a duality in feminine consciousness. The gaze of the Other is internalized so that I myself become at once seer and seen, appraiser and the thing appraised. ("Narcissism, Femininity, and Alienation," 38)

The feminist cultural critique goes on to note how self-objectification can in extreme cases develop into an obsession with physical appearance. Bordo argues that "arising out of and reproducing normative feminine practices of our culture," eating disorders such as anorexia and bulimia, which afflict certain sectors of women with alarming frequency, are "practices which train the female body in docility and obedience to cultural demands" ("Introduction," 27). When they enact these obsessive-compulsive behaviors associated with food, women submit to the cultural demands for disciplined female embodiment, disfiguring their bodies, depleting their vitality, and even risking death.

This debilitating process re-creates women as "docile" bodies, reproducing the prevailing and oppressive system of what Bordo has called, "gender ideology" ("Hunger as Ideology," 110). She argues that gender ideology is defined and perpetuated by commercially generated images of women that reinforces "gender difference and gender inequality" ("Hunger as Ideology," 110). It is this generally unquestioned and prevailing thought regime that compels so many women on a never-ending process of self-inflicted mortifications such as dieting, surgery, and over-exercise. The interconnection between consumer culture and the disciplined body is a widely explored topic by feminist theorists and others.[6] For example, Bordo affirms this connection by stating that eating disorders arise at the "intersection of patriarchal culture and post-industrial capitalism" ("Introduction," 32). Moreover, Mike Featherstone notes that commercial advertising "helped to create a world in which individuals are made to become emotionally vulnerable, constantly monitoring themselves for bodily imperfections which could no longer be regarded as natural" ("The Body in Consumer Culture," 175). Furthermore, consumer culture produces the conditions by which the seemingly contradictory impulses for discipline and hedonism combine to create the desire for "an acceptable appearance and [for] the release of the body's expressive capacity" (Featherstone, "The Body in Consumer Culture," 171). While some women may argue that exploring the creative and decorative potential of their bodies enables them to experience a kind of empowerment or enjoyment by virtue of their bodies, cultural critics counter that these responses are more attributable to the effects of sociocultural imperatives, media saturation, and enculturation than individual creativity and choice.

In sum, feminist cultural critics generally dismantle the neat modernist separation of body from culture by rendering the body as principally a site of cultural mediation. Ideology is regarded as being both inscribed upon and constituted by bodies; thus, oppressive regimes governing women's embodiment are simultaneously enacted upon women and enacted by women themselves in order that they comply with the cultural demands for appropriate female embodiment.

The Personal Is Political

While admittedly there are many feminisms, one collective effort of a broadly construed feminism is to render apparent women's sociocultural position by making women's disempowerment evident. Yet in a statement reminiscent of de Beauvoir's pithy descriptor of women, Bartky has stated, "to be a feminist, one has first to become one" ("Toward a Phenomenology of Consciousness," 11). Commonly referred to as "consciousness raising," this process of "profound personal transformation" entails self-reflexivity and the development of solidarity with other women ("Toward a Phenomenology of Consciousness," 11). According to Bartky, this transformative experience "goes far beyond that sphere of human activity we regard ordinarily as 'political'"; indeed it manifests itself in everyday performances of self:

> In the course of undergoing the transformation to which I refer, the feminist changes her behavior: She makes new friends; she responds differently to people and events; her habits of consumption change; sometimes she alters her living arrangements or, more dramatically, her whole style of life. ("Toward a Phenomenology of Consciousness," 11)

Becoming a feminist, then, is embodying the maxim "the personal is political." This aphorism, considered so important that Bartky calls it a "prime theoretical contribution of contemporary feminist analysis of women's oppression," consists of recognizing that

> the subordination of women by men is pervasive, that it orders the relationship of the sexes in every area of life, that a sexual politics of domination is as much in evidence in traditionally private spheres of the family, ordinary social life, and sexuality as in the things we do in the traditionally public spheres of government and the economy. The belief that the things we do in the bosom of the family or in bed are either "natural" or else a function of the personal idiosyncracies of private individuals is held to be an "ideological curtain that conceals the reality of women's systematic oppression."[7] (Bartky, "Feminine Masochism," 45)

Although becoming a feminist may occur in many ways and may result in various ways of being, it is surely evident that becoming a feminist influences the way a woman enacts her everyday self-performance. Indeed, as my own feminist consciousness developed, my acceptance of certain pervasive beliefs about gender, images of women, and gendered activities changed. I became less willing to take these normative assumptions for granted. Given feminism(s)' dual purpose—the intellectual endeavors of theorizing and critiquing women's social position on the one hand, and political activism on the other—becoming a feminist means, as Jane English has stated, that "fundamental attitudes *and* personal relationships must also be affected" ("Introduction," 3, emphasis added). Thus, for feminists, how we understand the world *and* what we do in the world are personally significant as well as politically exigent.

Femininity, with all of its connotations of "niceness," "frivolity," and "contrivance," has been revealed to be a social construction perpetuating women's subordination and has come in for special scrutiny by feminists (Brownmiller, *Femininity*, 16–17). When a woman participates in an act of femininity some feminists suggest that she is "male-identified" or that her consciousness is not fully raised.[8] Moreover, since acts of femininity are regarded by some feminists as actions that appease men and "perpetuate inequality between the sexes," the politics of the personal urge feminists to resist engaging in them (Brownmiller, *Femininity*, 19). The clarity with which Bartky articulates how femininity is both a social construction and how performing femininity is politically invested merits quoting her at length in two separate passages:

> Now the transformation of oneself into a properly feminine body may be any or all of the following: a rite of passage into adulthood; the adoption and celebration of a particular aesthetic; a way of announcing one's economic level and social status; a way to triumph over other women in the competition for men or jobs; or an opportunity for massive narcissistic indulgence. The social construction of the feminine body is all of these things, but it is at base discipline, too, and discipline of the unegalitarian sort. . . . [T]he imperative to be "feminine" serves the interest of domination. This is a lie to which all concur: Making up is merely artful play; one's first pair of high-heeled shoes is an innocent part of growing up and not the modern equivalent of foot-binding. ("Foucault," 75)

And in the following, Bartky articulates how women become habituated to self-surveillance and the disciplining of the body through complicitous enactments of femininity:

> The woman who checks her makeup half a dozen times a day to see if her foundation has caked or her mascara run, who worries that the wind or rain may spoil her hairdo, who looks frequently to see if her stockings have bagged at the ankle, or who, feeling fat, monitors everything she eats, has become, just as surely as the inmate of Panopticon, a self-policing subject, a self committed to a relentless self-surveillance. This self-surveillance is a form of obedience to patriarchy.[9] It is also a reflection in woman's consciousness of the fact that she is under surveillance in ways that he is not, that whatever else she may become, she is importantly a body designed to please or to excite. . . . Hence, a tighter control of the body has gained a new control over the mind. ("Foucault," 80–81)

Becoming a feminist, as the preceding section suggests, is a process in which taken-for-granted cultural scripts are interrogated and, in time, replaced with politically savvy feminist performances of self. Refusing to perform femininity is a strategy that some feminists enact to assert their agency and resist domination. Through overt enactments that oppose cultural expectations for feminine embodiment, these feminists refuse the abjectification the status quo would foist on them. Yet when a feminist engages in acts of femininity—such as enacting weight reduction—it is presumed that she is allowing the status quo to prevail by her apparent complicity. Furthermore, complying with these dominant expectations is believed to subjugate her will as she is presumed to struggle in her efforts. Thus she renders her commitment to feminism suspect.

Reading the Weigh-In through a Feminist Cultural Perspective

The insights of the feminist cultural critique offer one interpretation of my experience of the Weight Watchers' weigh-in as a public site where cultural expectations for female embodiment are socially evaluated and reinforced. The Weight Watchers' weigh-in is a public event yet tremendous care is taken to ensure that only the member and the leader learn the member's weight. While the appropriateness of a woman's embodiment is a socially negotiated and evaluated matter, a woman's actual weight is commonly regarded as a private matter, something we rarely discuss and never with strangers. Yet the Weight Watchers' leader, by virtue of her role as an official of the organization, has the authority to assess my embodiment even though she is little more than a stranger to me. The social taboo against making my weight public is simultaneously maintained and broken: The information is kept secret from the other members but it is openly acknowledged between the leader and myself. Thus, in the practice of the weighing-in the leader and I reassert cultural expectations and simultaneously perpetuate the evaluative and objectifying process of an internalized male gaze.

I have depicted the weigh-in as a liminal time, a point of arrest from everyday life. As such, the weigh-in is a time in which I make my body present to myself and explore how I experience my embodied being. The feminist critique augments that understanding by clarifying how the weigh-in perpetuates self-surveillance. This personal scrutiny of my body is not just a part of the weighing-in procedure, rather it is fundamental to the entire weight-loss process. Judgment and surveillance are disciplining practices encouraged through my relationship with the leader, the other Weight Watchers' members in the room, and to the scale.

Clearly the cultural ideal for slender embodiment guides my judgments for I state that I sense "liberty" in my body as I compare myself to the other women, women whom I take to be much larger than I. Although I am disappointed by what I regard as a minimal amount of weight loss, the leader encourages me. Of course, while she may indeed have a genuine desire to see me succeed at what I am attempting to do, her encouragement clearly benefits her for professional reasons as it helps to keep me a member. As Weight Watchers is a commercial organization it is founded upon the kind of "gender ideology" that Bordo indicts for perpetuating and capitalizing on gender inequality. The leader's efforts prompt me to continue to discipline my body.

Yet as it is the scale that functions as the final authority, my "success" or "failure" is not fully arbitrated by the leader or myself. Whatever experiential understandings of my body I have, they are muted and trivialized in the glare of the scale's power. The numerical value of my weight and its presumption of objective truth become the defining arbiter of my progress toward cultural conformity. We tacitly accept the cultural standard that small and implicitly powerless female bodies are the appropriate measures for the performance of women's weight loss.

This feminist cultural critique helps us understand women's social disempowerment and how women's bodies are used in the maintenance of contemporary regimes of power. Feminism(s)' significant social criticism is helpful in creating the critical space where such oppression may begin to be dismantled. Yet *how* women actually experience their embodiment and whether or not the way they perform femininity actually contributes to their disempowerment falls out from the feminist cultural argument. How then does embodied experience, specifically my embodied experience accord with this feminist perspective?

Lived Experience and Ideological Affect

The Political Is Personal

Susan Bordo provides an extensive examination of the cultural dictates exploiting and confining women's bodies (*Unbearable Weight*). Significantly, in the introduction to her book, the only time where she foregrounds her experience, Bordo announces that she "lost twenty-five pounds through a national weight-loss program" ("Introduction," 30). She notes how her personal choice to do something that seemingly supports cultural standards appears to contradict her politics:

> although my weight loss has benefited me in a variety of ways, it has also diminished my efficacy as an alternative role model for my female students. I used to demonstrate the possibility of confidence, expressiveness, and success in a less than adequately normalized body. Today, my female students may be more likely to see me as confirmation that success comes only from playing by the cultural rules. ("Introduction," 31)

Yet despite the meanings that may attach to her behavior, Bordo nevertheless tries to carve a performative space where personal choice and politics may coexist, however uneasily:

> Even though my choice to diet was a conscious and "rational" response to the system of cultural meanings that surround me (not the blind sub-

> mission of a "cultural dope"[10]), I should not deceive myself into thinking that my own feeling of enhanced personal comfort and power means that I am not servicing an oppressive system. ("Introduction," 31)

While she advocates a "healthy skepticism about the pleasures and powers" that apparent cultural conformity can offer, Bordo nevertheless ends her discussion with the following question: "since when has the feminist critique of normalizing beauty practice ever been directed against individuals and their choices?" ("Introduction," 31). Perhaps Bordo is correct that the analytic purpose of feminist thought did not intend for there to be repercussions against individual women. However, I want to respond to her question by suggesting that the political purpose of feminist thought surely puts the spotlight on every woman's performance of self. When the personal became political, the political became personal.

Daphne Patai and Noretta Koertge's book *Professing Feminism: Cautionary Tales from the Strange World of Women's Studies* is filled with personal narratives by feminists detailing the intolerance some feminists display toward other feminists when political strategies and personal performances appear not to mesh. For example, one of Patai and Koertge's interviewees describes how some feminists stomp their feet in women's studies and feminist courses in order to drown out voices of people, including the teacher, who articulate feminist viewpoints other than their own (14). Another interviewee recounts how a "kind of surveillance and a kind of mapping" goes on among feminists that often results in "devastating character assassination" (205). On a personal note, I recall presenting a scholarly paper about my weight-loss experience with Weight Watchers after which another feminist suggested that I had been "brainwashed" by the organization. She thereby impugned both my scholarship and my capacity for agency. When the personal is political, the political becomes personal for it becomes difficult to separate the person from the position. In my description of the weigh-in, I note my uneasiness in telling others that I was a member of Weight Watchers and that I was trying to lose weight. I stated that "I worry that my commitments to feminism may be brought under suspicion." Clearly, such concerns are not fantastic for when I declared my affiliation with the organization when I presented that paper, my scholarship as well as my person were made suspect.

The context of critique from feminists and others conditions my experience of the Weight Watchers' weigh-in. In my description of the weigh-in I keep a distance between myself and the other members and organizational representatives. I state that "even though we are together, we are all alone." While I experience some solidarity with the other women as we stand together semi-disrobed, I also worry that the women more overweight than I will feel I am not "'legitimately' overweight." The tensive ground I claim between not being entirely willing to admit that I am a member and not feeling entirely entitled to be a member may be the most comfortable space I can claim given the alternatives: On the one hand I fear being a hypocrite by embodying desires that contradict feminist principles; on the other hand as I sense "liberty in my body as I compare myself to these other more overweight women," I am surely admitting to the "pleasures and powers" that being in accord with the cultural mandate for female embodiment provide. The contested position in which I find myself is surely akin to the space Bordo seeks. Aware of both the cultural mandate that I be slim—which presumably at least in part compels me to lose weight—and the schism this compunction produces between myself and my political commitment to feminism, I feel my body to be doubly inscribed by overlapping and competing authoritative cultural "texts." Ideologically imbued affect inflects my performance of self. For example, one point where I allow myself to experience liberation with my body occurs at the point I seem to put my feminism to one side, embrace the cultural standard for women's embodiment at the expense of my solidarity with other women, and see myself as having a slimmer body than the other women at the weigh-in. This sense of "liberation" therefore comes at the cost of adopting an ugly competitive stance toward other women through embracing the cultural norms.

The feminist cultural critique clarifies how being a female and being overweight results in punishments for offending women. Similarly, performing a feminist identity mandates doing acts that are regarded as politically effective in challenging if not dismantling the system of oppression that produces those punishments, rather than doing acts that potentially reassert women's oppression. Thus, on an interpersonal level at the very least, social sleights, if not actual punishments, may be enacted upon "offending" feminists by other feminists. The fat feminist who tries to lose weight in order to escape the social abjection she experiences by being overweight is potentially rendered abject by other feminists who regard her weight loss as a performative example of her complicity with cultural standards for female embodiment. During the weigh-in I am poised between these possibilities for abjectification.

Refusing Abjection

To be sure, the feminist refusal to adhere to cultural standards is a way to erode the potency that these standards have for the demeaning act of assigning social worth to women on the basis of their embodiment. Nevertheless, large women who enact their being in defiance of cultural standards still do not, in general, escape the social censure their status attracts. In order to not be seen to be "servicing an oppressive system" should feminists therefore be overweight? When a woman endeavors to lose weight, even if she is not obsessional, the act appears to contravene feminist politics for it is regarded as an action that supports the standards of female beauty.[11]

Some feminists argue against contemporary standards of female beauty by citing cultures where large female embodiment is revered (cf. Bordo, "Hunger as Ideology," 102–03); however, doing so only serves to demonstrate the contingency, if not perverseness, of cultural values. Were the standard reversed so that large female embodiment was the ideal, the exclusion and debilitating effects propagated by standards of beauty would, I suggest, nevertheless prevail. Then, might not the feminist critique shift to those women seeking larger bodies in order to conform to that culture's standard of attractiveness? A contemporary example may support my point: NAAFA is an organization meant to "call attention to the exclusion, exploitation, and psychological oppression of fat people" (Millman, *Such a Pretty Face,* 4). Additionally, "fat admirers," those people—typically men at NAAFA gatherings—who are more often than not of average size and who are attracted to overweight people—typically women at NAAFA gatherings—also find a comfortable refuge at the organization's social events. In Millman's book, female NAAFA members complain that only the really large women find dance partners and that "those who weigh under 250 pounds are seemingly at a disadvantage" (*Such a Pretty Face,* 3).

Disrupting the economy of oppression that standards of beauty promote will take more than simply inverting the standards. While it may be a useful strategy for overweight women to disavow the cultural abjection they experience, in general their abjection is not eradicated in the process. Thus, the feminist argument against overweight women endeavoring to lose weight is, in my view, most effective when it is confined to a focus on the debilitating effects of female obsession with weight. How some women are compelled to conform to standards of beauty at all cost surely merits discussion and activism. Obsession notwithstanding, a politics based upon conformity to some feminist political standard of embodiment is too simple. It would fail to accommodate a more nuanced examination of resistance strategies, those strategies potentially capable of subverting normalized readings of women's bodies. I will return to my description of my experience to explore what other alternative strategies of resistance appear within it; however, first I consider performances by others that are paradoxically subversive in that they too employ conformity to cultural standards of female body size to enact their resistance to those standards.

Cindy Jackson: Giving Her Audience What It Wants and "Pushing Buttons"

Clearly there are many slim feminists who model strength, success, and political dedication. One notable example is Gloria Steinem. In order to write her article "I Was a Playboy Bunny," she used the fact that her body accorded with cultural standards to surreptitiously secure a job at the Playboy club and ultimately launch a searing feminist critique. That article forcefully advanced a feminist political agenda by bringing attention to the exploitation of women in that line of work.[12] Yet what should we make of women who perform femininity not as a subterfuge as in the Steinem example, but as a method for challenging oppressive cultural norms?

Cindy Jackson transformed not only her body size and shape but also her face by undergoing twenty-eight surgical operations (Jackson, Home Page). Modeling her transformation on an examination of the female form in art, theories of proportion, and that idealized image of girlhood, Barbie, Jackson, now in her mid-forties, has spent the last twenty years repeatedly under the knife ("Becoming Barbie"). Her operations include three face-lifts, cheekbone implants, two nose jobs, several dermabrasions to remove wrinkles, and liposuctioning the fat from her entire body. Unlike others who undergo plastic surgery, Jackson has built her reputation and an apparently lucrative business on her technologically aided transformation. She markets books and a video detailing her experience of becoming a "living doll" and outlining her rationale for doing what she has done (Jackson, Home Page, *Living Doll*).[13] What distinguishes her activities from others who have had cosmetic surgery is the fact that Jackson capitalizes on her transformation and has essentially parlayed her surgeries into a successful career. She claims throughout an interview on ABCs *20/20*, and on the pages of her website, that more than her body was transformed when she went under the knife; plastic surgery transformed her career, her lifestyle, and her entire way of being ("Becoming Barbie"; Jackson, Home Page).

Jackson proclaims that her experience is living proof of the correlation between looks and success.[14] In short, designing and creating her new self-performance has been an act of meticulous analysis of the cultural audience. On the *20/20* interview, Jackson admits that she was not unattractive prior to the procedures and counters any argument that she is motivated by an obsession with her looks by citing the cultural abjection awaiting any woman who is less than beautiful: "I was always satisfied with the gifts I had. It was the world that would not reward me for them." When correspondent Bob Brown asks if she is being cynical she retorts:

> I don't think it's being cynical. I think it's being realistic. It might not be politically correct. It might not be the way we'd design the world if we were God, but that's the way it is. Why fight it? Why deny it? And why blame me? It was like this when I got here. ("Becoming Barbie")

Her philosophy, which apparently disavows the possibility of positive cultural change and which appears to culminate in a sort of postmodern version of the

Serenity Prayer, admits to a recalcitrant world and an ameliorative science: If we can't be God and change culture, then let us change what technology enables us to, and let us have the realism to know the difference. For her, cultural abjection can only be escaped by conforming to cultural standards.

Moreover, she refuses feminist abjectification in the following exchange with Brown:

> BB: But if someone who was in the feminist movement said you shouldn't do this to your body just to please a man . . .?
> CJ: (interrupting) I didn't do it to please men. I did it to taunt them.
> BB: Is it a form of revenge?
> CJ: Possibly. Success is the best revenge, isn't it? ("Becoming Barbie")

Although earlier in the interview she sarcastically states, "Oh, it's terrible to be treated like a beautiful woman," she denies that she is motivated to appease men. Rather, she claims her actions have been motivated by the need to succeed. Moreover, she claims that she is not just manipulating her appearance, she is also manipulating men. To be sure, nowhere in the interview does Jackson claim to be a feminist. Many feminists would cringe at her logic, which is predicated upon and perpetuates stereotypically negative feminine attributes. Like the archetypical feminine symbol, the spider, Jackson trades on a kind of "mate and kill" behavior and appears to revel in the power she might have over males (cf. Hopcke, *Men's Dreams,* 36–37).

Yet, even if using feminine wiles and engaging in manipulation and revenge supports a prevalent negative female stereotype, Jackson is nevertheless employing a common strategy of resistance. James C. Scott's *Domination and the Arts of Resistance* outlines several strategies the dominant and the dominated use to negotiate their positions. History is rife with examples of the powerless adopting a "strategic pose" in order to make those in power feel secure in their position while subversive activity was carried out behind their backs (Scott, *Domination and the Arts of Resistance*, xii). The "step and fetch it" slave or domestic servant, feigning stupidity and displaying obsequiousness either to survive or to prevent discovery of some subversive activity, comes to mind. While I do not wish to collapse differences between diverse oppressed groups, Scott's claim rests on the possibility of strategic similarities among subordinate groups. Like the posturing slave, Jackson appears motivated by a similar need to "reproduce hegemonic appearance,"[15] that is to say, to appear to act in accordance with cultural expectations, while she is nevertheless quite conscious of her ulterior motives:

> I know that they [men] are responding exactly the way I have designed myself to evoke. They're giving me the desired response. It's just reinforcing

> what I did. I'm pushing buttons. And men are very easily manipulated by looks. It's frightening, really. It's so easy. . . . You push button A, you get B response. ("Becoming Barbie")

Additionally, it is important to note that like the slave example, aside from being deployed as a subterfuge, appearing to act in accordance with cultural expectations may have the counterproductive effect of reasserting negative stereotypes.

According to Scott, the dominant and the dominated have both "hidden" and "public transcripts." The "hidden transcript" is a kind of discourse oppressed groups typically engage in amongst themselves, which they conceal from the powerful. Distinguished from the public transcripts, the hidden transcript "represents a critique of power spoken [and enacted] behind the back of the dominant" (Scott, *Domination and the Arts of Resistance,* xii). The hidden transcript is the more honest expression of the subordinates' perspective. With Jackson, her *public* transcript is perhaps her compliance with the cultural dictates for female embodiment that appears to render her body as a body available for sexual objectification and that thereby seemingly supports men's social power. Her hidden transcript appears to be her self-aggrandizing motives.

Arguably, Jackson is a special class of "oppressed" person. Her position as white and upper-middle class surely affords her privileges denied many other people.[16] Notwithstanding that real and important caveat, my point here is not to debate degrees of disempowerment among groups, but, for the purposes of this argument, to place Jackson within the category of women and acknowledge that she too experiences some oppression by virtue of the general prejudice affecting women. When she claims that she "notice[d] how much easier it was for girls who had [good looks and that] this is what life rewards—the right look," this is a hidden transcript that all women know. What only women considered attractive know, and what is rarely openly acknowledged, is how easy it is to manipulate heterosexual men by means of women's physical appearance. The heresy in Jackson's claim is her apparent open disregard for how her acceptance of the cultural standards and her embodiment of them perpetuates this unjust system. Yet Jackson's hidden transcript is made public through the media attention she courts and an open acknowledgment of her motives. Thus, by making this hidden transcript public, this quintessentially idealized female is the whistle-blower evincing the prejudice against "unattractive" women and publicly challenging the standards that sustain it.

Perhaps because of her privilege or perhaps because of the implication of narcissism and opportunism that pervade her story, Jackson may be easy to dismiss. Noting how a given action's power depends upon the social construction of meaning Scott states:

> How an act . . . is construed is not merely a question of mood, temper, and perceptiveness of the dominant; it is also very much a matter of politics. . . . Thus the refusal to reproduce hegemonic appearances it is not entirely straightforward. The political struggle to impose a definition on an action and to make it stick is frequently at least as important as the action per se. (*Domination and the Arts of Resistance*, 206)[17]

After the interview with Jackson, Bob Brown discussed the story with anchor Barbara Walters who summed up her experience of hearing the story thus: "I don't know whether to say get real or poor soul." Walters then says, "I can see doing your eyes, doing your face, making yourself look better if you want, but to put yourself through months of surgery. . . . I don't know, Bob." During the interview Jackson continually indicts the cultural standards that compelled her to undergo these painful operations: "What I've been through was painful. Yes. But it was not as painful as living my life as a plain, ordinary, aging, Midwestern woman." Yet even though Walters admits that looking "better" by surgery is okay, she won't acknowledge the cultural indictment Jackson repeatedly makes. It would seem the excessiveness of Jackson's actions and the fact that she profits both interpersonally and professionally from her surgical procedures overshadows any political claims Jackson stakes.

Orlan: Making the Audience "Suffer"—"Speaking from My Body to Yours"

Orlan's exploits on the plastic surgeon's table could be regarded as just as excessive as Jackson's, if not more so, even though she has only had a mere nine operations.[18] Unlike Jackson, whose endeavors foreground her personal advancement, politics and art are central to Orlan's surgical transformation. Since 1990 in a project entitled "The Resurrection of St. Orlan: Image/New Image," Orlan has been using her own flesh as her artistic medium to engage in what she calls "Carnal Art" (Rose, "Is It Art?" 86). She works by transforming the operating theater into a multimedia performance space. Barbara Rose describes the performances in the following manner:

> The operation/performances are choreographed and directed by the artist herself and involve music, poetry, and dance. They are costumed, if possible by a famous couturier. Paco Rabanne designed the vestments for the first operation. All the accouterments, including crucifixes and plastic fruit and flowers, are sterilized in accordance with operation room standards as are the photo blow ups of preceding Orlan performances that decorate the operating room. Only state-certified surgeons operate. ("Is It Art?" 85)

These operation/performances are, needless to say, very expensive. To support her work, Orlan charges for the photos and videos that come from them as well as for the "relics" made during the performances, little vials containing some of her flesh and blood siphoned from her during the operations. Her work tests the relationships between body and religion, aesthetics and technology, and social values and politics. Rose epigrammatically sums up her work in this manner: "paradox is her content; subversion is her technique" ("Is It Art?" 83).

The operations are meant to transform Orlan into a living representation of select features found in artistic representations that Orlan believes epitomize the feminine ideal fabricated by male desire: These features are "the nose of a famous, unattributed School of Fountainbleau sculpture of Diana, the mouth of Boucher's Europa, the forehead of Leonardo's Mona Lisa, the chin of Botticelli's Venus and the eyes of Gérome's Psyche" (Rose, "Is It Art?" 85). Furthermore, because liposuction enables her to create the "relics" of her performances, and because liposuction is something that can be conducted away from her face and thereby allow her to speak during the performances, she frequently incorporates it into her performances (Orlan Panel, Performance).

The multi-faceted nature of Orlan's work extends beyond the scope of my interests here. What is salient, however, is how her work challenges and potentially subverts the power that standards of beauty have over cultural readings of women's bodies. In order to displace the potency these standards have, Orlan's strategy is to make the process of her transformation her subject and thereby evoke visceral responses from her audience. At a panel discussion at London's Institute of Contemporary Art entitled "The Body as Site," Orlan presented a seven-minute video containing "rushes" from the fifth and sixth operations.[19] Prior to beginning the tape she warned the audience: "Watching these images, you will suffer. But it is important to know that I am not suffering" ("The Body as Site").[20] Her warning is prophetic, for over the course of the event a couple of incidents occur that clearly reveal the impact the images had upon members of the audience. One of the panelists apparently swooned during the video and throughout the remainder of the discussion, whenever questions were addressed to her, kept referring to her nausea and her inability to regain her composure. After Orlan's presentation the floor was opened to questions from the audience. The first woman up to the microphone began with an attack of Orlan:

> Woman: Can you make sure this gets translated?
> Translator: Yes, I'm doing it right now.
> Woman: You're just the sickest person I have ever come across. And I'm ashamed at the other human beings in this room for clapping that.
> [Translator halts her so she can translate]

Orlan: [in translation] Perhaps we all do and make things that are crazy without being crazy ourselves.

Woman: It's not crazy; it's just crap.

Moderator: [responding to the murmurings beginning to rise in the room] No. I'd like to open up discussion. And we have to respect the diversity of opinion. . . .

Woman: [interrupting] It's not about opinion. I don't see how anything like that can be couched within an aesthetic debate. I don't know how anyone can clap watching that. I find it complete bourgeois excess. All you're doing is just shocking the bourgeoisie.

Other audience member in background: Apparently she's succeeded.

Woman: [backing away from microphone] I'm not bourgeoisie. I'd just like to smack her really hard. ("The Body as Site")

At another panel discussion devoted to Orlan's work, Sarah Wilson, an art historian, recounts how at a show containing videos of Orlan's work, women in Poland fled the room "with genuine shock and horror" (Orlan Panel, Performance). These reactions are precisely what Orlan hopes her work will solicit for she claims: "I like very much images that speak directly to your body. And that is why I wanted to start immediately with the video. So I can speak directly from my body to yours" ("The Body as Site"). Despite her desire to shock, she is clear that her intentions are not simply to shock: "There is no point in shocking just for the sake of it. What really matters is what you do with it" (Orlan Panel, Performance). Indeed, Orlan claims that her intention is to bring the social, the political, and the physical together in her work and "create something that will take the body beyond what it has been so far and for future generations too" ("The Body as Site"), a decidedly subversive intention. While she admits that "feminists are angry with [her] because [she's] using aesthetic surgery," and makes it clear that she is "not against aesthetic surgery," she nevertheless allies herself with feminists when in the same sentence she claims: "I'm against standards of beauty" ("The Body as Site"). While she admits that her work may not redefine the standards of beauty, she avowedly interrogates them: "I want to question the pressure linked to the standards of beauty and why these standards of beauty are so strong that this is how we define who's attractive and who's not" (Orlan Panel, Performance).

While I agree that Orlan's work may not redefine the standards of beauty, it is surely subversive. Exposure to the painful images from her performances and the knowledge of her physical constructedness certainly make it difficult to read her body with a standard sexualized understanding. Rather than developing a strategy of resistance that operates in opposition to women's socially constructed sexualized identity by, for example, refusing to perform femininity, her strategy is to subvert through public acknowledgment of women's already sexualized embodiment, to subvert through demonstratively revealing femininity as construction.

Obviously controversial, Orlan's work is simultaneously critiqued and celebrated.

As Sarah Wilson makes clear, Orlan "is not an exemplary person for French feminism but a recalcitrant, an obstreperous person who disrupts a lot of their practices" (Orlan Panel, Performance). Orlan herself notes the polarities her work evokes by stating simply: "For some my work is revolting, for others it is revolutionary" ("The Body as Site").[21] Perhaps the most significant critique levied at the political claims embedded in Orlan's work comes from those who argue that Orlan "never really made herself ugly" (Orlan Panel, Performance).[22] Orlan, however, rejects this critique: "It's not about improvement or the desire to appear younger. Up to this point I refused face-lifts. It's really about a complete change of image. It's about modifying the image, not about the quality of the image" ("The Body as Site").[23] Moreover, in a discussion about the seventh operation, which was conducted by a female surgeon, Orlan explained that her project is not simply an attempt to conform to accepted standards of beauty. Seeking to put large silicone implants usually used for cheekbones in her brows, Orlan notes that until she found the female surgeon, "no male surgeons would accept to do this because they wanted to keep me 'cute'" ("The Body as Site").

Whether one regards Orlan as simply an opportunist, a misguided artist indulging in "bourgeois excess," or a woman at the figurative and literal cutting edge of gender critique, it is hard to ignore the visceral response exposure to her work evokes. In the foreground of Orlan's work is the processual and temporal nature of embodiment. She claims that the results of the procedures are less important than the process:

> the result is not something that interests me on a day to day basis. What is not so important is whether the transformation is complete, whether it is as impressive as it could be. What really matters is what the work does and which questions we would then have to ask ourselves. (Orlan Panel, Performance)

Unlike Jackson, and other women who go under the knife, for whom the process of transformation is typically a "hidden transcript," Orlan's work unflinchingly demands it be public. In her "Carnal Art Manifesto" she underscores the processual nature and rhetorical purpose of her work by stating: "Carnal Art is not interested in the plastic-surgery result, but in the process of surgery, the spectacle and discourse of the modified body which has become the place of public debate" (Orlan, Home Page). In making her process publicly painful, she challenges the tyranny of beauty standards and the unreflective taken-for-granted assumptions that acts and facts of nature are morally supreme and are or should be beyond human control.

The Possibility of Bodily Transformation as Process Not Product

The process of bodily transformation so conspicuous in Orlan's performances and implied in Jackson's dramatic physical change makes the culture's taken-for-granted product orientation to bodily transformation unmistakably evident. For example, even though Jackson frequently refers to the personal and social benefits that have accrued to her life since making her physical transformation, the focus of the *20/20* interview is on the fact that she made the transformation.[24] The audience is continually provided with before and after photographs silently inviting us to calculate the presumed benefits of the changes she's made. Despite the show's angle, Jackson keeps arguing the significance of how being Barbie-esque alters her day-to-day being-in-the-world. Similarly, in my experience of the weigh-in, the leader and I focus on the body fact of my weight and very little on the process. I am disappointed that I have lost so little in the preceding week, even though I feel more agile. The weigh-in diminishes the importance of the ongoing changes in how I am experienced my being. I note that since I've begun to lose weight I walk differently, with more purpose and dynamism. I also note how my sensory experience of my body is often contradicted by the scale. Though these changes are important to my kinesthetic involvement with the world, and though I have joined Weight Watchers because of my *qualitative* experience with my body (i.e., my "body at this moment" is estranged from "habit body"), the weight-loss process is measured by a *quantitative* measure. A point of arrest is the arbiter of my process. This effacement of my bodily experience is perhaps best appreciated when we consider with paleoanthropologist Maxine Sheets-Johnstone that embodiment may entail a kind of "gnostic tactility," a kind of sensing through the body (*The Roots of Thinking,* 335). When the process of bodily transformation is understood only in terms of achieved results, our faith in the processual day-to-day development of bodily knowing is effaced. Our faith in the mechanical object and its objective measure obscures the epistemic power of experience; it negates how "the living body is more than a thing. . . . It is first and foremost the center of the tactile kinesthetic world" (Sheets-Johnstone, *The Roots of Thinking,* 16). A product-oriented procedure such as the Weight Watchers' weigh-in is, then, a disempowering process. The weigh-in process privileges knowing *that* I weigh a particular amount rather than knowing *how* it is to be at a particular stage in my process of bodily transformation. Thus, I am continually orienting to what I am not yet; the process defines me and I define myself by what I am not. I am positioned then as always already lacking. The weigh-in frames me in the negative, as still in breach of social norms. I continue to be encumbered with the stigma of being overweight given that the weigh-in renders my bodily knowledge mute.

Embodiment is not so much an obtainable thing or a stable position; rather it is a negotiation of a process. Thus, the fact that most people who diet gain back the weight they've lost within two years could be conceived less as a critique of the weigh-loss industry or a comment on the recalcitrance of the body than as an acknowledgment of the perpetual evolution of being. A particular weight is not so much something to be had as it is something one perennially negotiates over time through staying somatically attuned.

The Possibility of a Liberating Discipline

The feminist critique claims that women who engage in the dieting process disempower themselves by submitting to the cultural dictates for female embodiment and by becoming "docile" bodies through intense regimes of discipline. Yet it does not follow that refusing to engage in bodily discipline of any kind will prevent disempowerment. The pursuit of the fat-free body may be the subject of much feminist criticism; however, given that cultural abjection for overweight people is so prevalent and pervasive, I argue that generally there is no such thing as a free fat body, that is, a fat body free from cultural abjectification.

Some feminist cultural critics argue that women are socially disempowered by self-surveillance. Nevertheless, self-surveillance may not always signal the presence of docile acceptance of an internal male judge in a woman's consciousness. In my experience of the weigh-in, as I sense my developing agility and the dynamism in my newly rediscovered walk, the disciplining of my body empowers the development of a positive new self-performance. The reflexivity I have about my body, which may appear to be a kind of debilitating self-surveillance to outsiders, suggests to me a reveling in the gnostic tactility previously dormant in my overweight body and now re-awakened as I feel my "habit body" re-emerge. In a sense, such reflexivity is a remembering of the body. Drew Leder observes how "the body is remembered particularly at times of error. . . . It is precisely because the normal and healthy body largely disappears that direct experience of the body is skewed toward times of dysfunction" (*The Absent Body,* 86). This embodiment Leder calls a "dys-appearing body," to connote a body that is remembered in times of dysfunction and, simultaneously, a body "in the *dys* state, to use the Latinate sense: doubled, away, asunder from itself" (*The Absent Body,* 89). Similarly, Iris Marion Young describes in her depiction of pregnant embodiment, how the body in the "dys" state engages in a "double intentionality" ("Pregnant Embodiment," 165). It entails a process in which "subjectivity splits between an awareness of body and an awareness of aims and projects" ("Pregnant Embodiment," 165). Surely, the self-surveillance women engage in when they experience their embodiment as a breach with social norms is, as per Leder, a body being remembered at times of error. Yet as Young clarifies, the body is also remembered at times of pleasure. Thus, the abject body is an appearing body, a body remembered because it is in the "dys" state. Yet, when a woman loses weight and begins the process of discovering a different more dynamic self-performance, the body is also remembered. It is a body not forgotten and taken for granted, but rather, one remembered through the pleasure of these reawakened dynamics.

Perhaps some feminists would agree with Leder that a "normal and healthy body largely disappears." Thus they may view their argument against self-surveillance as a move toward a healthy absenting of the body. Yet, remembering the body may also be a way to find alternative positive self-performances. The split subjectivity I experience as my body changes does not hinder my developing belief in my capacity to accomplish my ambitions. Rather, the positive changes make me aware of my body and help me focus on my projects and aims, envisioning them now as performative possibilities. Self-surveillance then, is not necessarily always already a negative act. Self-reflection may be beneficial, even empowering. Focusing on the newly apprehended possibilities the changes in my body portend frees me from a rigid product orientation to my body; it frees me from a rigid acceptance of an arbitrary moment of artificial stasis; it frees me, however momentarily, from the cultural dictates. Instead, through mindfulness I focus on being and becoming, on the inevitability of change and the potential for possibilities.

During the weigh-in I note, like Cindy Jackson, how changing my embodiment has altered my experience of the world. Slimming down occasions a renewed vitality and keener sensation with which to engage the world. Similar to the women in Orbach's study who felt cushioned against the world by being overweight, I too experienced being overweight as a kind of insulation. However, unlike the women in Orbach's study, this insulation is not comforting to me. I happily discard the rounded, dull-edged, and guarded experience of being overweight in favor of the angularity of reappearing bones and a renewed contact with the world. I rediscover a dynamic self-performance ready to engage the world rather than hide from it. More than a confirmation of the way our experiences are mediated by cultural meanings, the absence of insulating fat creates a readiness, an opening up to new possibilities for engagement.

What is not apparent in my description of the weigh-in is how slimming down affected others' reception of me. While I note with discomfort how other women in the Weight Watchers' meeting room potentially view me, I only implicitly address the power and privileges that I possess by being slimmer than they. Surely, like Jackson, others treat me differently than they would if I were the size of the women in Millman's study of obesity. Yet as I am a fairly self-assured individual and as that dynamism increases with the loss of weight, I would no doubt be treated differently than would a more guarded, circumspect person. The performance of self emerges from sensory-kinesthetic awareness as well as from negotiating oneself with others. The bodily understandings we have from our own bodies, which are often taken for granted, affect how we understand others. If we consider someone to be lethargic, slow, lugubrious, for example, our apprehension of that individual draws upon our own embodied understandings of that motility. In order to understand that person, I might, for example, associate her or his deportment with how I drag when I wake up, how I feel heavy, and how my mind is not at its most insightful best. Such inferences may further inform how I understand this other person's perspective. Of course, we note surprise when someone contradicts such expectations; and they often are contradicted since motility is not simply the external reflection of some innate being. Yet commonly we use language that reveals our taken-for-granted, if un-nuanced, assumptions that embodiment connotes being: We say a person moves like a gazelle to indicate physical agility and grace, an angular but powerful physicality, and a quickness of spirit. We describe people as sluggish to indicate slowness of both intellect and embodiment. We point out people who are quick to pounce and in so doing draw upon an example from the natural world to describe an individual's attitude. How we present ourselves is always a negotiation of physical capacities and the rhetoric of embodiment. In order to present ourselves in what we deem to be the best possible manner, we scan our capabilities, our possibilities, and how our choices may be interpreted. We all make performance choices in the development of our self-performance, even if we are not as premeditated as Cindy Jackson or go to the lengths she has. Engaging in disciplinary regimes such as the weight-loss process may engender more liberated, vital, and empowering self-performances. Acts that are positively experienced as empowering women should be at the heart of the feminist enterprise.

The Possibility of Bodily Transformation as a Subversive Activity

Women whose bodies accord with the cultural standards for female body size are less apt to be culturally abjectified for their body size than overweight women. Yet such women, especially, of course, young women, may experience the abjection that comes with being sexually objectified. While feminists may try to resist sexual objectification by refusing to perform femininity—in this case, refusing to participate in the disciplinary regimes of weight loss–they may nevertheless be disempowered through doing so. First, social abjectification occurs when a woman fails to comply with the standards for female embodiment, and punishments for this infraction can have, as I've noted, material effects including loss of income and social acceptance. The feminist refusal has thus far been unable to significantly change this social stigma and its material effects. Second, while an overweight woman may not be sexually objectified, she may experience her embodiment as a buffer against the world, as in need of concealment, as insulated, rather than as capable, expressive,[25] and pleasurable. Were she instead to envision her body as one in process, I suggest that possibilities for a more vital self-performance may ensue.

It is easy to trivialize the value of expressive potential as simply narcissistic. Cindy Jackson easily can be construed as not only narcissistic but as self-servingly opportunistic as well. Yet she challenges these easy attributions when she openly declares her intentions and articulates her critique of standards of beauty. No doubt she reinforces the standards of beauty and even invites sexual objectification. But she simultaneously foregrounds her agency and subverts a normative reading of her body by aggressively declaring that she not be taken as an object to be toyed with.[26] However, since personal profit is so central to her performance, and because her transformation overshadows her politics, her performance is less subversive than it might be. Orlan's performance differs in this respect as politics are central to her performance through public displays of the transformative process. Orlan's intentions are declared verbally and in visual displays that palpably impart to her audience the visceral cost of her, and by implication others', transformation. Moreover, as she is conscious throughout the operations, and anything but a passive patient as her gaze is purposefully trained on her observers beyond the lens of the camera, her agency is unmistakably present. She may be a woman culturally defined by her body, as women typically are in Western culture, but it is she, not the surgeons, who orchestrates the drama being played out upon her body. Although their means differ, both Jackson and Orlan challenge the social norms. By making the hidden transcript public, unveiling the process of production, their performances demand that their bodies be reinterpreted outside the dominant cultural meanings. Insofar as their performances reverberate beyond themselves, they cannot legitimately be understood as solely narcissistic and self-indulgent acts. Their performances demand that we think twice about them.

Yet for some members of their audiences, Jackson and Orlan remain pawns of the status quo or victims of "false consciousness." Despite her protests to the contrary, the *20/20* team dismiss Jackson as a misguided woman obsessing about her looks. While Jackson is quick to disavow their assessment of her motives, she is incapable of getting the *20/20* production team to accept her political perspective. They are a recalcitrant audience. She appears to have more success in having her claims accepted when she addresses people with ambitions similar to her own, as she does on her website.

With Orlan, there are those, of course, who doggedly refuse to accept her political (and artistic) claims. By directing her performances toward the arts community, however, Orlan's political claims, nestled as they are within her artistic ambitions,[27] are more readily accepted there than they might be elsewhere. They remain contested even there; however, the power that art has for social critique, and the provisional social dictum that it do so, may prepare her audiences to accept or at least to entertain Orlan's blend of art and politics.

How might we understand the subversive potential of these performances? Like many critically resistant performances, Jackson's, Orlan's, and my own both reinscribe and challenge normalized readings of our bodies, confounding easy acceptance of our political claims. Marvin Carlson cautions that "The central concern of resistant performance arises from the dangerous game it plays as a double-agent, recognizing that in the postmodern world complicity and subversion are inextricably intertwined" (*Performance,* 173). This ambiguity makes it clear that for a critically resistant performer, deft analysis of the audience is of the utmost importance to furthering a subversive end. One way to do this, as Jill Dolan has argued, is to employ flexible notions of identity and subject positions, or "spectorial communities" ("Desire Cloaked in a Trenchcoat," 129). Playing to and against the expectations those spectorial communities hold may help challenge and/or subvert assumptions about gender performativity through, for example, ironic play.

Beyond a strategic use of audience analysis, let me further suggest that two interconnected conditions need to be present in order for the transformation of body size to be subversive. The first concerns reflexivity. The critically resistant performer needs to be reflexive about her being, the cultural and contextual meanings and the reigning systems of oppression within them, as well as how a given audience may interpret her performance. The second condition is that her challenge to the status quo be openly articulated through her body and voice.

Feminism has taught women to be reflexive, to be conscious of the systems of oppression and to question women's participation in sustaining them. That a woman may reinforce dominant values even while she wishes to eradicate them clarifies how robust those values are and how complex it is to perform woman and perform feminist. Performing weight loss without sacrificing feminist ideals begins with awareness, as Bordo has noted, how doing so can be both personally beneficial and politically problematic. But unlike Bordo, I cannot dismiss the idea that the "feminist critique of normalizing beauty practice [has been] directed against individuals and their choices" ("Introduction," 31). I have experienced those indictments and witnessed them directed at others. While not universal, such criticism by feminists is prevalent enough to hinder feminist goals by fostering divisiveness and dispersing critical and political energy.

That conflicts should arise in feminist thought is an unsurprising result of the necessary move in the feminist "third wave"[28] to dislodge the monolithic, white, liberal, and middle-class conception of feminism. Yet embracing multiple conceptions of feminisms has not resulted in respecting performative difference. Of course, there are more feminist corporeal styles than the stereotypical woman in Birkenstocks who does not shave her legs or wear makeup. However, the volatility of response I've already described makes clear the abject otherness to which traditionally feminine feminists are subjected. These critical responses appear to derive from a presumption that a surface inscription of corporeal style is the outward expression of core identity. The *personal* choice of clothes or activity is seen to make a *political* statement about the self, a statement of support or ignorance of the dominant cultural dictate that women be valued on the basis of standard notions of sexual attractiveness.

This logic used by these feminist critics is similar to that used by men who sexually objectify women who act feminine. They too are likewise responding to the surface inscription or corporeal style of traditionally feminine women; in this case, these women's bodies are believed to be constructed for their pleasure. For both the feminist critics and the sexist men, femininity is understood through what Judith Butler has called "primary identification" (*Gender Trouble,* 137); that is, they understand it within the socially constructed original meanings accorded to femininity. Even though femininity "has involved the arrangement of items within a *system* that gives them meaning" (Bordo, "Introduction," 24, emphasis in original), these feminist critics and sexist men fail to grasp it as a construction. Destabilizing that system and denaturalizing the original meanings makes the construction of alternative conceptions of femininity possible and opens the way for more performative choice. Femininity, then, may be regarded, as Butler shows, as one of many possible gender performances (cf. *Gender Trouble,* 128–41).

Femininity conceived as performance challenges assumptions about a woman's commitment to feminism or her desire to appease men. As with my own performance of weight loss, an act of femininity may be performed with a concomitant awareness of feminist theory and the political exigencies that attend on such an action. To take another example, lesbian femmes often wear makeup—a traditionally feminine act—yet their position in a heteronormative culture renders apparent the oppressiveness of that positioning and the taken-for-granted assumptions made about their sexuality. Yet they frequently articulate themselves in ways that challenge negative assumptions about their complicity with patriarchy and/or their commitments to feminism. They consequently wrest their performance of femininity from the primary identifications about femininity. Assessing whether or not a woman wants male sexual attention or whether or not a woman is truly patriarchy's pawn depends upon how a woman articulates herself.

My caveat that a critically resistant performer needs to articulate her intentions brings me to my second condition for an act of femininity to be subversive. The cultural and the feminist notions about feminine feminists are complacent conceptions. When the traditionally feminine appearing feminist resists the meanings accorded her, she challenges presumptive definitions of a feminist subject. She subverts through her ambiguity. She ruptures the system of meanings at the point where it seems most secure. Declaring that her body be read as a challenge to the status quo, despite the assumed stability of the meanings given to femininity, brings focus to her agency. She is a feminist subject who resists a monolithic interpretation of her femininity. She articulates her feminist identity, challenges feminist or cultural abjection, and demands her audience think more deeply by taking account of context. She may be an irritating presence, one not easily assimilated into prior categories. She may be cunning and charming, creatively circumventing and spoofing abjectifying attitudes and conceptions of her. She takes femininity out of the bedroom and makes it public. Hers is not an accepted feminist politic, but step by step, she makes it more difficult for anyone to presume her sexual availability. Incrementally, she makes femininity another possibility for performing feminist woman.

I have traveled a great distance from my experience of weight loss and my experience of the Weight Watchers' weigh-in. I arrive aware that insofar as women's bodies are always already ideologically inscribed, the process of revaluing women's social standing will take more than the micro-politics of performing femininity. Surely, "the metaphysics of culture shift piecemeal and through real, historical changes in relations of power, modes of subjectivity, the organization of life" (Bordo, "Introduction," 41). The possibilities I have explored here are offered in the spirit of encouraging alternative understandings of a feminine feminists' bodily transformation: By focusing on embodiment as a process and by making the act of transformation public, by articulating the pleasures and pitfalls of bodily discipline, and by resisting standard cultural interpretations and feminist misreadings of her body, the feminine feminist may contest and subvert problematic cultural and feminist norms.

CHAPTER THREE

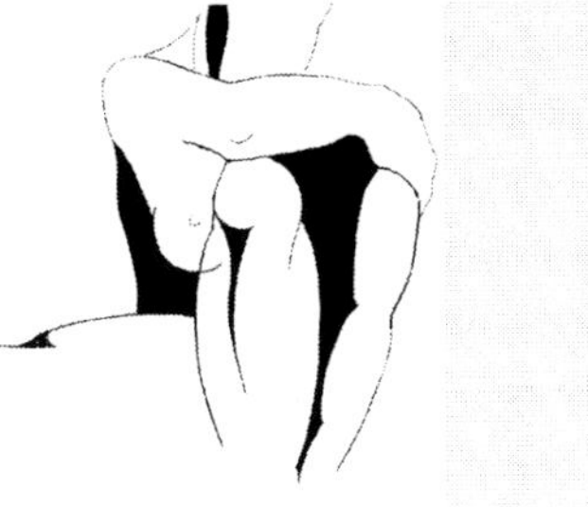

"Would You Do It?": Doing the Scholarly Striptease for Academic Gain

A woman who has no wish to shock or devalue herself socially should live out her feminine situation in a feminine manner; and very often, for that matter, her professional success demands it.

—SIMONE DE BEAUVOIR

Garter. n. An elastic band intended to keep a woman from coming out of her stockings and desolating the country.

—AMBROSE BIERCE

Femininity, it would appear, has vanished.

—KAREN LEHRMAN

Lessons in Femininity, Desire, and Social Acceptability

Lesson One

When Mrs. Bobincheck, chalk in hand, would stretch her arm up to the top of the blackboard in my fifth-grade classroom, her mini-skirt would hike up so far that we could plainly see the extraordinary girth of her thighs and the tops of her panty hose. Her white plastic zip-up boots strained at the seams and the tops were submerged under the visible roll of her fleshy knees. In 1968, fashion was brutal to every woman except Twiggy. And fifth graders are the devil's easy prey. Chris Martin sat to the right of me in the back of the class and would snicker every time our teacher's dress would hike up. I think I had a much misguided crush on Chris and perhaps that was why I was incapable of seeing him for the cretin he was. Marty Pinal, Chris's best friend, sat to the left of me and was too cool to snicker. Instead, in that way that young boys do, he would slyly smile toward Chris and across me with the glancing power of erasure. At the time, I think I wasn't yet fully conscious of the differences in status between boys and girls. Oh, I knew there were differences; I just didn't know that the social consequences were so implacable. Sitting between these two bad, and therefore fascinating, boys at the back of the class, I think I imagined I could insinuate a place in their clique by impressing them with my tomboy know-how.

Dotted around the room I could see my best friends, Julie Johnson, Sharon Turner, and Jana Dieckman. We would hold back our giggles with our hands over our mouths and our eyes bulging whenever Mrs. Bobincheck reached up to the top of the board. Her exposure was so revealing, so mortifyingly intimate, and she was so blatantly blind to its occurrence. I loved Mrs. Bobincheck and silently I prayed that she would save her dignity and not reach up to the high parts of the blackboard. My girlfriends and I would go red at the sight and simultaneously laugh and cringe. We laughed, for to laugh was to distance her humiliation from ourselves; we cringed because I think we knew deeply, though unreflectively, that our teacher's humiliation was our humiliation. The tools of her debasement were sharpened on the whetstone of male privilege; the boys' snickers and sneers fed on the overexposure of female fleshy excess.

I suppose I reasoned that if I could just be boy enough I might duck the burgeoning awareness that I was not entitled to the same power and immunity from social censure that boys were. But I suppose I also knew if I were too much boy, I couldn't play in the deliciously tensive game we shared, a game fueled by the fecund bloom of heterosexual adolescence.

That school year we discovered the cheap and scintillating pleasure of dirty words and base descriptions. Our newly discovered linguistic play was even more piquant when peppered with the names of our supposed adversaries. I do not know if we girls started it or the boys started it, but increasingly, our lunch hours and recesses were filled with alternating bouts of laughter and insults hurled back and forth between my friends and me, on one side, and Marty and Chris, on the other. During one afternoon recess, like a needle stuck in a scratch on an old LP, we landed on one particular abusive line as our favorite. Our overuse of this line was our boisterous but undeclared acknowledgment that this line was the best. Moreover, it was surely the most base, and we wasted little time in using it over and over and over again. Simply uttering this line made us all convulse in fits of laughter. The only thing that changed each time it was said was who said it about whom. The line went something like, Chris (or whoever), you'd better close your legs; you're attracting flies. Not a particularly humorous line as I now recount it, but at the time it was the funniest thing we'd ever heard. It didn't matter how many times it was said—and it was said a lot by the two boys and we four girls—we just thought it was hysterical. It was side-splitting hysterical, indeed almost pants-wetting hysterical, and the awareness of this possibility made the line even funnier, since whomever might have wet her or his pants might in fact have attracted flies in time. At the end of the afternoon's recess we could barely talk for all the laughter. I was doubled over in pain; it hurt so to laugh.

The next day just as we were letting out for morning recess, Mrs. Bobincheck asked for Jana, Sharon, Julie, and me to stay behind for a moment. After the other kids went outside, she told us that she wanted to see us during the lunch hour. She said that she had something special for us and asked that we plan to eat our lunches quickly and return to the classroom as soon thereafter as we could. We said that we would and went out to the playground for what was left of the recess. We filled the remainder of that recess relentlessly interrogating each other about what the surprise Mrs. Bobincheck had for us could possibly be.

After lunch, while the other kids played, my girlfriends and I knocked on the green wooden door of our bungalow classroom. We were contained but bristling with anticipation. Mrs. Bobincheck with her big blond back-combed hair and round smiling face answered the door immediately. She let us into the room, which was so uncharacteristically quiet without all the other students present. There was just the hollow hum of the swamp cooler stirring the hot desert air and the sound of distant screams of kids at play. Mrs. Bobincheck had placed a table at the front of the class and covered it with a table cloth. Around the table were five chairs, two on each side and one at the head. She asked us to sit in the chairs on the sides of the table and once we had done so, she asked us to close our eyes. We could barely wait for the mystery to unfold. We felt superior to the other students in our class who hadn't been selected by Mrs. Bobincheck for this special treat. She told us she had something that she wanted us to smell and touch while we kept our eyes closed. She passed around a bowl with some sort of grainy powder in it. We each touched it and smelled it. She asked us if we could smell anything. It was really hard to smell anything and so I shook my head. She then passed around another bowl and asked us to smell it. This bowl had a liquid in it, and it had a distinct odor. I wrinkled up my nose and said I thought it was vinegar. She then asked us to open our eyes and to put a finger in the bowl with the liquid and taste the substance. We all made faces when we tasted the bitter flavor. She then asked us to put our finger in the bowl with the granulated powder which we could now see had a white color. We weren't sure if it was salt or sugar and tentatively put our tongues to our white encrusted finger tips. As soon as we tasted it we recognized the sweet taste of sugar and readily licked the rest of the powder away from our fingers. Our teacher then asked us to describe the tastes of each of the substances. We, of course, said that one was bitter and yucky and the other was sweet and yummy. She praised us for saying the right answer. She told us that she too found sugar sweet and vinegar bitter. Additionally, she asked us if vinegar could ever be sweet. We all said no. She asked us if we preferred vinegar to sugar. Again, we all said no. She then asked us why it was, if we preferred sweet to bitter, that we produced language that was in such bad taste. Why was it, when we clearly had the choice to do otherwise, we chose bitter words when we could just as easily choose sweet ones. One by one, the lesson now dawning, we each began to squirm in our chairs. And one by one, riven with the realization of our fall from Mrs. Bobincheck's grace, we each began to cry.

I was mortified. Between stifled sobs I apologized. The other girls were apologizing too. We each sought redemption, realizing now how evil we had been and what an embarrassment we had made of ourselves. Mrs. Bobincheck was beatific. She calmed us and smiled at us and told us that we needn't apologize. She just wanted us to know that we had choices that we could make and that some choices were better than others. This of course, is to say, that we really had only one choice and it wasn't the one we'd made. We dried our tears, hugged our teacher, and filed out on to the playground, our heads hanging low.

Why didn't it occur to me to question why Marty and Chris were never asked to sample Mrs. Bobincheck's taste test?

Lesson Two

In the sixth grade, Linda Blackman's boobs were on everyone's minds. A whirlpool of whispers circulated among the girls in my class about the size of them. Someone said Linda had been wearing a bra since the fourth grade. Another girl declared that Linda was stuffing her bra. Someone else said she wasn't stuffing because she saw her change her shirt once when they were going for softball practice. We all noticed how the boys acted around her. What we failed to notice was how we acted about her and how much attention we gave her boobs.

That year the brassiere was added to my wardrobe. I had to fight my mother to let me get one as she could see by the contours of my chest that there was as of yet no physiological need for one. Eventually, however, I suppose she realized that there was a psychological need. All my friends were wearing them and to be without signaled the very uncool fact that I was still a child. I strained to join adolescence.

My mother and I went to Dunlap's, the locally owned department store situated in the College Shopping Center. There, my mother, the sale assistant, and I engaged in a tetchy tug-of-war. Compelled to both reject and seek my mother's counsel, I was a mess of conflicted adolescent nerves. The sales assistant only made it worse by somehow thinking she could offer help, where my mother couldn't. Having established that I would require what was ignobly dubbed a "training bra," my mother and the assistant debated the costs of various cupless brassieres. I think my mother saw it as a waste of money since she did not think I needed one. She probably also didn't like seeing her last child grow up. Whatever the reason, she was determined to spend as little as possible. I stood there to the side, unconsulted about a matter I regarded as of utmost importance to my social well-being, blankly staring up at the row of headless and armless female mannequin torsos, all managing to look quite jaunty, feminine, and elegant in their very pointy bras. This was 1969. Unknown to me, while I battled to don one, feminists were battling to doff theirs.

At some point during that year, after I had been wearing my training bra for a while, I remember standing in front of the bathroom mirror in that bra and my underwear. The door was closed. I diligently wadded up long ribbons of toilet paper, shaped the paper into a palm size mound and carefully shoved it into the left side of my bra. After a peek in the mirror to see the alteration in my contours, I did the same on the right side in order to get the full effect. Now sporting the shape to which I aspired, I slipped on my tank top in order to see how my "new" chest looked fully clothed. I had only stuffed my bra a little, so it wasn't like I looked stacked or anything. I just looked like I had a little something where I felt I had a lot of nothing. When I first started putting the paper in my bra I didn't plan to go out like that; I was just exploring how I might look eventually. However when I saw the transformation, I began to weigh the possibilities in my mind. Could I really get away with it? Who would know but me that my "boobs" were fakes? I rationalized that I would surely feel the falsies slip if I was in danger of being discovered. I took the chance.

Since I was planning on seeing my friend Julie Johnson that day, I really should have known better. In my crowd Julie was our "Eddie Haskell" (of *Leave It to Beaver* fame); you know, always demonstratively trying to insinuate herself into the good graces of my mother, while also being the instigator of the circumstances that inevitably led to trouble. In short, she was evil *and* a suck up. Her middle name was "Peer Pressure." As I think on it now, she was probably the one who originated the famous line that got us into trouble with Mrs.

Bobincheck. While we were walking down the street on our way to the park where we always hung out, Julie turned to me, pointed to the top of my scoop-neck tank top and said, "Look, you have toilet paper coming out of your shirt." With that instant look of mortification (which no doubt crossed my face), as I realized I either had to shove my humiliation back in my shirt or find myself having to reel the length of toilet paper out before the watchful and censorious eyes of my peer, I'm sure I gave the game away. A glint appeared that moment in Julie's eye, a secret sinister sneer that never abated in all the years I knew her. She had the goods on me and knew it and the silent threat of exposure hung like a poisonous vapor in the air.

Lesson Three

My sister is five years older than I and throughout my childhood she used her age and size to advantage. When my sister was twelve, my mother decided she was old enough to "look after" me for brief periods during the day if my mother needed to run to the store. My sister apparently regarded these occasional periods without supervision as times set aside for her to teach me the meaning of hierarchy and obeisance. She would pin me down, tie me up, and generally play domination games in which I was guaranteed to be the subordinated one.

A particularly favorite "game" of my sister's necessitated that she pin my much smaller body to the floor by sitting astride me. By placing the bulk of her weight on my thighs to keep me from kicking and by restraining my arms with her bent knees, she would tickle me mercilessly, painfully, until I would pee in my pants. Owing to her superior size and strength, no amount of squirming or screaming could dislodge her. She would exacerbate my debasement by adopting a devilish look in her eye and a sinister tone in her voice and query me with "What kind of underwear do you have on?" Then she would tickle me and say, "Let me feel! Let me feel! Let me feel!" She didn't say this because she was some sort of a pervert; she was imitating a pervert who had in fact nearly molested me when I was five years old.

Thanksgiving in 1963, after the requisite huge meal, I went for a walk by a deserted schoolyard with a family friend, a boy named Bobby. An ordinary looking white man happened upon us and asked us to help him find a missing girl. Once he had successfully managed to get Bobby to go in one direction to look for the supposedly missing girl and to sequester me off in another, he lifted my shirt, licked my belly and chest, and uttered the now famous line as he tried to pull down my shorts, at which point I managed to get away. After I found Bobby and we got back to his family's house where my mother and sister and his mother, brother, and sister were, the police were called. During the interrogation with the cops, the other kids were kept out of the room. With their ears plastered to the door they overheard me tell the cops the line that would subsequently haunt me. Forevermore whenever my sister or those other kids wanted to "get" me they would come at me and say, "What kind of underwear do you have on? Nylon? Cotton? Let me feel!"

I had met the Bogey Man. However, this child molester was like no Bogey Man I could ever have expected. He seemed very ordinary. Sure, I'd seen enough Hollywood monster flicks to know that it was females' lot to always be in peril. But this monster didn't have that immediately alarming demeanor of, say, the Creature from the Black Lagoon. In that picture when Julie Adams innocently swims in the lagoon and stirs the deep imaginings of the Creature, it seems more like the hapless conjunction of opportunity and responsible monster behavior than sinister premeditation. Nothing in my Disney and Universal Studios celluloid-filled childhood had prepared me for this schoolyard encounter. King Kong is tragic for his fleeting and fatal indulgence in his tender but impossible love for Faye Ray. The Wolfman is driven to kill the thing he loves most by a covenant he is powerless to overthrow. My monster, like the Wolfman, was driven. It was clear that he wanted me. And I felt sure he wanted to hurt me. His desire too was selfish. However, unlike the Wolfman, whose plight summons our pity, my monster's desire was driven not by circumstance but something altogether personal. Moreover, his drive for destruction masqueraded as affection, a strange affection from a stranger. And, of course, what made it altogether more incomprehensible to me was that I was a little girl. Saturday matinees had taught me that it was only the mature and svelte that drew the beasts. I had felt secure in my innocence.

By the time I was sitting around the dining room table with the cops, my mother, Bobby, and his mother, the seriousness of the conversation made it clear that I had been exposed to something more darkly dark than I had rights to know at that time. We were in hush-hush land: that musty corner into which all things profane are swept, the place where children are forbidden to go, where swear words and slang terms for bodily functions, and the truth about how babies are made are kept. And yet, with a lick of my belly and a tug of my shorts I had been catapulted into that place. In the eyes of my sister, Bobby, and his siblings, I was to be mildly awed for having gone where none of them had gone before and, moreover, I was to be castigated for transgressing, albeit innocently, the borders of propriety. I had been unnaturally desired. For some, the unblemished surface of innocence evokes, indeed invites contamination. I was somehow "dirty" now. And so my sister would sit on my chest and tickle and taunt me into physical and psychological abjection.

Public Display of Academia

If I had learned these lessons, if I knew the bounds of social acceptability, appropriate feminine behavior, and the sanctions against inappropriate desire, how was it I came to do what I did?

It was a dirty little secret. Whispers were everywhere but only a few people knew for sure. I even made the whisperers the topic for a conference paper and delivered it at a national convention, the subtext of which was "How could they think that? After all, what type of girl do they think I am?"[1] That paper was greeted with nods and applause more polite than approving. Of the people who knew the truth, one person guessed it; others, confidants all, were told when I simply couldn't keep the secret to myself. I had lied about it publicly and in a paper submitted to a professor; other times, as in the conference paper below, I obscured the truth.

The Fan Dance: A Peep at the Bare Facts at a Regional Academic Conference

"Researching Exotic Dancers: Just How Far Are You Willing to Go to Experience that 'Sensuous Way of Knowing?'"

In "Rethinking Ethnography: Towards a Critical Cultural Politics," Dwight Conquergood notes that doing ethnography "privileges the body as a site of knowing" (180). Furthermore, he emphasizes that "Ethnography is an *embodied practice*; it is an intensely sensuous way of knowing" (180, emphasis in original). In the field, as well as when ethnographic insights are taken to performance, the methodological assumptions informing performance-as-a-way-of-knowing support the claim that the doing is epistemic. Accordingly, if a researcher resists participating in some activity germane to the field she or he is studying, the researcher is presumably losing an opportunity to explore the epistemic power of embodied participation. However, a keenly experienced resistance to participation may nevertheless yield insights, providing that resistance is reflexively interrogated.

For more than a year I ethnographically researched the lifeworld of female exotic dancers, commonly known as strippers. Perhaps no activity better exemplifies the feminist critique of how a woman's body is positioned as an object for the male gaze than stripping. This issue led me to engage in that study about women who strip in male-dominated, heterosexual strip clubs. I was interested in exploring how women, who subject themselves to the male gaze, experience their subjectivity while under the gaze. During the time I conducted my research, which entailed numerous evenings in various strip clubs around the country as well as several interviews with women who strip, I was frequently asked by the women if I had ever been a stripper. When I would ask them their reason for their question, most often they responded that they had assumed, since I appeared to have such a keen interest in stripping, that I had previously been one. Similarly, as news of my research spread throughout my department, some colleagues questioned how long it would be before I found that I would need to close the gap between the researcher and the researched by engaging in the activity myself. As my fieldwork progressed, I became increasingly aware that the questions and concerns raised by my colleagues, advisors, and the dancers were becoming more pertinent. Moral questions aside, given that my research was to culminate in a performance of the narratives I was collecting, and though I was not actually going to strip as part of the performance, the question of how I could best bring an embodied understanding to the dancers' words, without having engaged the activity myself, became increasingly significant. This absence in my research was especially felt while I was in the clubs. Although I was in the field, I did not experience my presence there as a fully fledged participant/observer. As I was not stripping, I was not really a participant and as I was not a male member of the audience, I could not observe from the position of the typical spectator/customer. Women, of course, do occasionally go to male-dominated strip clubs; however, it is rare for one to go alone, as I most often did.

My presence in the clubs prompted a variety of reactions but never prompted the reaction it would have had I been male. While my intention had always been to stage the narratives that the dancers and I co-created in the interview situation, in time I began to question whether my articulation of their experiences could benefit from my own somatic engagement of their work activities. Without having experienced *that* "intensely sensuous way of knowing" I wondered if I might experience a distance between my embodied understanding of the strippers' experiences—which I was to recount performatively—and my own imaginative capacity to constitute their experiences. Moreover, I began to question whether or not my reticence to engage in the act of stripping was an effort to do precisely what Conquergood cautions against: He states that "When one keeps an intellectual, aesthetic, or any other kind of distance from the other, ethnographers worry that the other people will be held at an ethical and moral remove as well" ("Performing as a Moral Act," 2). Was my unwillingness to strip my way of ethically or morally distancing the dancers' activities from myself?

Early on in my fieldwork, I dismissed the idea of stripping as part of my research. I did not believe it was essential to my performatively constituting the dancers' experiences, and I continue to believe it is not a necessary condition of performance. Clearly, empathy, critical thinking, and imagination may permit a performer to create a fine performance without having previously experienced what the character has. As Clifford Geertz states in his discussion of Malinowski's posthumously published *Diary*, "you don't have to be one to know one" (*Local Knowledge*, 57). And yet, while bodily engagement may not be a precondition of good ethnography or good performance of ethnography, bodily engagement may enable the ethnographer or ethnographic performer to access some understanding that might not be readily grasped empathetically or imaginatively. Additionally, experience is the epistemological ground of ethnography and compels physical participation by the researcher. Nevertheless, the issue of whether or not I would strip during my research appeared moot since I did not look for work as a stripper as part of the study, nor did the situation where I might strip seem likely to emerge—until I met Amanda. When I interviewed Amanda, she challenged my preconceptions and predisposition against my stripping and alerted me to the distance I was erecting between myself, her, and the other co-participants in the research. Amanda pushed my accountability further than the other women I interviewed. It seemed that for her, trying to understand why I would be interested in researching strippers was not just a question of whether or not I had stripped before; rather, she seemed to recognize that if understanding strippers was my goal, then understanding the activity through bodily engagement was paramount. For Amanda, one is not born, but rather becomes a stripper, and one does so by stripping. Of course, she could have also just been having fun with me, testing me to see how far she could get me to go. Whether she was being genuine or was simply amusing herself is irrelevant. Her questions turned the table, effectively made me confront myself, and positioned me, however temporarily, as the subject of the research.

I first met Amanda at a New Orleans strip club on Bourbon Street called Big Daddy's and during the course of that initial conversation I invited her to meet me for a taped interview the following day at my room in the Marriott hotel. I was in New Orleans for a national academic conference[2] and was using the opportunity of being in a city replete with strip clubs to further my research. During the ensuing conversation, Amanda began to assert the viability of my going to Big Daddy's with her and taking a job there just for that one night. The part on the transcript where this first occurs goes like this:

Lesa: Is there anything you want to ask me?
Amanda: Would you do it?
Lesa: I don't think I could do it now.
Amanda: . . . Why wouldn't you do it?
Lesa: Well, I'm thirty-six and ah, you know. . . .
Amanda: . . . Well if you're doing something like this isn't that what you should do?

Lesa: Well, I mean. . . . ? Would I do this for a job . . . or would I go out and. . .?
Amanda: No. Would you work . . . ? Would you be able to work like this one night, to dance?
Lesa: Would I be able to. . . . ?
Amanda: Would you be able to go there and work? Tonight?

Throughout the remainder of the interview, Amanda doggedly countered every protest I mounted: I claimed I did not have the right clothes, she offered me some of her dance costumes—after all, "one size fits all"; I said I did not know what to say to the manager, she constructed a story for me; I said I didn't have the body for it, she cited examples of other dancers my age and shape, and so on. And so it was that the opportunity arose that, just for a night, I could cross the experiential limen and become a stripper.

Clearly, Amanda's interrogation brought to the surface a number of issues related to how I was positioned and how I was positioning myself in the research situation: ethical and moral issues, institutional and political issues, and methodological and epistemological issues.

Ethical and Moral Issues

In "Performing as a Moral Act," Conquergood identifies five possible "performative stances" that he believes an ethnographer can adopt toward the other. Briefly, the four problematic positions he delineates on the "moral map" are the "custodian's rip off," the "enthusiasts infatuation," the "curator's exhibitionism," and the "skeptic's cop-out" ("Performing as a Moral Act," 5). At the center of Conquergood's "moral map" is "dialogical performance," which Conquergood locates as "genuine conversation" ("Performing as a Moral Act," 5). It is the performative stance wherein the ethnographer "struggles to bring together different voices, world views, value systems, and beliefs so that they can have a conversation with one another" ("Performing as a Moral Act," 9). It is not so much a "definite position," as a "stance situated in the space between competing ideologies" ("Performing as a Moral Act," 9). Thus, I had to ask myself if my resistance to stripping was my way of "morally and ethically distanciating" myself from my co-researchers' activities. However "dialogical" I may have thought I was being, however much I thought I was bracketing off my judgment of these women for their activities, my unwillingness to participate suggests a double standard. Did my resistance signal my commitment to a morality that posits "Good girls don't do that kind of thing and therefore, since I am most assuredly a good girl, I mustn't"? Were my claims that "I don't need to do it to understand it" just a cynical rationalization that moved me toward the skeptic's cop-out? Furthermore, could I have really just been a custodian ready to rip-off some good performance material but never really willing to engage the culture, regarding it solely from the confines of my own ideological commitments? Or was my interest in exotic dancers due to a "curator's exhibitionism"? That is to say, was I somewhat exploiting these women simply so that I could associate my name with this exotic topic, all the while rigidly maintaining my difference from my co-researchers?

Institutional and Political Issues

Academics, no less than other professionals, are bound to certain ethical standards they uphold. As Amanda pressed me to join her that night, I knew that streaming down Bourbon Street outside of Big Daddy's would be most of the membership of my professional organization. The possibility of someone I knew seeing me while I was in the club would be fairly great. Having been in the club the night before when I met Amanda, I knew that casual observers stopped and peered in the open door from the street with regularity. If I did become a stripper for a night, aside from the possibility that I might have to explain my actions to people I knew, there was also the possibility that a man I asked for a tip might one day be sitting next to me at a convention panel or across from me at a job interview: "Gee, you seem so familiar. I just can't figure out where I know you from . . . !"

Amanda's suggestion that I join her that night challenged me by placing my role as ethnographer at odds with my role as academic. Working for a night with the women as one of them, spending time in the dressing room, experiencing what it is like to use my body for commercial gain, in short, availing myself of the opportunity to really become a participant/observer and gain experiential insights thus far denied me, potentially clashed with prevailing social mores and could in time reflect negatively upon me professionally, politically. How could I reconcile the demands of doing "good" ethnography with the demands of maintaining a "good" professional reputation?

Methodological and Epistemological Issues

Even if fieldwork is an "embodied practice" in which understanding the culture is developed somatically, no researcher should do something she or he doesn't want to do just because it is part of the culture she or he is studying. Yet I am interested here in what it is that stops engagement. Recent scholarship in ethnography and the performance of ethnography properly locate ethnography in the co-constitution of meaning between researcher and researched. For example, Conquergood's "dialogical performance"

("Performing as a Moral Act, " 9) clearly supports this view and Clifford Geertz likewise locates ethnography in the "moral interplay of contrasting mentalities" (*Local Knowledge,* 5). The illusion that renderings made by ethnographers are a "true" reflection of culture is now generally agreed to be just that—an illusion. Instead representations are "contingent accomplishments" that, as Melvin Pollner claims, require us to engage in a "radical reflexivity" in which our taken-for-granted assumptions are queried just as we inquire into the social activity under view ("Left of Ethnomethodology," 370). From this perspective, my un/willingness to participate by stripping shifts the discussion from a moral question to an epistemological one. Despite the methodological imperative that enjoins ethnographers to participate, what is learned by doing may not necessarily be anything like how the subjects of the study experience it. "The trick is," as Geertz says, "to figure out what the devil they think they are up to. In one sense, of course, no one knows this better than they do themselves; hence the passion to swim in the stream of their experience, and the illusion afterward that one somehow has" ("Local Knowledge," 58).

Would my becoming a stripper for the night help me to "figure out what the devil they think they are up to?" Perhaps. I believe so. However, I do not believe I would experience stripping as Amanda does. She walks through the world with an ease about her body I do not possess. She can surely dance better than I. While Amanda asserts that she believes she "has the upper hand" when she's in the club and she clearly negotiated herself with that certainty, I believe the feminist theory that I subscribe to could not allow me to experience stripping as anything other than disempowering. I do not believe I could be comfortable being nude on stage before a paying male public. I know I could not share the felt experience that she and other experienced dancers have. If I stripped, would those insights have told me anything about my co-researcher's culture that I couldn't have gotten by being in the club? Or would these insights have simply been about me? Yet my resistance to stripping made me question my taken-for-granted beliefs and challenged me not to see their experience only through my ideological commitments to feminism. Interpreting culture is surely a process where our conceptions are interrogated and should entail understanding within the framework of our subjects' view of what self-hood is (Geertz, "Local Knowledge," 59). As Geertz states, the interpretations we make are about "locat[ing] affinities and mark[ing] difference" (12). While embodying or performing indigenous activities is a way of knowing, there also is epistemic power in resistance. When coupled with radical reflexivity the body is potentially a site of knowing in the doing as well as in the not doing.

* * *

The Fan Dance: Undressing the Text

After I presented the paper—that now forms the above section of this chapter—at an academic convention, I was approached by a member of the audience, a young, yet widely respected performance scholar, who said she really enjoyed how in my paper it wasn't clear until the end that I did not strip and that I let that issue hang in the air unanswered for so long. I pointed out that while the paper surely is weighted against the affirmative, I do not actually settle the question explicitly since I do not say whether or not I did or did not strip. After she considered this and considered the issues I raised in the paper, she commented that with a performance studies audience I would probably receive more kudos for having stripped than not.

Perhaps.

Another member of that audience who is both a colleague and a friend told me that she believed I would not have been able to know the embodied understandings I relate in the paper had I not actually stripped.

Perhaps.

I put my body where my mouth was. I put my body where my reason was. I ignored the parade of convention rubberneckers lining the length of Bourbon Street. I ignored the wealth of feminist theory upon which I have cut my scholarly teeth. If understanding my topic begins with tits and ass then, I reasoned, I must engage it with my tits and my ass, not just the cold austerity of extraneous and distanced notions of professional decorum.

Since baring my body in that New Orleans strip joint, I have danced an academic fan dance. While I reveal a bit of what I found out, I also occlude from view the more sensational bits, revealing more or less depending on the audience. The higher the professional or personal stakes, the less I reveal. In the nine academic papers and/or performances I have produced from this ethnographic study, all but one obscure, shield, or alter the facts of my becoming a stripper for a night. As I flutter one lush fan and then the other in front of the naked truth, only the more socially acceptable parts are clearly visible. What the audience really wants to see, the prurient promise hovering around the topic, is shielded. I smile and wink and cheekily ask the question so evident on my audience's collective mind: What's a nice scholar like me doing with a topic like this? I dance secure in the knowledge that my dirty little secret is covered. I am coy. Surely, I am a nice scholar, one who would never actually bare it all, is the silent reply. Surely, I merely toy with the topic as I toy with my audience, a bit of winking and nodding fun. She's a good girl. She's a good scholar.

If not good, then what? Bad? A bad scholar? A whore of a scholar. A scholar slut. As I pursued this research, if the question that lingered around me was, "just what kind of girl do you think I am?" then I guess I'm just that kind of girl. I began to question if it is so wrong to be "that kind of girl." Maybe "that kind of girl" is just the type of girl to challenge the sexist ideology undergirding the restrictive binary of "bad" or "good" girls. Has engaging my research topic in the manner I believed best suited to exploring it meant selling out? I ask myself if I have compromised myself by showing my private parts to an anonymous audience. Having done it, do I compromise myself all the more by hiding the truth? Is dancing naked for commercial gain any more or less compromised than dancing naked in order to gain scholarly insights? If the colleague I cite above is right, there would be no alternate way to apprehend the embodied insights I did without my having engaged the strippers' world with my own body. Yet I wonder if there is any way to approach telling this tale without it coming off as naked self-justification. Like Betsy Israel, author of the confessional account *Grown-Up Fast,* I realize that "once you've said it you can never, ever take it back" ("The Original Bad Girl," 131).

The Full-Frontal Tell-All: Reflections of a Stripper for a Night

When Amanda sat across from me at the table in my $195.00 a night Marriott hotel room and doggedly asked me if I would strip if given the opportunity, and when she countered my every objection with solutions to those obstacles, she was implicitly challenging whether or not I was keeping her and her activities at an ethical remove. If I wasn't negatively judging her and her work, and since she had successfully removed any obstacles to my working in the club that night, just what was it that was preventing me from saying I would do it? Was I employing some double standard that permitted me to believe it was okay for her to strip but certainly not for me? Perhaps it's okay to have a double standard. After all, different people do different things and use their own sense of morality and judgment in pursuit of those interests. Yet by choosing to study exotic dancers I was asserting that I had an interest in the activity. And, as Amanda so pointedly and poignantly asked, "Well if you're doing something like this, isn't that what you should do?"—a point made all the more pertinent as I was intending to eventually perform the narratives told to me by my informants.

I went with Amanda to the club. On the way, Amanda took me by a shop on Bourbon Street to purchase a garter, which she said was necessary so that I had somewhere to keep and display money. The idea behind displaying the money was, she said, a way to give the guys the idea that they should tip. At Big Daddy's we told the "house mom," Barbara, a story concocted by Amanda and me about how I had just moved to New Orleans and was looking for a job. Amanda had told me that they would have a shortage of "girls" that night since many of the dancers had taken the night off to attend a birthday party and so, by Amanda's reckoning, it was the "perfect night" for me to try to get a job. Barbara asked if I had "danced" before. I told her I had not and when I saw what I thought to be doubt cross her face I strongly claimed that I knew I could do it. She sold me a g-string (called a "t-strap") for four dollars and told Amanda to tell me "how it worked" there. We went to the dressing room and while getting into our costumes Amanda explained what was expected of me: how I would first dance to two songs on the front stage, take a break for one song, and then move to the back stage and dance to two more songs; the order of the dancers and who I would follow; where the kick switch on the front stage was to change the lighting effects; how money for private dances was dispersed to the club and the "girls" and so on. She also coached me on how to get tips while on stage, and, generally, how to appear like I knew what I was doing. The secret she said was confidence. She said if you have confidence, "you can go up there and look like a complete whore and some guy's gonna fall in love with you." Many of the things Amanda told me had previously been told to me by her and by the other women I interviewed. However, once positioned to do these activities I was confronted with an epistemic gulf between my rational understanding and my hitherto untested corporeal capacity, a cleavage between my mind and my gut.

I get the job. I walk around the club in my skimpy costume hoping that the dim lighting helps to obscure clear inspection of my body. I stand next to an empty table near a wall so that I can hide my backside. I smoke a cigarette and watch the other dancers. As I wait for my turn in the rotation, I am riveted with fear. I stand in my cowboy boots, which make me stand tall. I am wearing lilac-colored-fringed-thong-bikini bottoms and a matching top that Amanda loaned me. It is the same costume that I saw Amanda wear on the night I met her. With my cowboy boots and the fringe on the costume, there is sort of Western motif to my stripper image that feels sort of corny rather than sexy. I chose this costume from the four Amanda offered to loan me. In the dressing room Amanda and I agreed that this costume suited me best in terms of my shape and in that it seemed to go with my boots—the only shoes that I brought with me to the conference that are remotely suitable. I wonder how many times this costume has been taken off on stage before. Under the bottoms of my costume I am wearing a brown t-strap with white fringe hanging down over the front triangular patch. Wearing the t-strap is an awkward sensation, sort of like wearing a rubber band up my butt. It is a sensation that is hardly comfortable and difficult to ignore. Amanda told me that the club owner always purchases brown t-straps with white fringe on the front because he believes that the customers will think there is nothing but white fringe hanging in front of the dancer's pubic area. Under the bikini top my nipples have been painted with clear-drying latex and then pinky-brown eye shadow has been colored over the latex. Amanda showed me how to do this in order that my nipples comply with the Louisiana state regulation that they be covered. While my nipples are in fact "covered," after this procedure they appear absolutely natural under the dim club lights. The latex is dry now and my nipples feel no different than usual. I am also wearing the recently acquired garter on my left leg and tucked in it are four one dollar bills folded lengthwise, seed money from my wallet for my expected tips. The garter is red and looks very tacky.

A very large bearded man sitting at a table with three other men calls me over to his table. I tentatively go over to the table and stand uncomfortably close from my point of view, but clearly I am not as close as these customers would like, or perhaps expect. Standing by their table I feel like a waitress only I don't dare ask "what would you like?" The bearded man looks me over and says, "We just want to know how tall you are?" I hesitate and say, "five six" This is, I am sure, my cue to work the table, but I just stand there incapable of finding the seductive little quips I am sure I am meant to spout. I know he's sizing me up for the obvious. As I look at him and his pals, I see in their faces that what they think I am and who I think I am are very different. In the gap that ensues the bearded man leans over, grabs my left hand and as I go rigid and resist, he tightens his grip and slips a dollar bill folded into a ring onto my wedding finger. I mumble something about needing to get ready to go on stage and leave the table. Boy! Am I not good at this. I silently wish I could just let go and get the most I can out of this experience. After all I'm here, what do I have to lose now?

Amanda is now confidently striding around the front stage, the customers literally (and, it seems, figuratively) at her feet. She looks down on them, towering over them. The men turn their faces up to her in apparent awe. The bartender waves at me to signal that it is now my turn to lie in the "swing." The swing is a well-lit, three-sided coffin-shaped box suspended from the ceiling with an angled mirror at the back. Dancers are expected to lie in the swing for two songs as part of the rotation. The mirror projects the image of the woman's bare behind through the open end at the front of the box out to the passing parade of people on Bourbon Street as a none-too-subtle means of attracting business. I walk toward the swing feeling like a person with a death sentence. I remove my top and bikini bottoms in a little area behind the bar by the ladder that goes up to the swing. After I disrobe, I am wearing only the t-strap, and as I climb up the ladder I feel utterly exposed. I feel the impact of being naked in a public place hit my body and my consciousness. I feel pale, flabby, old. I climb up the ladder, lie down, and feel the last hope for abiding dignity expire. I lie there caught, incapable of determining whether having my butt displayed like meat on a slab or having my face recognized by some colleague who chances to peer in through the door is the lesser of two evils. I decide that chances are good given this situation that observers will be less inclined to look at my face and I lie there hoping to be at the very least an anonymous exhibitionist. Nevertheless, I shield my face with my hair. From this bird's eye view, I cautiously peer around the club. The thought that some of the customers might be members of my academic organization crosses my mind. I quickly banish the thought, for if they are my professional colleagues, there is nothing I can do about it now. Moreover, I console myself with the thought that they may not recognize me outside of these circumstances, or if they do, they might be just as embarrassed as I to have it known that they were here. After I've been up there for a while, a man who looks to be some kind of manager or perhaps the owner of the club calls up to me to lie with more weight on one of my hips and to bend one of my legs at the knee. I interpret his direction as an indication that my butt doesn't look appealing enough in its current disposition. I adjust myself. He stares at the image of my butt in the mirror and seems only marginally satisfied by the change I've made. Nevertheless, he decides not to pursue asking me to make any other changes and he turns and walks away. I feel marginally relieved that he has relented in his pursuit of this indignity.

I look up and through the door of the club; I see the light from Bourbon Street streaming in the door. I can see the unrelenting flow of passers-by go past, some of whom must be my professional colleagues. Some individuals hesitate at the door before moving on. One late-middle-aged man who looks to be the quintessential tourist walks by; he is apparently caught by the image of my bare ass and he comes back to give it a double take. He then hurries away only to return a moment later with a woman whom I suspect is his wife. He stands there at the door pointing at the image in the mirror while his wife's jaw drops open. I decide to take my attention off myself and watch the woman dancing on the front stage that I can see quite plainly from this elevated position. She is wearing a red, white, and blue, star spangled, sequined bra and panty outfit with white leather knee-high cowboy boots and she barks every time a customer places a dollar in the garter on her leg. It is almost a howl. I am reminded of how bartenders will ring a bell in some bars when a customer gives a good tip. The moments I'm in the swing drag. Even the beat of the music seems slow. With flippancy I find I am incapable of mustering, Amanda calls lying in the swing, "mooning Bourbon."

Back on the ground, I put my top and bottoms back on and I am told to wait for my turn to go up on the front stage. I stand between the bar to my back and the steps up to the stage in front of me. Rachel is the dancer in the rotation just before me and I can see her on the stage directly in front and above me finishing the last of her two-song set. She is small, with a cute face and shape, and wears her hair dyed black and cut like Cleopatra. Her facial expressions and black outfit give her the air of a seductress with slight dominatrix overtones. I do not know the song to which she is dancing. I wonder how long it will be until I must climb the four steps to the stage and take her place. Standing here I am focused on how I am about to walk up the steps to the stage and enter the space where imaginative speculation must give way to embodied experience. Even though I was nearly naked in the swing, I experience this moment as liminal, a moment where my status as a non-stripper and my status as a stripper, or at the very least, a woman who has stripped will shift. I wonder what I will do once I am up on the stage. I suddenly have no idea. Even though I have seen many strippers dance, even though I can see Rachel dancing now, I do not feel myself capable of generating such movements with my body. I feel rigid and vulnerable. I don't know what I expected. I now know I agreed to do this before I really understood what I would be doing. I agreed to an in-theory imagining of what it would be like; now I have an in-body understanding and bodily "I cans" are evading me. I feel only bodily "I can'ts."

The steps to the stage have a brass rail on each side. The stage is raised up about four feet; it is about twelve feet wide and extends to the back wall about sixteen feet. The floor of the stage is red linoleum but there is a raised round revolving platform at the back of the stage that is carpeted. On the stage, just behind the brass rails and steps, is a vertical brass pole. It has a large brass ring at the top. I see Rachel grab the ring, lift herself up, and spin around the pole. She puts her feet down and ends her spin with her backside toward some customers on the right. There is a floor to ceiling mirror on the back wall and I can see Rachel reflected in it. She comes off the pole and struts around the stage looking down on the men in the audience. She does not dance, she walks or struts and intersperses the walking with some gymnastic moves on the pole. I have seen other women who really do dance, but Rachel struts.

Behind me is the bar that I rest my elbows on as I face the stage. I am trying to appear calm. I imagine that with my elbows on the bar and a strong attitude in my body I seem confident. The bartender has given me a glass of ice water that I repeatedly turn toward and sip as my mouth keeps getting dry. Despite the loud music I can hear the bartender behind me polishing glasses and setting up drinks. To my right but behind me and out of my sight line I know the DJ, Gary, is cuing up the CDs for my set. Further to the right of me, beyond Gary, is the open door to Bourbon Street. The light and noise of this street that never sleeps pour into the club. People continue to pass by, some looking in, others not, most moving on as soon as the bouncer approaches to encourage them to enter. A man looks in and gazes up at the stage watching

Rachel. After a second he looks past me to the woman hanging in the "swing" behind me to my left and above me. The woman lying in the swing is jauntily sitting up on her elbows, kicking one foot up in the air behind her, having a cheerful conversation with the bartender and occasionally throwing a comment to me. She is making favorable comments about Rachel's dancing. She seems unconcerned that her naked cheeks are being observed by the general public. I turn my head from the door because I fear that someone I know will pass by and see me.

I look around the club. There are three men sitting together at a table away from the stage to my right. On the left, in one of the chairs that ring the stage, one man sits alone. He looks like a professional person. Is he a conventioneer? Will he be in the audience for a panel I attend at the convention tomorrow? He looks up at Rachel, his elbows on the ledge with his drink and an ashtray. He holds a folded dollar in his hands but makes no move to extend his arms.

I shift in my boots and feel the fringe on my costume top swipe across my rib cage as I move. I wonder what would happen if I went back to the dressing room, changed clothes and left. I envision myself walking out the door. I am the next dancer. I am afraid of creating the disturbance that would likely ensue if I missed my place in the circuit. Barbara, the house mom, is behind the bar to my left. I cannot see her but I know she is there. I know that the bartender, the DJ, and Barbara all know that this is my first time. I expect that they are waiting to see how I dance.

Amanda is on the second stage, the back stage way to my left. She is not watching me. There are three men sitting around that stage intently watching her. There are two dancers sitting and smoking at a table to my left by the dressing room door. From where I am I can barely see their faces because of the dim lighting, but they are watching Rachel. They will probably watch me when I dance. There is also the bearded man and his associates with whom I spoke earlier, closer also to my left. The dollar he gave me is still on my finger. I wonder if he is waiting to see me dance. I stand there waiting for my turn, trying to look as cool as the other dancers do.

I feel the air conditioning waft against my bare thighs. I think about my thighs, they jiggle when I walk and are not slim and taut like Amanda's or most of the other dancers'. I feel my exposed rear against the coolness of the bar. Standing as I am against the bar, my rear is hidden for the moment. My lower half is in darkness as I wait there. I will soon have to put my body up on the stage and perform as if it should be looked at. I know from previous experience of looking at my body in a mirror that my rear and thighs are dimpled with cellulite and that I have stretch marks on my thighs. I wonder if these imperfections will be visible in the lights on the stage. Rachel has several large scars across her stomach and legs as if she was lacerated by a razor or knife at some distant point in her life. In this light, her scars are somewhat visible. Amanda has told me where the kick switch is to change the lighting to a lower light than the one Rachel has on. I plan to do this but am hopeful I can find the switch without looking like I am fumbling around for it.

Rachel struts over to where the man is holding out the dollar; she squats down with her legs apart so that her crotch is eye level with the man. He looks up into her eyes seemingly unable to look anywhere else and, as she looks into his eyes, she takes the dollar bill with her hand. She stands and struts away. The man's eyes graze over her body as she moves away.

Rachel's song is being faded out by the DJ and the song I have selected is being mixed in. Rachel quickly gathers up the various items of clothing that she has taken off during her set while the DJ calls for applause for her and introduces me: "Here she is, the one, the only, Lisa." The music to a song by Duran Duran called "Love Voodoo" blares loudly. I have never heard this song before but I requested it because when the DJ asked me what I wanted to dance to I could not think of any song title other than the song that Amanda had told me she sometimes dances to. I hope it is a short song. Rachel comes down the steps with her clothes in her hands. I step forward and walk the three paces to the bottom step. The music is blaring and the disco lights on the stage are flashing frenetically. As I move forward I feel the cold air from the air conditioning fly around my shoulders and arms, then my legs, cheeks, and stomach. I grip the brass handrail with my right hand. It is cold. I put my left hand on the other rail and go up the four steps to the stage. I feel the strength in my step as my feet are encased in the boots. With each step I feel the flesh on my thighs jiggle and I believe that I feel the eyes of the bartender, the DJ, and the house mom on my backside. I turn to face the audience and begin to move to the music.

I move as I usually do whenever I dance to pop music. I glide around the stage. I feel the air waft around my bare midriff, butt, and thighs. I can see the silhouettes of the barman, the DJ, and the house mom all at the bar, lit by recessed lighting above them. I cannot make out their facial expressions and I don't want to. I allow the faces of the people watching me to blur. I know they are there, but I let my focus go to how my body moves. I am reminded of how Amanda said she goes into her "own little silo" while she is on stage. I wonder if this is the same feeling, this sense of being alone yet exposed. I slip around the edges of the stage. I turn upstage and see my image in the mirror. I feel distant from myself. I know that image is of me, but I do not believe I am doing this. It does not seem quite real. This time feels like an island of time isolated away from the usual rhythm of my life. Without being fully aware of it now, I know that once this evening is over, I will never do this again. There is some distant solace in that unarticulated thought. While moving to the music, I take my hands up and down my stomach and onto my thighs. I dance again toward the edge of the stage. I make myself look down into the eyes of the men around the stage. Only one man by himself is really watching me. The others have started to talk among themselves. I know their lack of attentiveness must be because I am less than captivating. I partly don't care. I am not doing this for money; whether they tip or not doesn't concern me, though, it would perhaps enhance my understanding of this experience if I were to find myself having to negotiate the exchange of money. However, I also do not relish having to do that. I recognize that I am essentially a chicken. Yet partly I do care that these men are not utterly enchanted by me. Absurdly, I feel slightly hurt. It hurts, I think, not because I want these men to be attracted to me, but because their lack of interest confirms my fears about my body being out of shape and that it is being conceived as unattractive. It hurts because when they avert their eyes they have the power. I want the power to turn off to them. I decide to spin around the pole. As I've watched dancers use the pole, I've always thought spinning around the pole must be best part of dancing on a strip club stage. I decide to just hold on to it with my hands and lean into a spin with my feet on the ground. I know I could get myself into some trouble trying to do some more advanced gymnastic move on the pole; moreover, I am too modest to do so in this costume or rather, this lack of costume. I watch myself in the mirror again. I spin around the pole and try to watch myself while I spin on the pole. I have seen many dancers watch themselves in the mirrors while they dance. I wonder if they do so because they lose interest in trying to generate interest from the customers. I wonder if they do so because they, like me, are fascinated by the fact that they are actually doing this and find, like I do, that it feels unreal.

I know that before this first song ends I should take off my top; I was told that is the usual routine. Then the bottoms will come off with the second song leaving me dressed only in the t-strap and boots. I decide that it is time to take off the top. The costume bra is elasticated without any fastener at the back, so it has to be removed over my head. In my imagination I try to figure out how I can remove the top in a manner that will appear "sexy." I cross my arms in front and lift the brassiere up. As the elasticated back rolls up my back, the fringe on the top and some of my hair gets coiled up into it and pulls my scalp. Pulling my arms through the arm holes I get caught up with the fringe as well. The more I try to get it off of me, the more I just want to be rescued from it. Eventually, after a cringe-making tug-of-war, the costume top is off, wadded up into an elasticated ball with large tufts of my long hair caught in it. I put it down on the upstage area near the revolving platform. I audibly laugh at myself and give myself a sort of mental "fuck it." Any pretense I may have had for thinking I could do this with any grace must now be abandoned.

The next song is being mixed in. I didn't know what song to request when the DJ asked so I just told him to play anything. Annie Lennox's "Why" comes on. I know this song and I like it, even if the title and refrain ironically comment on my current situation. I am bare-chested and because of my "fuck it" attitude I refuse contemplation of the thought that the men are more than likely appraising my breasts. In fact, I don't care what they think. I am not here to please them, even though they may think so. I resist thinking about anything that might make me experience this as more humiliating than I already do. I hear Amanda's words explaining how a dancer must dance for herself. I try to dance for me. I move and watch myself move through the lights in the image in the mirror. I look my body over in the mirror and from this distance and in these lights I see it as a not unattractive body.

After a while I strut back toward the raised, carpeted platform at the back of the stage. I stretch back on it. I flip up the top switch and the platform begins to revolve. I turn on the bottom switch and the lighting effect changes to a more dramatic and more comforting darker light. I lie on my back and raise my right leg with my left foot flat on the floor with a bent knee. I slide the costume bottoms off from under me and over my knees. With my left foot I slip the bottoms off the rest of my right leg. I am dressed only in the t-strap and am praying that in the low lighting and while I am moving on a revolving platform the men cannot get a good look at me. My eyes are almost closed. It is as if, just like children will do, I somehow think that by not allowing myself to see, I am preventing myself from being seen. I will finish out the song on this revolving platform. Here at the back of the stage, I feel comfortably cut off from the customers. I am just putting in my time. It seems to take forever for the song to end.

At last, as the song is coming to a close, the DJ mixes in the song for the next dancer. I gather up my costume, flick the top switch and the platform comes to a slow stop. As I cross the stage to go down the steps, the man sitting on the ring of the stage on the stage left side holds out a folded dollar bill. I see the bill in my peripheral vision. I have to decide in an instant whether to carry on toward the steps and exit the stage as I am meant to do and as I want to do, or to claim my dollar. The norms of the situation dictate that I should get the money, so I walk over to the edge of the stage by the man. The DJ's voice over the PA is calling for applause for me and he then announces the next dancer as she climbs the steps to the stage. I am standing on the stage over and in front of the man with the dollar. I have my costume clutched in my right hand in front of me. He holds out the bill and looks into my eyes. I can't tell if he liked my dance or is giving me the money out of some sort of pity or sympathy. I take the bill with my left hand, say "thank you," and rush over to the stairs to get off the stage. The new dancer is already in full swing.

I have one song to rest, hustle for tips, and put my costume back on before going to the back stage where I will dance for two more songs. As all the other dancers do, I put my top and bottoms on while I am standing in the same spot in front of the bar that I stood in prior to going on the front stage. Getting the balled up bikini top sorted out takes some doing and leaves me standing there virtually naked longer than I would have had my costume been more compliant. I fold the dollar I got from the man and tuck it into my garter belt with the four dollars I had there before. I take a drink from the glass of ice water that I left there before I went on stage. The barman refreshed the glass while I was gone and the water tastes good. I feel like I have been dancing for hours. The barman leans on the bar and over the music says "Nice dance." I smile showing no teeth and say, "You're a gentleman."

I go to the back stage where I wait for Rachel to finish dancing her set. I can't bring myself to ask any of the customers if they want to tip me for my dance. I don't want to speak to any of these men or have to be face to face with them. Again I wonder what if the man I go up to is a member of my professional organization?

The back stage is much smaller and is not so high up. Unlike the front stage, the back stage is a good distance away from the bar, where the house mom and the other members of the club management usually locate themselves. The customers at the back stage are much closer to the dancers. I was told that for this stage, the dancers are to take off their clothes almost immediately. This was told to me by Amanda and emphatically reiterated by the house mom. Rather than a pole or a platform, in the upstage area of this small stage there is a wooden swing suspended by two ropes from the ceiling.

Rachel finishes dancing, picks up her discarded clothes, and collects some tips from two of the three male spectators who are sitting on two sides of the stage. The music for the next song comes on. It is a very fast song, again a song I am unfamiliar with. I move to the center of the stage. The entire stage is only about nine foot square. Stools ring three sides of the stage. Mirrors again line the upstage wall. Way off to my right I can see a room, somewhat darker than the rest of the club. This room is the "VIP" room where table dances are done. For the dancers, the VIP room is where the real money is. I take off my top and drop it down on the carpeted area next to the steps to the stage. The three customers, two together on my left, and one on his own at the front, watch me as I do this. I look away from them and let them look at my body. I feel some intangible power slip from me as I look away, and yet I am too embarrassed to watch them look at me. Unlike on the front stage, these viewers are so close that it is impossible to let their faces blur. I can diminish the heat of their gaze only by averting my own. As I turn away, I look into the VIP room. I see Amanda in the room sitting on a banquette next to a customer. She smiles at me and waves. Her customer is smiling and looks at me briefly then back at Amanda. I smile at Amanda. I wonder if she has told her customer the truth about me.

I begin to move with determination, refusing to let this situation get the better of me. I take off the bottoms of my costume and drop them next to the top I have already removed. I am dancing in the t-strap and my boots. The boots give strength to my step as I move around the stage, which helps to mask the fragility I feel as my flesh meets the air and the eyes of my audience. The lighting on this stage is brighter than that of the front stage; it has an orangey-red cast to it. I feel so exposed, so incapable of hiding anything. There is no kick switch on this stage to lower the lighting. There is no revolving platform to cling to. I look for the "silo" I felt when dancing on the front stage but it escapes me. Yet because I have already danced in next to nothing on the front stage, I feel more ready for this exposure than I did before I danced on the front stage. Also, on this back stage I am away from the judgmental gaze of the club management, which affords me a sense of some minor autonomy.

The two men on my left are no longer looking at me. They are clearly uninterested. They talk to each other, drink, and smoke. I flush with the awareness of the personal risk I am engaging in and I feel angry at these men who can so easily appraise me and dismiss me. I grab the swing, sit in it, and swing a few times. They are not watching. I stand and grab the ropes of the swing, then pull away from the swing letting the length of rope catch me. I look to my right and cannot now see Amanda and her customer. I hold onto the swing and spin on my heels again, letting the length of rope catch me as I twirl. The lone customer sitting on the front side of the stage isn't watching me either. I become more aggressive in my dance. I move over toward the side of the stage and dance right above and in front of the two men. I stare down at their faces. The largeness and deliberateness with which I move causes the men to look up at me. I know that my disdain and anger is thinly veiled in my face. The man on the left, a smarmy looking man in his late forties, glances up at me, picks up his drink in his right hand, and sips it while looking at his friend. He leaves his elbow on the ledge with the glass in his hand, held in the line of vision between his eyes and mine. He seems to be shielding his vision of me; perhaps he is irritated by my aggressiveness. I grin inside and hope so. I sense a mild victory.

At some point the second song is mixed in. I am again unfamiliar with this song, which is similar in tempo to the previous one, and so I hardly notice the change. I go back to the swing and pull on the ropes, lean away, and twirl. Anything to take up time in this song. I stay with the swing for a while, spinning, swinging, twirling, utterly uninterested in generating any interest in me. I begin to sense a kind of power in making them be repelled by me. I want to make them feel uncomfortable. I start moving and grinding my hips. I am sneering at them with the whole of my being. I begin to enjoy the idea that they might find my body unattractive. I start to want them to find it repellent. As I walk around the stage, I look down on these men and almost hate them. I *almost* hate them because they are not worthy of my hate. They disgust me.

The last song of the set comes to a close. The next dancer is preparing to come on stage. I gather up my clothes and quickly go down the steps. I start to head toward the dressing room weaving through the tables and chairs. Just then, another dancer whose name I do not know calls out to me, "Hey!" I look around and she yells at me that a guy wants to tip. She's holding his dollar bill in her hand. I go over to her. She gives me the dollar and points to the single man who has been sitting on the front edge of the stage. I turn to him and say "thank you." He smiles. I turn away, crumple the bill in my fist, and head back to the dressing room.

In the dressing room, Rachel is sitting on a hard chair smoking a cigarette. Getting back into my costume, I note the silence between us. I'm thinking that I should go back out there and try to "hustle" some tips from the other customers. I also think that if I was really doing this, I should probably go back out to those customers that did tip and see if I can "hustle" some table dances. I sit down on another hard chair in the dressing room and light a cigarette myself. My thigh muscles already feel a little sore from dancing. Rachel gives a sigh on an exhale as she puts her cigarette out and sums up the customers: "They're dead tonight." I catch her eye in the mirror; I exhale and give a little nod. As I sit there I wonder if I should just get dressed and go back to my hotel. The privileged and polished comfort of the Marriott seems a world away. Yet I sense a resemblance between the club and the hotel insofar as they are each unabashed bastions of mercantilism. Rachel asks me if I've ever danced before. I tell her "no" and I am aware that I have to be careful not to blow my cover. I say to Rachel that I guess I'm just not very good at this. In my mind I'm paving the way for leaving early. I want to make sure that when I leave everyone will just think I decided against it. I don't want Amanda to get into any trouble over me. Rachel starts telling me how beautiful I am. She is giving me a pep talk. She is quite languid about it; there is little pep in her pep talk. Yet I suspect she is languid about most things. This effort, however, is clearly her way of trying to comfort me. I look down and notice that the five dollars I had tucked into my garter (the four I started the evening with, and the one tip I got for the set on the front stage) are now missing. I am embarrassed that I should have been so stupid as to lose that money. I try not to let Rachel see that I am aware of having lost it. I fold the single dollar I got from the guy who tipped at the back stage and slide it under the garter.

Sitting in the harsh light of the dressing room Rachel's scars are highly visible. They are all over her stomach, thighs and lower back. Clearly they were once quite deep lacerations. They must have been done when she was much younger. I can only imagine what happened to her. I feel so middle class, so privileged, so sheltered despite being a good fifteen years older than she. I feel vulgar, like a tourist.

I make myself go out into the club again. It would be so easy to sit in the dressing room all night. I am still not sure if I will go through the rotation again. Perhaps one set on each stage is really enough. But, I believe I should go out into the club at least once more since once I put on my street clothes and leave I will not have access to this club again. I go up to the bar and get my glass of ice water. The barman refreshes the ice for me. He smiles and says, "How are you doin'?" I say, "Oh, all right." He leans both his elbows on the bar and says, "I don't know about you, but I'd rather be home with a bottle of wine." There is something avuncular about the way he says this; it does not feel like a come-on. As he looks into my eyes, I believe he is empathizing with me and I take his meaning to be a subtle suggestion that I go home. I mumble something in agreement with him and walk away.

There are still a few dancers ahead of me in the rotation. I look around the club. Amanda is still in the VIP room. I talk briefly with a couple of the dancers standing together by the dressing room. I know that if I were doing this for "real" I would be trying to hustle table dances right now. I go back to the dressing room. The room is empty. I stand there looking into the mirrors that surround me on two sides under these harsh, unforgiving lights. I see me standing in this absurd costume. I look like and feel like a fish out of water. The room is filthy; cigarette butts and ash pepper the floors. Cigarette burns and trash are scattered over the counter. The chairs are falling apart. There is a torn ragged and sagging couch in the entry way. The mirrors are cracked and filthy. I see my clothes folded on the counter. I decide I've done enough and I've had enough. I decide to get dressed and go. I glance at my watch. I think I can still make it back to the hotel early enough to attend a party I was invited to. The party is being held by the faculty of the department where I attained my Master's degree. Before I decided to meet Amanda's challenge, I told others I would attend the party. I would quite like to go since a number of friends and acquaintances I haven't seen in a long while will be there. I pick up my folded jeans and as I do so, five single dollars folded lengthwise fall to the floor. I realize that these five bills are the ones I lost from my garter. I pick them up and think that one of the other dancers must have seen me drop them and returned them to me. I am struck by the honor of that act by a stranger who could easily have pocketed the cash. I hastily dress. I place the costume Amanda loaned to me and a quick note of thanks under her stack of clothes. I leave the dressing room and walking with a deliberate pace, I cross in front of the bar without looking at the barman, the DJ, or the house mom. I know they must be watching me leave. I consider that it is not the first time they've witnessed such a departure.

I step out the front door of the club into the brilliance and cacophony of Bourbon Street. Even though it is almost 10 o'clock at night, my eyes squint from the light. People are everywhere, some come toward me from various angles, others walk around me, all move with varying speeds. It takes me a moment to adjust my walk to the slightly frenetic pace of this street. I feel immersed in a kind of bubble; everything seems other-worldly. I feel so aware of my being and what I've just done. Yet I feel a kind of "not me/not not me"[3] experience with the performances I've just given in the club—both the performance of stripper on the stage and the performance of neophyte stripper-not-researcher throughout my being in the club. As I walk down Bourbon Street all the faces seem bigger than usual and all the colors of things seem more vibrant yet virulent. I feel so contained, so encased in my clothes. I also feel free of the club. I feel free in the same way I've felt free before when I've left a job, that freedom from expectations of managers and customers, freedom from responsibilities, even freedom from other employees. The feeling is a sense of returning autonomy.

As I near the corner where I know to turn to go to the Marriott, I stop in a small store to buy a pack of cigarettes. I had been in this store a couple of days earlier when I also purchased a pack of cigarettes. The woman behind the counter says, "Three dollars." I say, "They were two-fifty when I was here two days ago." She says, "Okay." I hand over the money, walk out, and laugh to myself. Everyone is on the make. Guess I look like a tourist.

I push open the heavy glass doors of the Marriott lobby entrance and head toward the bank of elevators. Despite the late hour there are still a lot of conventioneers milling about. Many of them haven't changed their suits and business outfits from the day's sessions. Some still display their convention name badges. Some are standing around talking to other members. Some are in the bar in various degrees of animation. Some are sitting on lobby couches looking into brief cases, reading conference papers, or engaged in tête-à-têtes with other members. As I enter the lobby, the most impressive feature of this scene that I notice is the sound. Everywhere in this vast hall are the ambient sounds of people, lots of people talking.

As I wait at the elevator, I overhear two men also waiting for the elevator talking about a session from the day. One man is saying how impressed he was with so-and-so's paper today. The other man says that he heard a similar argument made better by another so-and-so at last year's convention. He then goes on to say how his own paper on blah-blah-blah argues the point as well. He tells the first man that he'll send him a copy of his paper. The first man smiles. The elevator car comes and we all go in. After we press the buttons for our respective floors, the first man, as if struck by a thought says, "Oh, I think I saw you there. Did you hear so-and-so's paper on blah-blah?" The second man hits his forehead with his palm and cries, "Yes! I couldn't believe it." He lowers his tone. "What a waste." The second man and he both shake their heads in dismay. I get off on the floor where I know the party is being held. The doors close behind me. Guess I don't look like a conference member.

When I arrive at the party many people are still there. The party is being held in a suite whose occupant is a man who holds an executive administrative position with the national organization. There are several old acquaintances from my Master's program as well as many former professors. There also are a number of conference attendees whom I do not recognize. I am offered a drink. I take some ice water. People are talking about their respective research interests, publicly displaying academia. A group of graduate students I know begin to ask me questions to make small talk: What have I been doing? What are my perceptions of the university where I am now studying? Am I presenting at the conference, and so on. I find it difficult to answer these questions and find myself tending to give one- or two-word answers. I say something about how I've been spending a lot of my time in New Orleans working on my ethnographic study. When I say that I am exploring the work performances of exotic dancers I see the rubber-neckers crane into view; I see some bemused and some incredulous expressions on some of these faces. It kind of angers me that these people should so quickly come to judgment about the value of studying people who do that kind of work; it angers me that they seem to come so quick to judgment about people of whom they know nothing except perhaps some received notions about sex work and sex workers. Some of the crowd is genuinely interested to find out more from me. I find I cannot muster the energy to explain why I am interested in this phenomenon and choose to just leave it there.

The conversation thankfully moves away from me. Another person begins talking about his work. Others chime in about how they are looking at something similar to him. Soon, various others begin teasing us with their academic pursuits and publicly displaying their well-shaped academic arguments. I am being unsociable; I know it. I am told several times by different people how tired I look. That makes me even angrier because there is nothing more draining than being told you look drained. After the third time I am told this, I become disagreeable. I refuse to produce a performance for their pleasure. I didn't know how my experience in the club would affect me. I am clearly trying to process all I've done tonight. I thought coming to this party would be a way to reconnect. Instead, as I listen to the talk about our work and disciplinary interests—the main topic of conversation—I feel peevish. I find our talk so privileged and so petty.

Speaking from the Feminist Circle: Scholarly Abjectification of Sex Work

How could I let myself be so dirty? Why would I let myself be so dirty? That I have kept it so quiet surely suggests the guilt and shame of someone cognizant of her transgression. Even if it was done in the interest of research, I had gone beyond the Pale. Now that I have made myself abject by participating in the activity, must this filthy laundry be aired publicly? Now that I am beyond the Pale, now that I am outside the borders of usual scholarly and feminist provenance and traditional decency, now that I can speak from abject space, how can I not make it public?

Before I began the research I was not blind to the dirt that adheres to sex work and sex workers and that would possibly accrue to me if I became a stripper for a night. The wealth of scholarship critical of sex work had convinced me that inequities exist for women who engage in sex work and that inequities for all women are perpetuated by the trade in women's bodies and by women's participation in the sex trade. As I noted above, I began this research from a theory-informed perspective, with an avowed feminist consciousness. My scholarly voice spoke passionately from within the circle of feminists and with arched tones and aptly righteous indignation I pointed to the sex trade as quintessentially both a product of and productive of patriarchal oppression. Arguments like the one below made by Susanne Kappeler in *The Pornography of Representation* filled me with anger and informed my position. Kappeler notes a trinity of themes that motivated my feminist interest in strippers and sex work.

1. The objectification of women is pervasive and debilitating:

> Turning another human being, another subject, woman, into an object is robbing her of her own subjectivity. . . . In cultural historical terms, it is the male gender, unified by a common sense, who assumes the subject position; as the authors of culture, men assume the voice, compose the picture, write the story, for themselves and other men, and about women. (*The Pornography of Representation*, 57)

2. Women potentially perpetuate women's cultural devaluation through complicitous behaviors and internalization of male standards:[4]

> The fact that women, as individual subjects, have inserted themselves into the cultural audience (not without a struggle), have apprenticed

to the male viewpoint which surveys women as objects and as products of fine art, is itself one of the most fundamental sources of female alienation: women have integrated themselves, have internalized, a permanent outpost of the other gender—the male surveyor. (*The Pornography of Representation*, 57–58)

3. Culturally, agency is a male prerogative:

> The male gender, in turn, has extended into the whole space of subjectivity and self-expression—the available "human" right to freedom of expression. . . .[M]en have spread into and usurped the available space for agency, for power and for action; patriarchal culture validates and replicates this expansion of male gender into human space. . . . The patriarchal subject constitutes himself through the discourse of culture. (*The Pornography of Representation*, 58)

Before someone challenged me to consider that the women who work in the sex trade might not consider themselves to be as disempowered as Kappeler and others argue, I accepted this feminist view. I believed that in the clubs I would surely find women who felt as Aisha Hakim-Dyce did when she nearly took a job as a go-go dancer:

> A flood of sordid images inundated me. The reality of what I was about to do hit me full force, and I could no longer steel myself against what I knew would be, for me a humiliating, degrading and spiritually depleting experience. . . .
>
> I sat there, contemplating the enormity of the mental, spiritual and emotional healing I would need after engaging in such a depersonalizing activity, one that would surely require me to become distant and removed from my body. ("Reality Check," 236)

Although I began with these assumptions, I knew I had to interview strippers myself and hear the voices of the women first hand. Moreover, I knew I had to go to the clubs to experience their lifeworld in situ. I justified my research by considering sex workers as a kind of muted group. It wasn't until after I began interviewing dancers and going to the clubs that I became aware of the literature that had been published by sex workers. Indeed, much of that literature has been published in an effort to temper feminists and conservatives who tend to pathologize sex workers in their efforts to make their respective rhetorical and political arguments against pornography.[5] Sex workers were muted, given that they have traditionally been silenced by the threat of social punishments that acknowledgment of their activities attracts and that others have talked for them throughout history.

Once I began interviewing dancers, going to the clubs, and reading books by women working in the sex trade, I came to see the diverse range of responses to sex work. I learned that sex workers and their supporters voice their concerns through a variety of activist organizations.[6] Most of these organizations are united only through their common interest in altering the social, legal, and/or employment regulations that circumscribe sex work. The nature of the changes they seek and each group's individual goals vary greatly. Some organizations see sex work as essentially a class issue and argue that if the economic situation were different there would be no need for sex work. Implicitly, their argument rests on the mainstream belief that sex work is wrong and damaging, but given economic conditions for women it is currently necessary. Since sex workers are not to be blamed for wanting to make a good wage, these Marxist-based organizations and their allies argue that sex workers should not suffer the social abjectification from the stigma that adheres to their world. Other groups and individuals advocate a sex-positive, sometimes called a pro-sex, feminism,[7] a liberatory yet resolutely feminist ideology. These organizations and these women do not regard sex work as innately problematic. Rather, they believe that there are problems associated with the work and economic class is but one of the problems that contributes to the existence of and difficulties for sex workers. Race, gender, heterosexism, patriarchy, unjust laws, and other factors also contribute to the problematic, sometimes dangerous working conditions confronting sex workers. Principally, sex-positive feminists advocate that "women have the right to determine, for themselves, how they will use their bodies, whether the issue is prostitution, abortion/reproductive rights, lesbian rights, or the right to be celibate and/or asexual" (Alexander, "Introduction," 17). Largely, this feminism has been "associated with a group of sex-industry workers and their supporters who identify as feminist and who work within traditional feminist organizations to advance a choice-based agenda" (Queen, "Dykes and Whores," 183). Moreover, they oppose censorship, support decriminalization of prostitution, and encourage dialogue about the issues which pertain to diverse sexual expression, including sex work, reminding other feminists that there is more than one experience of sex work, and not all are negative (Queen, "Dykes and Whores," 183).

If I once had an essentialized notion about women who strip, I found as I encountered sex-positive feminism embodied by the sex workers I met that I had to abandon those conceptions, however discomforting abandoning them might be. By adopting the lens of sex-positive feminism, I came to better understand my subjects' lives and to accommodate a more complex vision of the overlapping impulses for feminism and sex work than I had prior to the study. Yes, I saw some women in the clubs do things that were debasing. I met and interviewed women who had nothing but bad things to say about their experiences as exotic dancers and whose viewpoints and experiences support mainstream feminist arguments against sex work. Yet I also met women who emphatically tell me they love working in the clubs, women who say they experience the work as anything but abjectifying, women who are quite resolutely feminists. I met women who argue that they are not being sexually objectified but rather, if any objectification is going on, they are the ones who are financially objectifying the customers. I met women who argue convincingly that their work environment is no more circumscribed by male ideals than almost any other business environment, and argue, furthermore, that they have more autonomy and economic freedom than most women workers. I met women who loathe the conditions under which they work but do not find the act of stripping necessarily debasing; I met women who find stripping empowering for how it teaches them about their bodies, and for how it teaches them about the power of desire, and for how it helps them to love themselves and even to love men. Moreover, I came to see how strong many of these women are; despite the threat of social censure these women would willingly speak to me and agreed to allow me to put their stories in print.[8] I came to learn that understanding how these women experience their working lives meant that I needed to understand sex-positive feminism.

Over time I began to ask how these women could experience their work in ways so contrary to what my ideological beliefs had led me to believe in as right. To see them apparently feel so free with their bodies in contexts that I regarded as laced with sexism, sexual objectification, and oppression challenged the righteousness of my beliefs as well as my taken-for-granted understandings about my body. I felt in my tissues and marrow the tingle of vulnerability such exposure would give to me. Some of the women I spoke with and the words of some of the sex workers' publications I read articulated clear feminist defenses against the arguments feminist theorizers voiced in opposition to their work. These were strong, independent women; moreover, they were in control of the clientele.[9]

When I spoke with Amanda it was clear that in general she believed she was in control, that she was not being debased. Furthermore, with the reluctant voice of a woman of her so-called post-feminist generation, she demonstrated her ignorance of feminism when she dismissed any arguments I raised in favor of feminism on the grounds that she didn't approve of policies or politics that sought preferences for one group over another. She spoke like a person who feels sure she plays on a level playing field. She spoke like a woman who feels no debt of gratitude to the feminists who came before her and who worked to give her that feeling of security, however elusive or illusory that security may in time prove to be. Though she surely is not an activist for feminist causes *per se*, I consider her a *de facto* feminist. Her avowal of strength and her proactive determination to pursue an independent livelihood accords with feminisms' fundamental purpose of empowering women economically and psychically. Although each dancer will experience the work differently, for me Amanda is representative of the strong, independent, feminist dancers I encountered.

Speaking from Experience: Reflecting on Stripping

I was never fully a participant/observer until the night I stripped. Yes, I could observe, but being female I could never be a participant/observer with the rest of the spectator/customers. Without stripping I wasn't fully participating from that side of the stage lights either. Yet I also knew that my becoming a stripper for a night would not bridge the differences between what Amanda and the other strippers experience and what I would experience. My experience could only be a momentary sampling of what it means to strip. During and following the experience I would remain a graduate student with a stipend and student loans and an ongoing course of study; and although there are graduate students who fund their studies by stripping, that was not my intention. Like Carol Rambo Ronai who danced in order to collect data for her Master's thesis, my intention as a researcher would not be erased while I danced (Ronai and Ellis, "Turn-Ons for Money," 274).[10] In my description, I do not reflexively consider myself as simply a stripper, but as a researcher who is stripping for her first and only time.

Like Hakim-Dyce, I mostly found stripping "humiliating, degrading and spiritually depleting." Arguably my experience supports Kappeler's arguments I've cited earlier, for I felt sexually objectified and debased. Moreover, I felt complicitous in my debasement and, by implication, complicitous in other women's debasement by engaging in the activity. Rent with fear, I was incapable of giving myself permission to do anything but be a conflicted unwilling/willing participant. I continually appraise my body and the bodies of my co-workers with the appropriated gaze of an abiding male judge. And finally, I let my agency slip away as I foundered under that assessment. I felt vulnerable, acquiescent, and utterly exposed. I felt myself to be abject and I abjectified myself. In short, I got what I came for. I got what I came with.

Speaking from beyond the Pale: Sex-Positive Feminism as a Variation on Sex Work

A pale is literally a pointed wooden stake intended to be driven into the ground and used with other pales to create a fence. Over time, a pale came to be known as a "boundary or limit," a "defence or safeguard" (*The Compact Edition of the*

Oxford English Dictionary, 390). In time, a figurative sense derived from this literal sense to denote any place proscribed by jurisdiction or established bounds (391).[11] When one is said to be beyond the pale, she is thought to have transgressed established norms, morality, or law. To speak as a sex-positive feminist is to speak from beyond the pale; in fact, it is to speak from beyond a double pale, for no matter how ubiquitous feminism is within academe, it is hardly mainstream in the broader cultural milieu. Yet a sex-positive feminism speaks beyond the traditional circle of feminists. It speaks beyond the beyond.

A sex-positive feminism challenges several assumptions that operate within more academically valorized feminist viewpoints. When the strippers I spoke with and spent time with voiced feminist concerns and argued that they find no contradiction in holding those positions, they spoke from sex-positive feminist positions and challenged the feminist beliefs I held. Though Amanda forswore feminism, her position of strength implicitly argued against the feminist arguments I might have made that she was being victimized or degraded by her work. I held my views in check, did what I could to not simply fit my views to these women's lives, for I did not want to contravene personal and ethnographic ethics. I felt I had a responsibility to think beyond my feminist culture so that I might better understand her culture. Throughout my fieldwork I knew I could not entirely escape my culture or my ideology, but I did not realize until I danced that night how deeply my feminist beliefs are held in my body. In obvious contrast to my experience in the club, these women move through the club and through the world with a confidence and a sensual and sexual bravado I am too shamed or too reluctant to explore. While I may have undertaken the study in order to understand how strippers experience their subjectivity in the clubs, it was by stripping myself that I found out how I experience my subjectivity in the club, or more precisely, how I experience my body given the network of surveillance and self-surveillance that pervades that situation for me. By stripping I came to understand *in my body* the truth of HopKins's aphorism that locates performance as agency and the many resistances I had to negotiate in that performance.

Where Amanda felt confidence, I felt vulnerability. When Amanda danced she negotiated exposure; when I danced I negotiated concealment. Where I abjectified myself, Amanda abjectified the clientele. Where I averted my gaze and relinquished my power; Amanda looked the men in their eyes and took control. Furthermore, any abjection I may feel for having stripped effectively invites abjectification, for it is by disavowing my experience that the dirt of the work clings to me; whereas Amanda eschews the dirt by refusing to let it attach to her.

Understanding how Amanda and I differ in our performances as strippers means accounting for these differences in resistance; it means returning to, as

HopKins has called it, the "squirming," and the "turning and tossing" that characterize the negotiation of my agency in my performance of stripper ("The Performance Turn," 235). If performing gender is a routine accomplishment (cf. Garfinkel, "Passing"), then the discomfort I experience and the incompetence I display as I dance is perhaps at least partly attributable to the situational exigency that urges me to perform my gender differently than I am accustomed to doing. As I dance, I strain to convince the customers and the club management that I belong there and am capable of performing some recognizable category of stripper femininity. Similar to Agnes's experience in Garfinkel's study,[12] I find myself having to undergo a kind of "secret apprenticeship"("Passing," 146): I very quickly have to appear to be at ease in the club and appear to know what I'm doing on the stage.[13] As I know my body to be older and fleshier than most of my dancing colleagues in the club, I feel myself to be less than adequate to the task since status is affected by physical shape. While a hierarchy of bodies exists in both the world at large and in the strip club, its effect on social standing is especially felt in the strip club—for obviously, there is no way to disguise one's body when doing a strip tease.[14] Bodies in the strip club are the currency by which status among the dancers is negotiated with the clientele.[15]

Any new stripper might experience discomfort and fear. But since I was figuratively (though obviously not literally) undercover as a researcher, the fear of exposure I underwent was more than the fear of exposed flesh. As my description shows, I was more fearful of being found out as a stripper by my professional peers than being found out as a researcher by the clientele, the other dancers, or the club management. My fear, discomfort, and incompetence, then, derive from a felt conflict between my role as stripper and my role as researcher, from my awareness that what I am doing contravenes how the role of researcher is supposed to be performed. Like Agnes, I fear the social punishments that might affect my livelihood and professional reputation if my "true" identity is discovered.

Unlike the other strippers who are motivated by the expectation of financial remuneration, I am motivated by a desire to understand the experience, by a desire to "get" some useful field material. I appear to care little if the customers tip or not. The "fuck it" attitude that I develop on the front stage when I so indelicately remove my top develops into a pronounced antagonism at the men on the back stage. As I move from one stage to the next, I move from fear to loathing. Once I am at the back stage removed from the palpable gaze of the club management and the passing parade of possible rubbernecking convention attendees, I perform abjection as a strategy to offend those men who so cavalierly dismiss my presence. I am in their faces, literally and figuratively. At that point, although I am performing stripper, I am not adequately or appropriately performing stripper femininity—as the meager amount of tips I receive for my pains would suggest. Absent then in my performance is a basic condition for constituting femininity in the club—that is, a demonstrated, even if insincere, sexual interest in the male clientele. How I experienced stripping is colored by my being a committed feminist and a researcher, and by the awkwardness I feel in my newness as a stripper, and by my anger at the clientele.

And so I begin to understand the resistances that affect my performance. Yet clearly, Amanda is not encumbered as I am; her experience exceeds my understanding. To understand Amanda's performance I must learn how unlike my own it is. I must engage how she says she experiences her work and how I observe her engage her work from a different perspective than the feminist position with which I came. I must sense what it feels like to be a body that does not experience the kind of vulnerabilities I felt. I must challenge the assumptions I take for granted.

I know that the feminist and gender research I brought with me to this experience would help me to catalog what strippers do sociologically. I know that it can give me several analytic tools to use to explore what happens in strip clubs. The knowledge I would glean through those scholarly insights is important and rigorous. Yet I also know that looking through the academic lens the skin and sinew of the experience vanishes. It doesn't help me understand what I came to learn, to know how Amanda, I, or more generally, other strippers perform their agency in the club. To understand that I must drop those tools, set aside the lenses I came with, and I must return to our lived experiences and explore the concepts that shape our perceptions. To get to a place where I can understand sex-positive feminism, I must reflect upon and feel into how Amanda negotiates her performance.

Dancing with Amanda

The elevator doors open at the lobby and a blanket of noise smothers our conversation. Amanda, her boyfriend Bobby, and I exit the elevator and snake through a sea of bodies toward the side door of the Marriott hotel. Suits are everywhere. Conference name badges catch the light, briefcases click open and shut, glasses clink in the bar. Fragments of conversation are caught and discarded as we move through the pack. Eyes snagged by a peripheral glance at the length of her leg, the shape of her torso, the flippancy in her walk turn toward us and refuse to relinquish the sight of Amanda. They do not see me or Bobby. With her lithe easy walk and tousled, short, dirty-blond hair Amanda slides effortlessly through the gawking gazes of male and female conference attendees. The jeans are not tight, but she wears them so well. The top is striking as it is black suede with long bell sleeves and laces up the front of the bodice. Her midriff is mildly exposed. Although she is an inhabitant of this city—unlike the crowds in this lobby—she is an outsider here. No one thinks for a second that she is a conference member.

Amanda appears at ease. The turning and gazing is so pronounced she cannot help but notice, but she does not acknowledge it; nor does she appear to enjoy it particularly. As men turn and stare at her I wonder if she is thinking about how, as she told me in the interview, she could teach them a lesson if they came into the club. How she could make them fall in love with her. Or perhaps she is simply tuning them out, regarding them as utterly unimportant. Could this game of looks from others and her refusal to acknowledge them just be the taken-for-granted way for Amanda? I am struck by how easily this presumably liberal group of educators is transformed into voyeurs.

After leaving Bobby at the club where he is a stripper, we arrive at Big Daddy's. In the dressing room Amanda and I select our costumes from her bag full of options. In front of the cracked and smudged mirrors and the harsh lighting of the dressing room, Amanda stands only in her t-strap as she pulls costume after costume from her bag. She is twenty years old with a lovely face and slim, polished body very close to the "ideal" female form. She has long legs with tight firm thighs. Her rear is smooth, shapely, yet small. Her breasts sit high on her chest and are neither remarkably big nor noticeably small. Her short hair is perennially disheveled. She wears no face makeup. She is both professional and jovial as she considers each costume option that I might wear: This one is cute but she cautions me that it irritates under the arms after a while. Black leather and chains won't go with my boots and, as she smiles, she points out that I might not want that "look" my first time out. The red outfit she says she rarely wears and it's just too whorish. Surely her smile as she says this is fed by her amusement at getting an academic to strip. For herself she decides on a beige leather micro-mini-skirt and matching bra top. She pulls out a pair of thigh-high, low-heeled boots that are also beige to complete her look. The lilac-colored costume I select meets with her approval. Amanda's choice of costume is not made according to how much money she assumes it might help her to make; rather, Amanda chooses her costume according to how she feels, what feels good to her today. As I touch up my face makeup she gives a cursory glance at her face, runs her fingers rather than a brush through her hair, and spies a red mark on her shoulder. She reaches in her bag for a tube of Durablend creme concealer and as she looks at her back's reflection in the mirror and smears some of the concealer over the pimples on her shoulders and back, she exclaims, "The body needs Durablend." The gaze is hers.

We go out on the floor and Amanda sticks by my side until she is called to go up in the swing. She is comforting and coaxing without being maternal. We smoke cigarettes and she gives me the lowdown on all the "girls." I'm told to be careful about what I say to Carol because she tells management everything. I'm told to watch out for Natalie because she likes to steal customers. I nod and smoke and feel as if my body is glowing in neon, cold with exposure, in the wrong place at the wrong time. Amanda exudes warmth and calm. She moves with the ease of a gazelle at home in her habitat. As I look at Amanda, I cannot help but *look* at Amanda. I cannot help but look at her body, for it is beautiful. There is something simultaneously comforting and frustrating to know that there are bodies such as Amanda's out there. Hers is not the pampered and produced perfection of the media's models. Hers is an easy beauty, achieved without worry, without much economic expense. She is twenty, I remind myself.

She leaves me to take her place in the rotation. It is her turn to "moon Bourbon." Before she leaves me she tells me to remember to dance for myself. She looks so self-contained as she walks away. I think how much easier it must be to dance for oneself when one has a body like hers. I am heavy with the weight of my culturally ascribed bodily imperfections. I watch Amanda slide out of her micro-mini-skirt and bra, slip up the ladder to the swing without hesitation, and disappear from my view.

Later, when Amanda takes to the front stage there is a conscious premeditation in her movements. The easiness in her gait has given over to a more studied style. She seems to prance and glide. I sense a kind of careful willingness in her dance. She is beautiful and skilled. Rather than demanding compliance, she coaxes her audience into adoration. Perhaps she is thinking about sex as she dances, for she has told me she does this and that it helps her to move and helps her to garner customers' interest. Men dotted around the stage look up at her on the stage and follow her every move. She strides downstage toward the pole and leaps up grabbing the ring up on the pole. Hanging from the ring, she wraps her legs around the pole and once her legs are gripping the pole she releases her hands from the ring, leans back and stretches her torso out from the pole. She swings her arms behind her head. Using all the strength in her stomach muscles she pulses her torso up and down keeping her torso, head, and arms perpendicular to the pole. I imagine she is thinking that this pose is a sure-fire crowd pleaser and is reveling in the power she has to grab and control their gaze. The pose demonstrates her remarkable physical strength and skill and also conveys a sense of her sensual and sexual power. She pauses there, then, slowly, using her stomach muscles she rises, grabs the ring, and then lets herself slide off the pole. A man at the rim of the stage, stage right near the pole, has fallen into the vision of Amanda. He cannot, nor does he want, to extract himself. As she comes off the pole, the man proffers a dollar in his outstretched hand. She offers him her leg with the garter on it; he slips the bill under the elastic as their eyes meet. The dollar now secure, she breaks the gaze and strides away. She knows he's hers if she wants him. She doesn't.

She places herself strategically beneath the beam of a light. Light saturates the top of her head, shoulders and breasts. As she moves to the music she reaches behind her neck with one hand and behind her back with the other and unties the strings that hold her leather bra in place. She lets the bra fall from her breasts to the floor. As the light spills over her contours she is stunning. She strokes her breasts with her hands. Her skin looks smooth, soft, silky. She invites us to want it. Her skin, now golden under the light, being touched by her hands sends a flutter through me as she flings her head back in what appears to be sensual delight. She may be in her "own little silo" as she calls it, but she knows she's in control. I imagine her thinking about that control, strategizing what new move she can make that will rouse the desire of the men in the audience. She told me that dancing is like playing Stratego and that around the stage are all these forts, which she says are the men's wallets, and all she is doing is looking for the key that will unlock the forts. I imagine that as she moves she is asking herself which move is the "key" that will give her what she wants. As she moves, her body is like silky liquid. She moves with an obvious comfort in her skin, a comfort that I long for but have never known.

The money comes.

When she removes all but her t-strap she doesn't so much seem naked, with all the awkward exposure that the word connotes. In fact, she seems appropriately attired. Her dance invites us to want her nudity; it comes as a culminating moment to all that's come before. Again, I sense the ease of her being. She struts around the stage returning the gazes of the men in the audience and as she does so, they seem more out of place than she. She looks down on them more than simply literally. I imagine her feeling the power of her victory over them.

At the end of her set, she stoops to collect a few rogue bills as she leaves the stage. It isn't as much as I've seen dancers collect after their sets in other clubs. But the crowd is small and it feels reluctant and cynical. Perhaps the glitz and sleaze particular to Bourbon Street with its too-hyped reputation keeps the punters' money in their pockets. I reckon these men are largely tourists, not regulars. Before I leave the club, Amanda is seated in the VIP room with a smiling and seemingly contented companion. She has gained access to the room where the real money is made, the room I cannot bring myself to try to enter. Her companion looks like he's in his early forties, not unattractive, middle class. He smiles first at me and then looks back adoringly to her. Amanda waves to me smiling. Is she happy to see me, or does her happiness come from the knowledge that now she will make some good money tonight? If you ignore Amanda's provocative costume, she and her client look like a picture of a happy couple.

The next night I leave the conference alone; I walk to the Silver Frolic to meet Bobby where he dances to the whoops and hollers of a paying female clientele. He has long jet-black hair and wears vampire teeth to add a bit of local spice to his act. While I wait for him to get off work, I sit in the back and watch women peel off dollar bills when he squats down beside them at the ring side, opens his mouth and tilts his head back, and lets the lights glint off his artificially elongated pearly whites. When he sticks out his tongue the women yelp in delicious pain. Still, while they are more vocal, women fork out less money than men generally do; Bobby always makes less than Amanda. We leave the Silver Frolic and go to a bar down a side street from Big Daddy's. Together over drinks we wait for Amanda to get off work. When it gets to be three in the morning, we decide that she must have a good customer and can't get away by two as she had planned.

Bobby and I talk of many things. Mostly he talks about Amanda. It's clear he adores her. He attributes to her all the best in his life, that she got him back on track after a miserable adolescence during which his parents' violent divorce and his prolonged bout with drugs systematically devastated him. The talk shifts to me as he asks about my "love life." I tell him I am bisexual and that I am currently in a relationship with a woman. His eyes light up and he sits back on his bar stool as if moving a little farther away will give him the appropriate perspective with which to comprehend this unexpected news. As he lets a long "Ooh!" escape from his lips I wonder if he's decided that my sexuality somehow explains my interest in the topic of exotic dancers. Or, I wonder if perhaps he's wondering if my interest in Amanda is more than friendly. Or, maybe he's imagining something far more salacious. He asks a few questions about my girlfriend and I make a few vague comments about her, preferring not to speak too specifically about a relationship that is currently faltering in large measure because of the growing differences in our feminisms. Despite the earnestness of his questions, Bobby is clearly not the right audience for that discussion.

Amanda finally saunters into the bar. She is in jeans and a big floppy white blouse, her hair is its usual tousled mess. She is surprised but happy to see me. She gives Bobby a peck on the lips and gives me a quick hug. She is happy to be off work. According to Amanda, unlike other dancers, she is not a stripper twenty-four hours a day. It's her job, not her life. Now that she's away from the club she's not interested in thinking about the club. Bobby orders her a beer while she settles onto the bar stool in between Bobby and me. Quick details are given about how work was, what kind of money she made, how the house mom reacted the night before when I walked out. "I guess Barbara saw you leave and just told the next girl to fill in the gap." She is dry, direct, and brief in her tale. She is not a narrator who embellishes for effect. Though I want more details of what happened after I walked out of the club, they are simply not forthcoming. That's yesterday's news.

Amanda is hungry and they both want to smoke some pot so they invite me to go with them to their apartment. We drive in their car to the apartment, which is in an old building with a huge veranda that runs along the front. The living room and bedroom are huge with high ceilings but the bathroom and kitchen are tiny, evidently the product of some landlord's plan to convert an old single dwelling into multiple units. I'm quickly introduced to Hannibal Lechter, their ferret, who is so excited at Amanda and Bobby's return that he speed races all over the apartment for the duration of the time I'm there. Bobby cooks while Amanda rolls a joint. While they are reserved in public, in the apartment they are unabashed in their affection, cooing and kissing openly while rashers of bacon sizzle in the frying pan. There are almost no furnishings, only two chairs, a table, and a mattress on the floor. Though I decline breakfast, they insist that I sit in one of the two chairs while they share the other chair. Amanda sits on Bobby's lap as they eat. When they're not kissing or touching, they sometimes talk in baby talk to each other.

Amanda tells me their future plans and how they are saving their money so that they can go back to school. By way of explanation for their meager surroundings, she says that she could buy more furniture or decorate but going to school is more important. She wants me to know that she knows the limitations of her current employment. Bobby holds her on his lap and seems content to agree to anything Amanda has planned. I catch myself saying that I hope they make it and note as I do so that I somehow anticipate that they won't. I wonder why I underestimate them. Certainly they have time on their side, they both (although Amanda particularly) appear ambitious and determined, and they seem fortified by a powerful and abiding commitment to each other. I wonder if my cynicism doesn't derive from some preconceptions about the nature of the work they do, that somehow I cannot shake some buried notion that they are losers because they are sex workers.

When we say goodbye we are all laughing. I wave as they drive off having left me at the side door to the Marriott. They are happy together; they have money and plans and are young and beautiful. I know I'll never see them again. As I enter the now almost vacant lobby at this early morning hour, I once again feel like a tourist.

Lessons in Desire, Social Acceptability, and Feminism

As I consider how the image of the tourist inflects both my description of my experience of stripping and my description of Amanda, I am reminded of a particular tourist I encountered as part of a coach tour I once took behind the Iron Curtain. At the end of a month-long bus trip through the (then) Soviet Union, Poland, and East Germany, we finally entered into West Berlin through

Checkpoint Charlie. As we stood outside the bus taking the air, taking a much needed break from being cooped up in the bus, the retired RAF captain filled his lungs and exclaimed, "Can't you just feel the difference?!" The implication was that now that he was back in the West he felt more relaxed. He claimed that even the air felt different. Perhaps because he had put his body on the line during a horrible war, he experienced the trip as he did. Clearly he and I had very different experiences of the Eastern bloc countries we had just visited. As commonly used, the image of the tourist conjures antipathy for it suggests a stance productive of the most loathsome form of voyeuristic (dis)interest. The image of a tourist suggests someone with a cold stare, lacking in sensitivity to others, with little tolerance others' differences, or possessing much emotional or bodily investment in the place he or she is visiting. Like the retired military man I describe above, the tourist is curious but only curious to the point of having his or her presumptions confirmed. We all, perhaps inevitably, do this to some extent. But the tourist resolutely resists being touched by what he or she encounters. Of course, actual tourists may not accord with this pejorative stereotype, for not all people who engage in tourism are so recalcitrant and reactionary. There are those who travel in cultures other than their own who do seek to be touched, moved, challenged, and engaged by the worlds—though different from their own—that they earnestly and openly seek to encounter. To do so can be a life-changing event, for assumptions may be challenged, taken-for-granted values may be subjected to critique, alternative visions and possibilities may be opened up, and possibilities that may or may not jibe with individual comfort may ensue.

This pejorative vision of a tourist's quick and ready interpretation of a culture is antithetical to the deep engagement usually associated with scholarly inquiry. Refusing to be a tourist when scholars investigate cultures or topics away from our own comfortable experiences, implies adopting a place similar to Conquergood's center ground on his moral map for ethnographic research. That space, the dialogic center, is located "between conflicting ideologies"(Conquergood, "Performing as a Moral Act," 9) where appreciation for difference permits deep questioning. There divergent rationalities, to use Richard A. Shweder's term, are given room to be tussled out and debated and where conclusions are resisted and where empathy is not the aim (Conquergood, "Performing as a Moral Act," 9). When we scholars explore other cultures and topics beyond our own experience or proclivities, it is not enough to employ our own understandings and moralities as guiding interpretive reference points. Anthropologist Shweder clarifies my point when he notes that "the idea of divergent rationalities helps us see that there may be more than one conceptual reference point from which to construct an objective ethic" ("Divergent Rationalities," 190). Given how morally contested the participation in sexualized activities is, that dialogic space where those contested ideologies and divergent rationalities may be engaged appears to remain elusive for some. Yet I argue that as we are scholars, find that space, we must, even when considering people whose behaviors challenge our own views of propriety. Gayle Rubin urges consideration along the same lines when she notes that "We have learned to cherish different cultures as unique expressions of human inventiveness rather than as the inferior or disgusting habits of savages. We need a similarly anthropological understanding of different sexual cultures" ("Thinking Sex," 284).

To open myself up to an alternative vision of what goes on in strip clubs I have had to try to set aside some of the feminist assumptions I bring to the scene. I have had to set aside a singular conception of the men in strip clubs as distanciated voyeurs ocularly consuming women's bodies and consider the notion that there are multiple ways of looking: In addition to the predatory gaze, there are some men who adore, some men who worship, some men who need strippers for entertainment, enjoyment, contact. To honor the women who work in strip clubs, I found I had to bracket off the feminist assumption I came with that women who work in these clubs are victims of economic and sexist oppression. I needed alternatives. To respect the women and men who inhabit the strip clubs, I found I had to explore what energizes the place. I found I had to understand the economies of desire.

Lesson One: Desire Is Desire Is Desire

Now that I have danced with Amanda, now that I have put myself in what I preconsidered to be an abject position, I find I have been invited around a very different moral table than the one at which I was originally seated. As I sit at this table I find I am no longer comfortably cloaked in the safe habits of my taken-for-granted ideological commitments. Rather, I find I my ideology revealed, laid bare. At this table I find sugar is not innately good and vinegar is not innately bad. Sugar is sweet and vinegar bitter, but one's preference for sweet or bitter has little to do with preconceptions of goodness and badness and more to do with what hungers are being stimulated by a menu of contextual factors at a given time.

As I sit at this new moral table, I envision abandoning a hierarchy of desire. The values embedded in that hierarchy are no longer appetizing to me for they produce a good deal of hate, and hate is not something from which one should take nourishment. Today, homophobia is still commonplace. Some people, many of whom are gay or lesbian, are biphobic—that is, prejudiced against those who claim bisexual identity. Other people are simply "erotophobic,"[16] for they possess a "fear of sex and sexuality"(Queen, "Everything that

Moves," 45). Rubin has characterized this hierarchy; at the top, of course, is the most accepted form, heterosexual monogamous coupling. Below this and in declining order resides queer desire, desire expressed in S/M, masturbation, desire aided by pornography or sex toys, promiscuous desire or with more than one partner at a time, desire for partners from different generations, and desire expressed or fulfilled via commercial sex.[17] As I imagine abandoning this hierarchy of desire, I feel a belt loosen and more comfort settle in. For without such a hierarchy, a variety of sexual discrimination articulated as righteous moralizing would likewise have to fall away. Abandoning a hierarchy of desire would remove individual or social judgment from consenting adults' beds. It would remove the cultural stigmatization of sex workers. It would mean that I would meet Amanda's hopes and aspirations as well as her activities without cynicism. Abandoning a hierarchy of desire would allow a greater range of desire that exists to come out of hiding; there would be no reason that consensual adult desire would ever be accompanied by shame. Abandoning a hierarchy of desire would let desire be in the I of the beholder. Abandoning a hierarchy of desire means the customers in the clubs do not merit my sneers simply by their presence there. It would also help me recognize that the struggle I had as I stripped had more to do with that hierarchy and how it bound my bodily freedom with cultural conditioning and ideological influence, than due to some innate immorality to the act. Indeed, as Rubin points out, hierarchies of desire or as she calls them,

> hierarchies of sexual value—religious, psychiatric, and popular—function in much the same way as do ideological systems of racism, ethnocentrism, and religious chauvinism. They rationalize the well-being of the sexually privileged and the adversity of the sexual rabble. ("Thinking Sex," 280)

As I find myself at this new moral table, I ask if instead of adhering to the values of a hierarchy of desire, I could take on an attitude of honoring desire?[18] Honoring desire would mean the most important question in adjudicating the rightness or wrongness of a given act would be whether or not it is consensual (Queen, "Everything that Moves," 47). Of course, as Jill Nagle points out, insofar as consent may be "based upon an abstract notion of equality but is applied to situations of social inequality" it can be a problematic criterion for judging the politics of desire ("Introduction," 14). Rubin clarifies how best to apply the concept by noting that "A democratic morality should judge sexual acts by the way partners treat one another, the level of mutual consideration, the presence or absence of coercion, and the quantity and quality of the pleasures they provide" ("Thinking Sex," 283). Honoring desire requires that each partner receive honorable treatment. By discerning the nuances of consent within actual situated experiences, rather than through application of general rules, we feminists could engender more equitable gender and sexual relations. It is far easier to discredit wholesale an activity like commercial sex than it is, for example, to help women assert their right to withdraw from enforced or even unsatisfactory sexual relations with their husbands. Consider how a blow job negotiated for a good price may leave the individuals feeling far more honored by the experience and more mutually content than the debilitating politics of sexual entitlement that some intimate partners exact on each other. Consenting to sex for financial remuneration (whether that reward be in the financially explicit negotiations of a brothel or in the implicit financial dependence and economy of a marriage) may suit the participants just fine and be experienced quite happily as an equitable arrangement. Far more insidious than the exchange of money for sex or titillation are the social and legal conditions imposed on sex workers by a morally indignant voting majority and their legislative officers who do not legislate on behalf of sex workers for the protections most of us take for granted as terms of our employment. Discerning the social inequities that may lead a woman to engage in sex work because she has little other opportunity for making a decent living wage, and who takes that work though she would prefer not to, would reveal nuances of coercion and consent within society that truly merit our attention. Of course, in order to discern the nuances of consent and to honor desire, the voices of those involved need to be listened to; it means that sex is honorable. Honoring desire means seeing sex as positive by means of the

> simple yet radical affirmation that we each grow our own passions on a different medium, that instead of having two or three or even half a dozen sexual orientations, we should be thinking in terms of millions. [Even if one's imagination does have limits, the point is that being] "Sex positive" respects each of our unique sexual profiles. (Queen, "Introduction," xviii)[19]

Honoring desire means abandoning notions of good girls and bad girls, or more accurately, good and bad women. Adhering to a hierarchy of desire keeps that binary in place and keeps an allied system of punishments and oppression in place. Honoring desire means abundance on the moral table; each of us needn't partake of it all, but at least the choice is there for us all.

Lesson Two: Without Desire, Social Acceptability Is a Drag

Like toilet paper popping out of an adolescent's bra, openly acknowledging desire is socially unacceptable. It is potentially socially unacceptable in two ways. First, it is unacceptable because social dictates deem that it should be kept hidden and because desire funds a symphony of sneers from the moral elite when made public. Second, if the desire under scrutiny is socially abject, its social unacceptability is compounded. Yet however abject the desire may be, as with the adolescent who fakes a bigger chest, only she knows in her sinews and psyche the power of her desire, what is at stake, and how sanctimonious and vacuous the voices are who admonish her to accept who she is and to do without the padding. She may still love the sight of her bolstered figure, however false or deviant it may seem to some.

When I danced naked before a paying male public, I dragged the heavy mantle of preordained notions of social acceptability and an anticipated chorus of disapproval behind me. I was weighted down with my socially enculturated understandings of strip clubs as abject space and by doing what I preconsidered to be abject activities. I cowed under the weight of the unacceptability of the place and the act. Amanda with her freedom to be herself unencumbered by the fear of sexism, stigmatization, and victimization rises above the abject. She is capable of subverting the potentially abjectifying situation by refusing to give credibility to those who, by deeming her work socially unacceptable, would stigmatize her.

Having danced with Amanda and found myself wanting, I am left wanting an ideology that will bolster my appreciation for the diversity in the world; one that can, in time, become fleshed out, embodied, habituated. I envision a world where desire is not something sneaky and furtive. I imagine a society where a person's social acceptability and behavior are judged by that individual's capacity for humanity. Current public policy tends to want to keep the issue of non-normative sexual preferences in the dark and mostly out of public debate. Such silence would work fine if people's desires only accorded with the norm; when they don't, when sexual preferences that deviate slip into public view, it matters in sometimes quite devastating ways. In short, for those whose desires transgress, social norms of social acceptability require that these desires are dressed in confining clothes, in clothes that mask its true identity. Non-normative desires are made to dress in behavioral drag, if you will. Of course, unlike the drag that can be campy fun, behavioral drag is just a drag.

Passions are very powerful things and when they are secreted away, they sometimes ferment until they emerge in potentially damaging ways. I wonder, what if the drag was removed from non-normative desires and they, like other tastes, became something we accept as just part of people's lives? I wonder, what if we chose not to judge others for liking bondage, or porn, or strip shows, just like we accept their preference for the color blue, or banana and peanut butter sandwiches? If we agree there is no accounting for taste, then how can we reasonably judge others for liking one thing over another? What if desires were permitted to become more public? What if they became a more publicly acceptable and even significant part of our being, as something less circumspect and subject to misunderstanding? Wouldn't the more our desires became public, they would matter less to others? In a curious paradox, wouldn't the more they are subject to our scrutiny, they would be less subject to judgment and misunderstanding?

Of course, the world I am imagining here through this series of questions is far from our reality. Some must see my vision of a world free of sexual judgment as utopian fantasy or just naïve. But I wonder, haven't we moved toward the possibility for such a world through the cultural analyses of gender currently in circulation? Once we moved away from "sexual essentialism—the idea that sex is a natural force that exists prior to social life and shapes institutions" (Rubin, "Thinking Sex," 275) and moved toward a constructivist alternative—seeing it as a human product, in terms of social and historical analysis—then a more positive and realistic cultural view and political understanding of sex and desire becomes possible (cf. Rubin, "Thinking Sex," 277). Moreover, as it is with Amanda, perhaps it now becomes more possible to live more comfortably in our bodies, to ignore strict codes of ideological or social appropriateness that aim to ghettoize parts of our bodies and beings within dubious and restrictive categories of good and bad.

Lesson Three: Desire Is Fundamental to All Feminisms

Like a big sister sitting astride her younger sister and pinning her to the floor, some feminists use their social stature and rhetorical weight to dominate the sisterhood of feminist voices. When a singular notion of feminism was replaced by the notion of feminisms in the plural, feminists appeared to be opening up ourselves and our ideology to the idea of diversity and pluralism. Despite this positive step, the destructive idea that there are good and bad feminists and good and bad feminisms continues among feminists. It has surely been appropriate and right for feminists to acknowledge diversity, yet given the prevailing reaction to feminist sex workers, not all diversity is tolerated and respected. In our acknowledgment of our diversity we have focused so readily on difference—and decided that some differences are tolerable while other differences are not—to the exclusion of a focus on the commonalities that link us as feminists. Thus I find myself wondering, if feminism is fundamentally about equality, why do feminists argue for a hierarchy of desire? If feminism is about women's agency, why do feminists impugn other feminists simply because they exercise their agency in ways that challenge conventions of social acceptability? I want to know, if feminism is about taking control of our bodies, why must feminists only do so in prescribed and sanctioned ways? If feminism is about women asserting themselves for what they want in defiance of a cultural script that would make women demur, why do feminists encourage women not to demur in the boardroom but then shirk away from women who are not afraid to demur in the bedroom? If feminist scholarship catalogues sexual expression into good and bad categories, even in realms where there is mutual satisfaction and no coercion, aren't we pathologizing sexual variation and expressions of desire simply because they lie beyond our experiences or conceptual frameworks? Classifying that way makes tourists of those feminist scholars. Being outside the culture they purport to analyze, their rough and ready interpretations seem cavalier, like pot shots taken at a great distance at other people's experience.

What's particularly interesting in this form of feminist theorizing is that much second-wave feminism gained its critical impetus by arguing against the dominance of male interpretations of women's experiences and arguing for a critical space wherein women could voice and interpret their own experiences. For example, Maria C. Lugones and Elizabeth V. Spelman writing in 1983 in *Women's Studies International Forum* introduce their essay thus: "Feminism is, among other things, a response to the fact that women either have been left out of, or included in demeaning or disfiguring ways in what has been an almost exclusively male account of the world" (573). They go on to question how scholars should position themselves when interrogating fields outside their own experience:

> What should the relation be between a woman's own account of her experiences and the theorizer's account of it?
>
> [. . .] Most of the time the "interpretation by an outsider" is left understood and most of the time the distance of outsidedness is understood to mark objectivity in the interpretation. But why is an outsider as an outsider interpreting your behavior? (Lugones and Spelman, "Have We Got a Theory for You," 577)

The distance of outsidedness so patently evident in some feminists' arguments against sex work of course does not mark objectivity in interpretation; rather for those whose experiences are being scrutinized, such interpretations are often demeaning and disfiguring. The sex negativity implicit in some feminist biases fuels a culture of sexual misunderstanding, guilt, and shame; the result of which is stigmatized identity for the women and men who transgress social norms and, potentially, even results in violent reactions against them. Moreover, this stance of outsidedness is complicit in the politics of secrecy that pervade discussions of sex and sexual desire at an historical moment when open discussion about sex is not merely politically important but critical to people's lives and safety. Of course, no one individual or feminist perspective has the corner on desire (cf. Queen, "Fucking with Madonna," 112). When acknowledgment of the diversity of experience for women and men who transgress social norms is absent, and instead the most exploited forms of sex work or the most shocking examples of pornography or sexual expression are cited, ideology becomes demonology for desire is misrepresented in all its variation (Rubin, "Thinking Sex," 301).

The work of feminist scholars who positively explore desire, sex, and the enjoyment of sex (not just "palatable" discussions of erotica) tend to land in a kind of scholarly tenderloin[20]; that scholarship is sometimes demeaned as frivolous and self-aggrandizing. Sex, and by implication desire, is always political. It is worth remembering that when educated feminist voices opt out of discussions of sex and desire, the theorizing of these issues is left to people who may not have women's interests at heart, to people who may wish to maintain a system of sexual oppression. Increasingly, I've come to see the feminist argument against sex work as a ploy devised for political efficacy that effaces a more complex reality. Rather than making sex work and other forms of sexual variation the negative target of feminist activism and scholarship, I cannot help but believe women's interests are better served by combating sexism and other forms of oppression whether they occur in a strip club, a brothel, the classroom, or the bedroom of a monogamous married heterosexual couple. If feminists only challenge sexist and other oppressive acts against women when they occur in mainstream or socially acceptable contexts, aren't we implicitly supporting the same fallacious argument historically used to vilify women who've been raped when they wore what were deemed to be suggestive clothing, namely that these women "asked for it"? Isn't our silence an insidious form of complicity?

Demonizing sexual variance puts a demon in the heads of feminists for potential pleasures are stripped from consideration in the theatre of our desire. When desire and politics collide on the bulkhead of sex negativity, this inner feminist demon creates guilt in those unwilling to resist their politically incorrect desires; or worse, in an effort to silence the dissonance, some women abandon feminism or never join its ranks. The increasing number of young women who dismiss the name "feminist" when applied to themselves implicitly, if not explicitly, impugns feminism as a constraining perspective, even if that increasingly common conception is a misconception. When politics or scholarship takes the pleasure out of desire, it's surely time to take politics and scholarship out of pleasure or better yet, construct politics and scholarship so that pleasure and desire may flourish. If feminism is about empowering women, then what could be more empowering for female sex workers than eradicating the stigma of sex work? What could be more fundamental to feminism than for the criminality and marginality that undergirds the sex industry, and that keeps sex workers vulnerable to economic if not sexual exploitation, to be eliminated? What can be more feminist than a sex worker who embraces feminism despite the abjectifying stigma, despite work conditions unacceptable in any other line of work and that tend to exploit her, and despite a legal system that gives power to the business operators and little, if any, legal protection to her? What can be more feminist than this woman who is strong, resolute in her refusal to be abjectified by these conditions and who nevertheless actively finds her work satisfying for the financial remuneration and autonomy it provides, and who even finds it just plain enjoyable?

When I danced with Amanda I quickly learned that it was I who experienced abjection and not she. Moreover, I learned that the abjection I experienced was not simply the product of spectators' potential abjectification of my less-than-ideal body. I saw other women who danced that night, women who dance there regularly, and I've interviewed and seen other dancers who were as plump or as old as I who do not appear to experience the activity as I did. I feel now that the abjection I experienced then was as much a result of socialized expectations for female embodiment as it was due to my awareness and hence my anticipation of these expectations through my exposure to feminism. When I danced and found myself to be ignored by the men at the back stage, I believe it was my feminism that rallied my agency into action, that enabled me to get in those men's faces by performing abjection and thereby to deny them the power to dismiss me. Yet my feminism could not give me permission to explore the sensuality and enjoyment in my body, to dance for myself as Amanda urged me to do, to learn to love my body through dancing as one of the other women I interviewed asserted it did for her. Having danced with Amanda and, in some ways, having ideologically danced with all the women I interviewed, I learned again that feminism (in all its variations) is a critical perspective, and as such it must be perennially scrutinized lest its tenets reify into dogma.

When, after much deliberation, I finally answered Amanda's question, "Would you do it?," by taking to the stage, I thought I was stripping for academic gain. What I didn't know then, but came to realize, was that stripping revealed more about my ideology than it did of my body.

CHAPTER FOUR

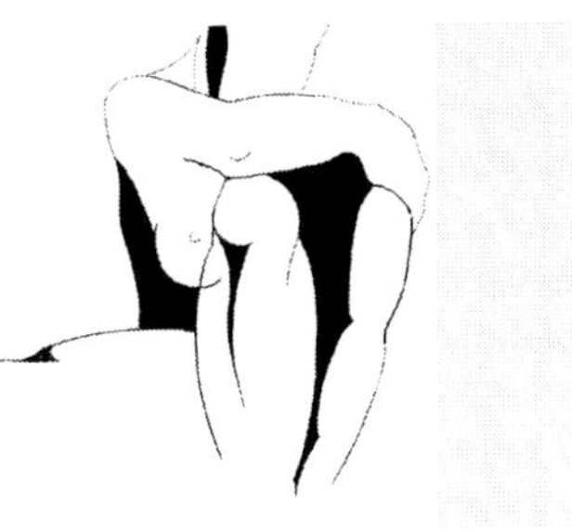

Reading the Body: Consuming the Feminist Scholar

The world is not so much a noun as an adjective.

—GASTON BACHELARD

Do we see the real, concrete world or do we see our own system of rubrics, motives, expectations and abstractions which we have projected onto the real world? Or to put it very bluntly, do we see or are we blind?

—ABRAHAM H. MASLOW

Our yesterdays follow us; they constitute our life, and they give character and force and meaning to our present deeds.

—JOSEPH PARKER

The Pleasure of Your Company Is Requested

We are what we eat, or so the saying goes. Therefore, we should beware of what we consume. We must choose well. Tastes cultivated early may affect us later. We may grow fat and confident on a regime of the acceptable and tasteful staples of academe. We may take soporific comfort among the mainstays, safe from risk of offense or indigestion. The flavors that we savor, others may not stomach. There on the margins of scholarly acceptability, we may dine alone or with few others. We may starve or grow tetchy and tense by indulging in that which refuses succor, grow ill by savoring only the unhealthful, or we may grow robust on that which others refuse.

I have cut my scholarly teeth on what some call the tasteless. That which has piqued my scholarly appetite perhaps holds little or no appeal to others beyond the curiosity that difference (to some, aberrance) may prompt. "What is past is prologue," Shakespeare reminds. To savor the scholar that I've become, I must re-read from the table of my academic past, the place where my scholarly identity was wrought. I invite you to read and re-read with me, beside me, opposite me, as me. As with any well-mannered guest, you are expected to eat what is put on your plate. As your host, I hope you will savor what is put before you, and that you will willingly sample these offerings with more than the compunctions of etiquette.

Readings: Spinning the Ideological Bottle

I am standing waiting to do a performance, a risky performance. The risk is in the raw. The raw presence of my body, my unclothed body, will be on display. The raw presence of a body made abject, willfully presented for their consumption. I anticipate the heat of their gaze. Skewered on the tangled forks of abjection, I expect they will read me. The readings surely will be multiple, possibly irreconcilable, often contested. There will be readings I did not expect and readings I could not imagine they would make. As points on a compass they hold their abjectifying gazes steady and aim them toward the plane of my body. **"She is standing . . . ,"** *I believe I hear them begin. No, wait for that. First, read from where I stand. Read with me. Close the divide that separates us. Change the script and see a different text:* "You are standing . . ." *Yes, read from here.* You are standing, your calf muscles made taut and pert from the black suede stiletto-heeled shoes you are wearing. Black stockings cover your legs, silky and smooth. A white alpaca wool wrap-around full-length coat comfortably cloaks the rest of your body from view. Your face is made up and your shoulder-length hair is pinned into a provocative style. Around you is a circle of chairs that you have placed on the playing space of the department theatre of the university where you study and work. A familiar place, a mutable space, made alien by your ministrations. Your blood-red lips boast a beaming, though insincere, smile. You are standing in a pose reminiscent of a mannequin, motionless, except for occasional quivers of nerves which run up the length of your legs. You are anxious about the performance, a usual and expected sensation bolstered all the more by the anticipation of risk in this performance. In your hands you have a placard that says, "Please take a seat in the circle." You feel the tightness of the short, black skirt, and a tight, black, low-cut, knit top under your coat. You warm at the thought that you look every inch the cheap stereotypical sex object. Beneath the skirt and top you feel the slink of the black full slip, and the pinch of the black garter belt and black panties you wear. A white push-up bra creases the skin on your back and pushes up your breasts into significant cleavage and your breasts are enlarged by the foam falsies that augment them. After standing here, waiting, for several minutes, your eight colleagues, your current lover, and the two professors for a class in Ideology and Performance file in; they read the sign you hold and seat themselves in the chairs around you.

When everyone is assembled you break your motionless stance by putting the placard down. You break the silence by switching on one side of a dual cassette tape deck that rests on a stand near you. Your never break your smile until the very end of the performance and its vacant and plastic disposition makes the muscles in your face tight. When you move, you are like an exaggerated spokesmodel or a sort of motorized mannequin. The beginning of Eartha Kitt's version of "Love for Sale" plays. You strut around the circle and tease the audience by seductively taking off your coat to reveal that underneath it you are wearing the tight short skirt and top. Eartha stops and a male voice-over begins from the cassette player. The voice tells the audience a few things about the "game" they are about to play, a "game" they did not know they were going to play until this moment:

> `Welcome to "Spin the Ideological Bottle." We're sure you know the rules, but just in case you need a little recap, the game is played as follows: First, the assistant will spin the bottle. Then, a pre-recorded question will be asked by either myself or the opposition. Whomever the bottle is pointing to will have the opportunity to answer the question. Thank you for participating. Have a good time.`

During this you hold a full Coke bottle aloft and display it to the audience. You are the "assistant." Tom Waits' "Step Right Up," a song about rampant commodification, plays on the cassette. You squat down in your tight skirt, carefully teetering on your heels, and spin the bottle on the floor. It spins then slows and stops. You pause the music, start the other tape, and the male voice asks a question from traditional American history: `"Who sailed the ocean blue in 1492 and discovered America?"` You pause this tape and with exaggerated gestures and a big beaming open-mouthed smile you point to the man to whom the bottle is pointing. It happens that he is one of your professors. He noticeably squirms a second in his chair and states that he objects to the question because he disagrees with the answer implied by the question. However, he says, **"Columbus"** and declares that he is giving that answer because he expects that is the answer you are looking for. Throughout this, you do not alter your body or facial expression. You release the pause button on the tape and the male voice confirms that the answer is "Columbus." Tom Waits continues as you strut around the inside edge of the circle in celebration and hold up a placard that says "**Correct.**" You feel like the woman who prances around the boxing ring with a numbered card marking the beginning of each round as you do so, despite the po-faced expressions of your audience. You put the placard down, face your professor—that question's "winner"—and while looking directly in his eyes, you grab the bottom edge of your top with your hands and raise it up over your head and slip out of it. You are revealed to be wearing a black slip, the bottom half of which is still covered by the skirt, and your white lace bra peaks over the edges of the slip's bodice and around the armholes. The first flush of exposure hits you. You somatically realize that there is no turning back now. You feel the circle of eyes slam against your newly exposed body. You twirl around as you twirl the shirt above your head doing all that you can to look and feel in control. Then you strut toward him. You award him the shirt by dropping it in his lap, which he takes reluctantly. You turn to walk away after dropping a sexy little wink lingering in your wake.

You spin the bottle again. It stops this time in front of a woman. Again, the male voice-over asks a question from traditional American history:

> Warned of the British decision to send troops to Concord by a prearranged signal in the North Church, this man rode through the night warning the Minute Men. He was captured before he reached Concord. Who was he?

You pause the tape and point to the woman awaiting her answer. The woman hesitates and meekly asks, "Paul Revere?" The tape reveals that "Paul Revere" is indeed the right answer and you strut around the circle again in triumph with the placard that says "Correct" held up high. You unzip your skirt and seductively step out of it. The full-length of the black slip is now exposed and you are still wearing the stockings and high heels. The cool air-conditioned air slaps against your bare shoulders and arms. You twirl the skirt on your finger as you slink over toward the woman who answered the question and drop it in her lap, making sure to look provocatively in her eyes as you do so.

Another spin. A woman's voice on the tape this time, "**Who was the woman in the American Revolution who successfully rode two days through enemy territory and past enemy sentries carrying vitally needed intelligence dispatches to General Washington?**" The bottle is pointing to a woman, a woman you know to be a feminist, a woman you know to be well-read in feminist thought. The woman is your lover. This is the woman who lovingly helped you dress this morning in preparation for this performance. She is the one person in the room who was told in advance what this performance would entail. Surely she will answer this question correctly. You know she wants to subvert the game and move it toward a feminist conclusion. You point and pause for her answer. At last, with sudden bluster she says, "I don't know." You release the pause button and the woman voice-over announces that the answer is **"Deborah Champion"** and that she was never captured.

You start the music again and strut around the inside of the circle exactly as before only this time the card you hold says "**Not Correct.**" You sit on a black box in the circle, unhitch your garters from your stockings, remove your shoes, and languidly roll the stockings down your legs as you look into the eyes of the "loser," your lover. She is the one person here who has seen you disrobe in intimate space. She is now being made to watch you do so publicly. She is restraining an embarrassed smile. You allow a hint of pain, as an indication of your debasement, to cross your face beneath your painted smile-emblazoned mask. You slip your shoes back on before standing. Then, after you stretch the length of the pair of stockings between your hands above your head and after they are pulled tight, you release them, "shooting" them over to your lover, the "loser." You glance back at her as you turn to go spin the bottle again.

Shift the text and re-read the story from the opposite place in the circle. Can we calculate the abjection here? Can we imagine what rankles in this *soul? What reading is possibly being given license?*

She is spinning the bottle again. Oh, it is stopping in front of me. What's the question going to be? It's a woman's voice on the tape this time: **"Who was the woman in the American Revolution who successfully rode two days through enemy territory and past enemy sentries carrying vitally needed intelligence dispatches to General Washington?"** In order to subvert the striptease I must answer this question correctly. She is looking at me and waiting for the answer. She is beaming a big red fake smile and pointing at me. The rest of the class is looking at me, waiting. Most of them know I am having a relationship with her. I know I learned that somewhere in a women's studies class. If I answer it right, it will change the game. Even though in my bedroom as I helped her dress this morning she told me the rules of the game and how I can prevent her from disrobing if the feminist questions are answered correctly, even though only she and I alone know how this performance may unfold, I can't help feeling manipulated.

Oh, god, I don't know the answer. I don't know it! God! I should know this. She's waiting, the class is waiting; I have to speak: "I don't know!" Dorothy Champion?! I don't remember that name. Why don't I? Why do I remember Paul Revere and not her? They both rode across enemy lines, but unlike him she was victorious. Well, I know *why* I don't remember her and do remember him . . . !

She's taking off her stockings. Ugh, I don't want to watch this! It's so painfully public. How can she do this in front of all these people? I feel like I am objectifying her. I guess I am objectifying her. She is making me. Is that possible? Can an object be the agent who provokes objectification? I don't want to do that to her, especially to *her*. I know that's what she wants in this performance, but I feel myself resist!

She's giving the stockings to me; I hate this. How can she let her body be read in this way? It's moments like this that make me aware of how very different from each other we are. Do I have to catch the stockings? What do I do with them now that I have them? Should I hold them? Maybe I should put them on the floor. That seems inappropriate. I'll just sit here with them in my lap, I guess. My face is burning. Well, at least now all the eyes are back on her as she turns to go for her next victim.

Another view. Again a re-reading of that moment. Another re-turning. Possibilities and probabilities arise amidst questions. The abject performing body and the spectator body now felt as abject tug at each other. Push and pull. Acceptance and rejection. Another point in the circle. What possibilities might we read here?

No. I don't want the bottle to point to me. I really don't want to participate in this. Good, the bottle is pointing at someone else. I'm okay to watch. A woman's voice asks a question this time. Yes, okay, there is a gap. I don't know what women helped in the Revolution. Why should I? We all learned American history but not women's part in it. I suppose I could have taken women's studies classes and learned it there. That idea never felt comfortable. Would I have been welcome in a women's studies class? Would it have been meaningful to me? Perhaps. But why isn't this information part of the general curriculum? That is part of her point, of course. But look,

A WOMAN IS SET TO ANSWER, AND EVEN SHE, A FEMINIST, CANNOT. EVEN SHE, AN INTIMATE OF THE PERFORMER'S, CANNOT. IS THIS PERFORMER PURPOSEFULLY MANIPULATING US BY ASKING QUESTIONS THAT ARE DELIBERATELY OBSCURE? I MEAN IF A FEMINIST CAN'T ANSWER, HOW COULD I?

IS SHE JUST GOING TO STRIP NAKED? IS THAT WHERE THIS IS LEADING? DOES IT MATTER HOW THE PERSON ANSWERS THE QUESTION? OR WILL SHE TAKE SOMETHING OFF NO MATTER HOW THE QUESTION IS ANSWERED? THIS IS HARD TO FOLLOW.

SHE'S TAKING OFF HER STOCKINGS. SHE'S SHOWING US HER LEGS. LOOK AT HER LEGS. SHE WANTS US TO LOOK AT THEM. FROM WHERE I SIT I CAN SEE HER CLEAVAGE. A PROMISE OF MORE? THIS IS WEIRD. THIS IS A CLASS. I CANNOT RESIST LOOKING. I . . . I . . . WISH I WAS SITTING CLOSER TO THAT SIDE OF THE CIRCLE. SHE IS KIND OF . . . SEXY. FLESHY. SOFT. ROUND. GOOD. SHE'D BE. . . . WHAT AM I THINKING? CAREFUL. I DON'T WANT TO THINK OF HER THAT WAY. I KNOW BETTER! SHE WANTS ME TO. . . . SHE WANTS US TO SEE HER SEXUALLY. OR DOES SHE? CAN I GET AWAY FROM THINKING OF HER THAT WAY? STOP. I DON'T WANT TO PARTICIPATE IN THIS. I UNDERSTAND HER CRITIQUE AND SHE'S MAKING ME LOOK AT HER IN THE WAY SHE IS ARGUING AGAINST. THIS IS . . . AWFUL . . . OVERWHELMING. IT IS . . . INTERESTING, A STRONG PERFORMANCE, BUT AN UNCOMFORTABLE EXPERIENCE. I GUESS . . . I AM OBJECTIFYING HER. I KNOW THAT'S WRONG. I THINK SHE COULD MAKE THIS POINT DIFFERENTLY. I THINK SHE SHOULD MAKE THIS POINT DIFFERENTLY. THIS PERFORMANCE IS INAPPROPRIATE FOR A CLASS. WILL SHE GET NAKED? I HOPE SHE GETS. . . . I DON'T KNOW IF I SHOULD KEEP WATCHING. STOP IT. CAN I STOP WATCHING? I, I, . . .IS IT I WHO'S INAPPROPRIATE HERE? I'M SUPPOSED TO WATCH AND YET TO WATCH EXACTS A COST. IT'S NOT FAIR OF HER TO PUT US IN THIS SITUATION. STOP LOOKING AT HER LIKE THAT. STOP IT. THIS IS A CLASSROOM PERFORMANCE.

Read on. Read from the sidelines. Is there comfort in the distance? Is the abject body more easily viewed with a distance that permits silent abjectification? Read me from there.

I spin the bottle for the fourth time. A question from traditional American history. The "contestant," a woman, gets it right. Of course. Any American would get it right. We know the answers to those questions so easily. Is it that my audience is answering those questions right because they don't want to look stupid? Or more likely, they are trying to find the codes for appropriate audience response and they are not sure what those are. So they answer dutifully what they know. I take off my garter belt. Don't they want to subvert the game? Don't they want to at least try to subvert the game? Or maybe they do want to see how far I'll go?

I spin again. It is a question from American feminist history. Another woman, also a feminist, gets it wrong. I pop out the falsies and give those to her. She is flushing in embarrassment. Inside I am like jelly, I am so nervous.

But I do love how this is going. I hope they go all the way; I want to get to the ending I have planned. I am getting more excited as it looks more likely that they won't subvert the game. If they do subvert it, the ending I have planned is not as spectacular.

I spin the bottle again. And again. And again. And each time they answer all the questions from traditional American history correctly and all the questions from American feminist history incorrectly. It is going so fast. My shirt, skirt, stockings, garter belt, falsies, bra, and panties are scattered about the circle in the various hands of my audience. I am barelegged standing in my heels and if they have been keeping track, they must think there is little other than my slip left to come off. They have one more chance to subvert the game. I am shaking at the thought of what I am about to do. I know what is about to come and I am worried about how it will be received. I worry about revealing my body. The hairs on my arms bristle with cheek and with fear.

This final contestant is a large red-headed man who, I know from previous discussions, regards himself as a feminist—not just pro-feminist, but as a feminist. I release the pause button on the tape and the female voice asks another question: "Who wrote the Declaration of Sentiments as a feminist version of the Declaration of Independence?" I point to the contestant and beam him my best Vanna White smile. He is slumping in his chair and nervously fingering the bra I awarded him for successfully identifying the Declaration of Independence a few questions before. I am standing about four feet away from him. He looks up at me, sheepishly. The redness in his skin tone is beginning to flush from his neck upward. His voice is almost a cry as he says, "I don't know." There is an expectant pause. They all know that I will remove some article of clothing; are they wondering if I will be naked as I take off my slip? Do they think I will take off my shoes instead? Do they want to see my naked body, or are they hoping for some more acceptable resolution to this question?

I do not need to turn on the tape to confirm that he has been unable to successfully answer the question. Silence. I dip my chin and peer directly into the eyes of this contestant, my last "debaser." There is accusation in my gaze. He cannot get out of this. I know it. He knows it. I cross my arms across my chest and with each opposing hand, I slip the straps off my shoulders. I uncross my arms and the slinky nylon slip slides down my body to the floor, revealing that my breasts and crotch are bound in surgical gauze. The white gauze is blotched with red dye as if I have bled beneath it. I do not bend to pick up the slip. All eyes are on my body. I extend my arms out shoulder height and walk slowly toward my debaser. My smile vacates my face. My body confronts his gaze. Look. Look. Look, I silently implore. He does not shift his eyes for he either *will* only or *can* only look into my eyes. I am momentarily arrested by a flashing glint deep in his eyes of what seems to me to be the flush of shame, horror, fear.

Shift, turn over the page. Examine the image overleaf. Read from me; come over once more and cross that divide that separates us yet again; sense if you will the power and the pleasure in performing abjection.

You slip away from your debaser's discomfited gaze and begin a slow prowl around the circle. Your stiletto-heel encased feet feel sure and sharp as your step meets the floor. Your body is your defense. As you pass by each person, you insist that each one look at your body, moving slowly, methodically around the circle, arms outstretched insisting they behold your bandaged self. Eyes meet eyes as you navigate the circle. They will not break your gaze but instead, they wait, breathlessly, for you to move on. Your fear of exposure gives way to a deliberately antagonistic performance of victimization. Self-imposed abjectification. Performed abjectification. Willful ruin. Your desire is to hopefully impress your body's cultural wounds on the bodies of your audience, to in some way make them feel your abjection through the power that the image of your body exudes, through the ghastly horror of the display you make. Are you successful? How can you tell? Is your answer in their eyes?

Change the view. Another reading. How might it feel to be made abject as a spectator, as an abjectifier, while the body before you is degrading herself?

I am a woman and she is confronting me too. I don't want to look. But I feel like I am being forced to. It's hard to look away. And I do want to look at her body. Yet I must wait until she passes me and releases me from her gaze. Then I will get a chance at a better look at her bandages and the messages she's written on her body. There. I can see now that on her front side she has written "We Get What We Pay For." What does she mean? Who is this "we"? Is she saying that her body is all women's bodies? Her body is my body? Her body is not my body. She is too close to the feminine ideal to make this critique, for this critique to be taken seriously from her. My body is more damaged by the cultural standards than hers. I wear the wounds she only pretends to wear. I am not complicit in her debasement but I feel she is accusing me too. She is just an exhibitionist.

Turn, turn, shift, move along the circle. Another possible inscription. Different markings to read.

I am a man and I suppose she blames men. I don't want to look; I want to look. She is demanding that I look. I want to break the circle and leave; I want to, but I must be a good student in this class and stay. I can see that on her back side she has written the words, "Damaged Goods." What does she mean "damaged"? She was looking quite beautiful a moment ago. She looks damaged. Who is she saying damaged her? I didn't damage her? How am I complicit? She blames me. I have done nothing. This is inappropriate for a class.

Different reading. Different script. A shift along the circle. As the teacher, do you feel you have lost control of the class while you worry about my loss of control?

I am her teacher. I want to stop this performance. I am worried about how this performance is affecting her. She looks to be in peril. I think she wants to stop. I have a duty to stop it. Should I? Should I? I don't want to be paternalistic. Should I?

Re-turn. Center view. Gaze from the circle, from the comfort of your chairs. Look out.

I am exposed. I have completed the circle and pressed the vision of my abject body into the eyes of every member of the audience. Do they feel that abjection? Is it churning in their beings? Or have I missed my mark? I feel the coldness of the air-conditioned room on my exposed flesh and the coldness of their gaze. Clinical cold. The circuit now complete, I move to the center of the circle. All eyes are on me; they are anxious, antagonistic, amazed, angered, amused, apologetic, appreciative. There is a hush as I fall to my knees next to the Coke bottle which is lying on its side on the floor. The grime of the gritty stage floor stains my knees and grinds uncomfortably along the length of my shin bones as I kneel there. The gauze around my breasts and crotch slip and I pray my private parts are not being revealed; I steel myself against the impulse to check. Let be. Just let be. If I am exposed, just let be. I place faith in the power of the performance; it feels like a magic carpet, flimsy and mysteriously powered. I ride in holding onto the frayed edges of that faith.

I take up the Coke bottle and hold it up above my head with my left hand, gazing reverentially up to it. With my right hand I pull a bottle opener from the folds in the gauze around my crotch. The bottle opener is attached to me by a string long enough for me to reach up to the bottle and pry open the top. As the top pops off, it flies to floor; I drop the opener, and the shaken liquid squirts out the top. With both hands gripping the bottle I quickly turn it over into my expectant mouth. I hold the bottle upright as the splash and fizz bursts in my mouth and exceeds the bounds of my lips. The sticky fluid runs down my face and splashes onto my chest, my legs, and the floor. As I gulp, the liquid trails along the length of my forearms and drips to the floor from my elbows. I gulp furiously, continuously, forcing the liquid down. The foaming cola comes out my nose; my eyes are watering; the gulps are painfully huge and the carbonation expands and burns as it goes down my throat. I did not rehearse this part of the performance and am rigid with surprise by the magnitude and force of the experience. Every instinct tells me to pull the bottle away and take a much-needed breath. I force my mouth to continue to suck it down. My belly swells with the carbonation. My esophagus feels raw and ripped. I burp in between gulps, which causes me to choke. It is as if I am crying, my eyes are watering so much. It seems the bottle will never empty. When, at last, it is spent, so am I. My arms come down in relief. I place the bottle down. I am sticky, wet, bloated, repeatedly and uncontrollably belching, and can barely see as my makeup has run into my eyes, which sting and are full of tears. There is only the sound of the heaves of my breath punctuated erratically with the ceaseless spontaneous burping. I am grotesque. My self-abjectification complete.

I get to my feet toppling and tripping on the absurdity of my spiky heels. In the silence, I walk slowly, waveringly, out of the circle.

Making Sense of Body-Sense: Reading and Writing Performance, Identity, and Subversion

Sacred space. Performance space. The voices of a thousand performances, done in pursuit of some scholarly ideal, have resounded here. I, sticky wet by the product of my own doing. Space now defiled. My body, gorgeous in its grotesqueness. This profane performance now complete, done to my satisfaction. Satisfyingly profane.

I push at the seams of academic performance. The seams strain yet admit me, admit the seamy. I, a body, an unseemly body, a seamy body. A body scarred by the ragged edges of mismatched interpretive remnants sewn together helter-skelter. Piecemeal abject body. "To be a body, is to be tied to a certain world" (Merleau-Ponty, *Phenomenology of Perception*, 148). My body tied to academe. Academic bondage that is more than academic. Though, "our body is not primarily <u>in</u> space: it is of it" (Merleau-Ponty, *Phenomenology of Perception*, 148). I, the profane; I, the abject; I, though bound, am of this space. Academic jurisdiction, tight, often unforgiving, pervasive and partial, god-like though partisan, inveighs upon me. I challenge, prod, provoke. I hope for positive appreciation but am unsure how or if I will find it.

"We live in a bodily way in our situations" (Gendlin, "Thinking Beyond Patterns," 49). I find myself, my body, in this situation, that is, a "crossed mesh of implied behaviors and events" (Gendlin, "Thinking Beyond Patterns," 175). My situation is constituted by others as it is constituted by me. My body. Their bodies. Sensing my body, sensing my body in a situation. I have a "body-sense," that is, the "implicit situation"; it is "not just internal, private, nor subjective" (Gendlin, "Thinking Beyond Patterns," 105). My body. Their bodies. I am of this situation; and a situation is more than a space (Gendlin, "Thinking Beyond Patterns," 104). I attend to my body and inevitably I need to define my situation (Gendlin, "Thinking Beyond Patterns," 105). The situation confines. The situation does not accommodate my body. I feel tight in anticipation of the defining. I am exposed. There is no taking back the performance. I steady myself, sure in the power of the performance. The situation I find myself in calls for action, for actions explicate situations (Gendlin, "Thinking Beyond Patterns," 119). The situation implies actions. The situation also implies a change in possibilities (Gendlin, "Thinking Beyond Patterns," 119). Alternative possibilities that potentially subvert the situation. New situations are implicit in the original. Let the actions clarify the situation, or change the situation.

Colleague, friend, peer, identities all, in the wake of this performance give way to new identities. Scholar whore. Inappropriate body. Abject body. Abject colleague. Abject friend. Identity is constructed and relational (Conquergood, "Rethinking Ethnography," 184). I feel the scaffolds being built around me. I brace for it as I am being braced by it. I feel caged behind a scaffold of abjectification. I am looking for a way out.

I enter the post-performance critique filled with my performance—I can't hear the comments. The cola on my body dries and sticks me to my seat. I force my body into postures of attentiveness while the others try to talk about my performance.

Focus. Blur. Pull back. Here. Now.

Under the dressing gown that I quickly covered myself in, the gauze, still wrapped around me, now cuts deeply into my damp skin.

Focus! Attend not to the body but to the critique!

I strain for the time to pass. I hunger for the knowledge that I hit my mark. Occasional voices pierce the veil of my internal replay of the performance. What I do hear resounds mostly as comments upon individual's experiences. Some eyes are wide, some mouths are shut. A teacher begins. An academic voice, a voice that cuts away from the visceral impact—which lingers still in the wake of my performance—to the intellectual level. He guides the discussion to the purview of the course: **"My first response was to want to leave the circle. But, of course, it is impossible to leave the circle. Just like with ideology, it can never be left; there is no opting out."** I note the positive assessment buried beneath what I take to be an implicit denial of the visceral engagement he experienced and which the performance I cannot but believe produced. Propriety, academic propriety finds a foothold. Or perhaps it is the only comfortable foothold available to him when other stable ground is absent?

Another teacher's voice cuts through: "My response has more to do with personal risk. I wanted to stop the performance. I was worried about the performer."

Worried? Why worried? No. No, I was in control. It was what I wanted.

"You were shaking. You looked like you were in trouble."

I protest silently. No. I always shake in performance. And yes, it is risky. But I knew what I was doing.

"Well . . . I don't know. I just felt that. I don't know."

I am caught by surprise. I am caught by the surprise of the complexity of readings. I hold tight to the somatic knowledge of the power of the piece I have just performed. We are all straining to make sense.

A peer, a student speaks: "**I wanted . . . I wanted to get the question right. I didn't know how to stop her. I felt powerless. And then, I didn't know what to do with the bra. I had this bra. I mean, what do you do with it? What were we supposed to do with these things?"** I didn't fully anticipate how the performance would impart powerlessness to my audience. In this student's eyes I see a duality of resistance and awe.

Others' eyes. Mute mouths. Full heads. Bodies that twist in their chairs. Gaps of silence filled with unspoken things. My body. Their bodies. Disgust and loathing, fear and anger, rejection and abjection fill the space between our bodies. The situation gets defined.

Class ends, their bodies leave the space. Brief exchanges with my lover before she leaves. She praises me for the work. Without saying so, I see that she is conflicted. As she walks away I know she is struck by the power of the performance and I know she aligns with the rhetoric of the piece. Whether the means justify the ends seems to be the question that drags in her wake. I wonder how or if we will process this moment together later.

Clean-up time. The gathering of props, the changing of clothes. Empty space, reclaimed space. Profanity swept up into neat little piles with the other litter of the day. One body other than mine remains. This colleague who is glowing, who holds herself back from the pack, breathlessly exudes her appreciation for the work. Our history of turmoil has cleaved us apart. Yet here now, she gives me her love. This *rapprochement* pleases me. Her realm of academic approbation encloses me, embraces me, enfolds me. We cleave together, momentarily. Appreciation for the performance elides into appreciation for the performer. I beam.

The hours, days, and weeks that follow, tell other tales. Few cohorts speak directly to me about it. A teacher in the class encounters me in the hall later in the day. He is positive about the performance and effusive as he registers his appreciation and concomitant horror. He also tells me that **"That final image with the Coke bottle was pornographic."** He doesn't want to elaborate. I ask for clarification, but I know we are caught on the jagged hooks of decorum. We cannot wiggle around the inappropriateness of a teacher and student discussing the subject in the graphic terms necessary to clarify the point. "It was pornographic," he says. I ponder the word and the final image in my performance. A flood of voices haunt me:

> As a substitute of what cannot be seen, the money shot . . . whose name derives from the mainstream film industry slang for the image that costs the most to produce (porn producers pay their male performers extra for it), the money shot can also be viewed as an ideal instance of commodity fetishism. Finally, as the most blatantly phallic of all hard-core film representations, the money shot can be viewed as the most representative instance of phallic power and pleasure. (Williams, "Fetishism and Hard Core," 95)

> Pornography institutionalizes male supremacy the way segregation institutionalizes white supremacy. It is a practice embodying an ideology of biological superiority; it is an institution that both expresses that ideology and enacts that ideology—makes it the reality that people believe is true, keeps it that way, keeps people from knowing any other possibility, keeps certain people powerful by keeping certain people *down*. (Stoltenberg, *Refusing to be a Man*, 129, original emphasis)

> I had to step back from societal opinion, including feminist opinion, and decide for myself what I thought. I decided there was nothing wrong with the *concept* of sexual entertainment, but most of the actual films reflected this sexually shame-based society and its negative attitude toward women. I saw that there was nothing wrong with what I had done, or with the notion of pornography inherently, but rather with the underlying societal attitudes toward sex that were revealed in pornography. (Candida Royale, in Nagle, "First Ladies of Feminist Porn," 156, original emphasis)

Porn, complex and excessive, cannot be contained in a single interpretation. "Commodity fetishism," "ideology of biological supremacy," "sexual entertainment." Multiple interpretations map themselves across my body. "It was pornographic." My teacher's words linger unaddressed as we move awkwardly onto other topics.

A student who returns to the department from teaching elsewhere in order to defend his dissertation, a person not present at the performance, makes reference in his defense to "issues of exposure." He says as an aside, "I understand the department is currently dealing with those," as he looks into my eyes across the table during his defense. It is not said unkindly. I had not spoken to him about my performance.

Beware. Hard hat required. You are entering a construction zone.

I run into a student from the class smoking a cigarette outside our department's building at the same time as I. She looks like she thinks I expect her to say something. She and I avoid the topic of my performance as we speak obliquely about the class. As she stomps out her butt she turns to me and says: "Your performance. It was eerie. I didn't know what to expect." She leaves quickly.

Other students see me in the hall and they seem to me to be avoiding my eyes. As I round corners unexpectedly, I catch whispers. My performance, the object of whispered discussions. My body, the object of whispered analysis. My identity is being refashioned in the ante-rooms of my presence. I am raw with desire to hear their tales. This rawness only amplifies what seems to be a furtiveness in the voices and a sneakiness in the glances I catch. I begin to feel that what positive evaluations there may be are being kept more hidden than the negative ones. Distinctions between performer and performance seem to be appearing to blur. Performance in the theatrical frame becomes part of a larger frame, another act in the performance of everyday life. I slide around the department, a body with prone ears. I catch whispers.

"She just wants to show off her body."

"She just wants to shock."

"She is just an exhibitionist."

I catch whispers. Sh, sh, shshshshshshsh . . . She. Sh Sh Show. Sh Sh Shock. Sh She She is . . . She is . . . She is an X. An X. XXX. X-I-bi-Sh-on-ist.

Stop. Reflection in the midst of experience. Stop. These are misreadings. Perhaps I am misreading. Situations imply actions. Shift from noun to verb; the object objects: Don't you understand that I was critiquing the cultural objectification of women? Don't you understand that I was suggesting that the devaluation of women is systematic, pervasive, and impossible to escape? Don't you understand that I am arguing that women are damaged by this objectification, cultural silencing, and devaluation? Are you conflating the message with the means? It's a feminist performance, I mutely announce. I encase myself with body armor. I become rigid as I move through the gauntlet of the other voices. I become resistant. I refuse to admit the misreadings. In my private moments I flinch at the recollection of negative appraisals; I try to take succor in the few positive evaluations articulated to me. I know I protest too much. I am too raw, too vulnerable from the performance to tune in to their assessments with clarity. Or am I?

Norms are like spiders' webs. They mostly go unnoticed. Yet when even a gentle, small wind kicks up and vibrates the tiny filaments, they catch our eyes and in that instance announce their presence. They are so fragile and so easily disturbed. Once seen it is hard to believe they could escape our sight. They lurk there, resilient.

"It was inappropriate for a class."

"It was unethical for her to subject us to that performance."

"It was vulgar and rude."

It, it, it, it, it, ick. "Being ethical is easy when you have power" (Pelias, *Writing Performance*, 151). I vacillate between feeling powerful, sure that I have not transgressed any ethical boundaries, and feeling meek, fretting that I've offended my colleagues, teachers, and peers. I ponder on whether I should make amends. But to whom should I make amends? Nothing negative has been explicitly articulated to me. I would be responding only to whispers and gaps. I reconsider. I am not sure that contrition performed in the halls between classes would pave the way for acceptance and understanding. That might even fuel the fire. Should I let them off the hook, give credence to whatever misreadings there are?

For those in my audience, for the silent, the muted, the vocal antagonists, I transgressed. But, for these critics, the analysis stops there. They resolutely decry the means as incapable of justifying the ends. For them, I realize, the performance is not subversive, despite the avowedly feminist angle and despite the avowedly political edge to the performance. There is a thin line between complicity and critique. I wonder silently what stops their analyses, what makes them miss the body and see only the theoretic and the conventional.

Robert Murphy tells a story about a faculty party where a woman wore a "wide-mesh net dress and nothing else" (*The Body Silent*, 121). While people could not help but observe the woman, the tone of the party remained quite formal. The norms had been transgressed, but not subverted. Was she just an exhibitionist? Or was she silently poking fun at the formality of the event in an effort to make those taken-for-granted norms apparent? Did her intentions have to be made more explicit for her to be subversive? Or does the presence of sex or sexiness obscure a critical intent?

There is a gap between the act and the effect. Individual conceptual boxes across a critical gap divide us. Norms. Theories. Performance conventions. Manners. Morality. Conceptual boxes, cozy and warm. We snuggle up inside them. Though everyone's boxes are more or less the same, there are some differences. Some are standard issue in the halls of Academe, handed out or taken up like shelters to nestle in against the fiercest blasts of a critical chill. Standing outside these boxes is risky. It is a novelty. Doing so you will be subject to the harshest blows. I feel the chill and the isolation. **"Research [is] a strenuous and devoted attempt to force nature into conceptual boxes supplied by professional education" (Kuhn, *The Structure of Scientific Revolutions*, 5). "Novelties"** are suppressed **"because they are necessarily subversive" (*The Structure of Scientific Revolutions*, 5).** The subversive body is suppressed, made to "**dys-appear**" as Drew Leder observed **(*The Absent Body*, 69).** Social dys-appearance is a "**rupture in mutuality**," a clash of ideological agendas **(Leder, *The Absent Body*, 97).**

Mute mouths. They avoid my eyes. My abject body is present through its absenting. My body is excessive. My meaning is excessive; it runs over the borders of the "imposed order," beyond the **"conceptual box."** "She is just an exhibitionist." We make sense with these external forms; we cut them out and paste them on where they seem to fit; we avert our eyes from the unkempt edges that sneak out beyond the form and pride ourselves on how well it all fits. In that ignored excess lies the possibilities for new meanings (Gendlin, "Thinking Beyond Patterns," 178, 183). I am compelled to dig my feet in and endure what feels to be an icy blast. I am resolute and turn my back on those unwilling to read and re-read the space that divides us. Come out of your cozy boxes, I cry. I lean in and try to see across the divide. I wonder if I could have performed this piece differently, performed it with as much power and complexity, and not offended some. Maybe offense is balm, a homeopathic remedy, a taste of the illness with which to effect a cure. Maybe it is I who needs to step out from the box of my own resistance.

What ruptures our mutuality? What halts the move toward understanding? *"Analogical apperception . . . has its origin in the biological disposition to use one's own body as a semantic template—in the specific context under discussion, to understand the behavior of other creatures on the basis of one's own corporeal experiences" (Sheets-Johnstone, The Roots of Thinking, 308, original emphasis).* My body, woman's body; your body, man's. My body, slender body; your body, large. My body, young body; your body, older. My body, older body; your body, younger. My body, white body; your body, brown. Your body, not like my body. My body, not like your body. My body. Your body. Is it that your body doesn't like my body?

Inappropriate body. Eerie body. Shocking body. Exhibitionist body.

I find myself seeing you as recalcitrant bodies. Rigid bodies. Reactionary bodies. Though whispering, a very loud, yet small, student body.

Hold. Let her stoop to conquer. Breathe. Aaaaahhhh. Come down from your righteous place. Remember there are some people in that audience who got it. Focus there. Remember, **"If you're trying to please everybody, you're doing something wrong,"** as Bette Davis once quipped. I am overstating the case. I know I am making too much out of the negativity I feel, making too much because in my post-performance rawness I crave their articulated critique. Even if those critiques were to sting, I yearn to hear them. I need them to come through this. But I feel some inexplicable changes. I feel I am being read differently. I sense a template of understanding through which others interpret my comments in class. The sting of silent rejection lingers longer than the embrace of approval and understanding. I tightly wrap my abjection around me and seek comfort in isolation. I have the power of the bogey man. Others seem to look at me, wide-eyed and silent, ever fearful of what I might do.

Other bodies. Appreciative bodies. Admiring bodies. Critical bodies, alternately resistant and willing bodies, exploring with me the elasticity of the borders I transgress. These are bodies willing to at least momentarily suspend their judgment, to stand for an instance out of the box that prevents them from analogically apperceiving and instead, to think twice. As they bracket their resistance, I feel them negotiate the distance between our bodies. I lean toward them and am sustained. I pause to remember the ones who loved my performance. I reflect on the woman who waited to speak to me after the performance with her breathless exuberance. In her I could see the power of engagement being reflected; in her I saw the subversive power for which I hoped. I think on my lover's eyes, and the struggle I see there, her struggle to love me and her struggle to contain her inner conflict. She, and I assume others like her, are working hard to accommodate the destabilization my performance has evoked.

> To close the distance between the perceiver and the perceived is to take on a different sensory-kinetic stance in face of everyday objects and events, and correlatively, to enter into a different but not altogether alien sensory-kinetic world. (Sheets-Johnstone, *The Roots of Thinking*, 355)

Your body, man's body; my body, woman's. Your body, large body; my body, slender. Your body, older body; my body, younger. Your body, younger body; my body, older. Your body, brown body; my body, white. Your body, not like my body. My body, not like your body. Move into my body. Your body, my body. Different body. Not altogether alien body. Experientially approximate body. Our body. Empathizing bodies. Somatically understanding bodies.

Feel in your body how "fundamental concepts are corporeal concepts" (Sheets-Johnstone, *The Roots of Thinking*, 330). Feel in your body the cultural degradation I feel as a woman. Feel the imposition of social order on flesh. Feel my body fall into the void; my mothers' stories vanish from the historical account of America. Feel the objectification of my body. Feel the use and lose that's been made of my body. Feel the dehumanization of my person. Feel the abjectification of my body. Feel consumption gain momentum; it gobbles towards my body. My body is consumed for and by your pleasure. Feel yourself explore that pleasure and denounce it. Feel my body as a performer's body, a rhetorically powerful body. Articulate abjection. See my body as a body that not only transgresses, but because it makes you query the taken-for-granted norms you sometimes unproblematically abide by, see it as a subversive body. Know my body. Know my body somatically, kinesthetically, as a body unrestrained and in control.

I see that you emerge changed.

So do I.

CHAPTER FIVE

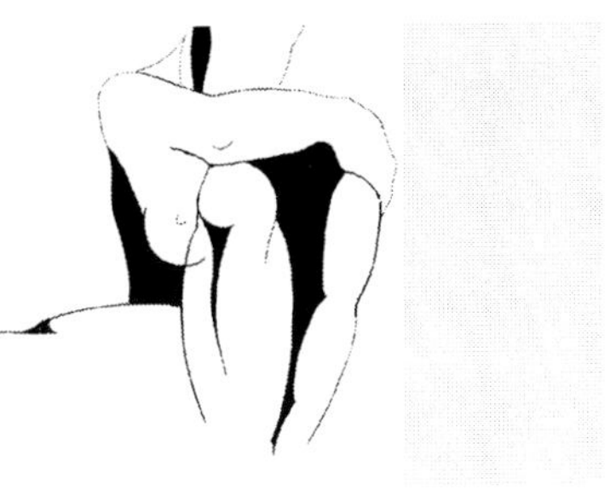

Reading Pink: The Beauty Persuasion

One loves ultimately one's desires, not the thing desired.

—Friedrich Nietzsche

I would rather lie on a sofa than sweep beneath it.

—Shirley Conran

It is abundantly clear to the traditional dyke, as it was to medieval church fathers, that the seed of all insurrection lies in the femme.

—Carol Queen

When I was little my mother would tuck me in and kiss me goodnight. I could smell the perfume of her lipstick on her breath. I don't know when they stopped perfuming lipstick, but if they do it still, I think it is rare. I would pucker up my lips, wrap my small arms around my mother's neck, and kiss her full on the lips. She used to call me "pillow lips." She would say, "your lips are like little pillows. You're going to make some man very happy. Goodnight, pillow lips." I would giggle, roll over, and fall asleep smiling, speculating on who that "man" would be.

Once upon a time, femininity was uncontested. It was comforting. It was the rush of warmth I felt when I curled up on the floor of my mother's closet in the late afternoon amidst the sea of high heels and the smell of Shalimar that wafted off of her raccoon coat. It was a beautiful promise made to little girls. Femininity signaled liberation. When I'm old enough I won't have to ask for permission. When I get to wear shoes like that. . . . When I get to wear makeup. . . . When I have dresses like these. . . . When I'm a woman, I won't have to get home by dark.

I walk down the halls of my department, red lips, painted eyes.

I could never lose the desire to wear lipstick. Good feminist arguments against the cultural objectification of women and about the cultural compunction that urges women to fill the coffers of the cosmetic industry, and for taking action against the cultural war on women, could not dissuade me from coloring my mouth. Colored lips, colorful words. My mouth demands your attention. Look here! My mouth asserts my presence; I enunciate and articulate my being here, with my mouth. I dab the color on the fleshy cushions of my mouth. I smack with color. Pillow lips, yes, but what comes out between them is often biting, occasionally sharp, sometimes flawed, sometimes intelligent. The rouge is only a ruse. The ruse is perhaps only rouge. Do not be lulled into traditional assumptions about femininity, about women. If wearing lipstick invites objectification, then I object. There are as many nuances in this scenario as there are shades of red in Revlon's lipstick display case at the local Wal-Mart.

I walk down the halls of my department, red lips, painted eyes, a woman whose brand of feminism is suspect.

Over coffee after a meal out, my mother will pull out her lipstick and touch it up. Always pink. Over the years she's become quite adept. A quick flash of color and it's done. It's done before grumblers can catch her and point to it as an example of the decline of proper social etiquette. Invariably, her slightly buck front teeth will catch some of the color too. I point to my teeth and she understands. She makes a quick dab of her front teeth with her napkin. She looks up to me, flashing her teeth. I nod, yes. Yes, it's gone. Nonverbal femininity. An erotic connection between mother and daughter. Audre Lorde reminds me, "In touch with the erotic, I become less willing to accept powerlessness" ("Uses of the Erotic," 212). My mother has always been a formidable woman.

I walk down the halls of my department, red lips, painted eyes, a woman whose brand of feminism is suspect. I walk the halls of the department as a woman known to be researching exotic dancers, a woman who has been challenged by some of her feminist peers for doing so. Challenged overtly and covertly, in little unsuspecting moments of conversation, on occasion I feel the sting of the little barbs that slip out and strike me, coming from between clenched teeth and tense, indulgent, smiles. I walk the halls of my department, a woman whose sexuality is suspect. I feel the pervasiveness of heterosexism and erotophobia, aware that, generally, others prefer the topic of sex and the performance of sexualities other than heterosexuality to be kept hidden. I walk the halls of my department as a woman known to have given a controversial performance in which she at least partially disrobed, a woman who calls herself a feminist but whose self-performance is not easily recognized as such. I slink and slope around the department feeling the glances of abjectification slice at my body. I sometimes feel them as glancing blows; they weigh upon me as I sometimes seem to invite these assessments. Nevertheless, they pull me away from myself. I pause and reconnect with myself. I select defiance as a response and elect to wear an even brighter color for my mouth. "Recognizing the power of the erotic within our lives can give us the energy to pursue genuine change within our world" (Lorde, "Uses of the Erotic," 213). There should be a lipstick color called "Defiance."

Persuaded that I might be promoting women's cultural debasement when I wore makeup, I decided in the name of feminist solidarity not to wear it for a time. But soon I wondered why I should put down my color box? Why should I let it be taken away? When women feel that they can not walk out of their houses without their "face" on, as, for example, many women of my mother's generation feel—although some women of my own feel this as well—I believe they are responding to a social conditioning, if not oppression, by cultural imperatives. And yes, those women who went against the norms of the 1970s by choosing not to wear makeup marked their sexual independence by refusing to comply with male fantasies of feminine beauty. But the terrain has shifted. Polarities are not so easy to recognize. Naomi Wolf, a beautiful woman by cultural standards, wears lipstick and mascara in the photograph on the back of her nonfiction bestseller *The Beauty Myth: How Images of Beauty Are Used against Women.* Mind you, it is only a pale pink shade. Is makeup more acceptable in the popular realm of bestsellers than in the more "serious" domain of Academe?

When I open my color box, it offers me possibilities. It gives me a chance to play. There is power in the unexpected. Maybe I'll wear this color or that. Maybe I'll wear no color at all. Opening my color box is not compelled by habit but by mindful choice. To choose comes after a moment of arrest, after an assessment of how I shall move through the next few hours of my life. Some colors antagonize. Some excite. Others placate. My color box brings me in touch with touch. With the erotic "not only do we touch our most profoundly creative source, but we do that which is female and self-affirming in the face of a racist, patriarchal, and anti-erotic society" (Lorde, "Uses of the Erotic," 213). I open my color box and I can be subtle or loud, gentle or strong, political or not. I can close the box too and choose not to wear any color. I experientially learn the meaning of color, the shades of being. The issue is a matter of context and the ability to read that context effectively.

I am told a story about a woman I know, an academic woman, who attended a local arts festival without makeup. Standing in a line she found herself among nothing but earthy, unadorned, Birkenstock-and-tie-dyed-wearing women. She drew out her lipstick, applied it, and announced to her companions that she "had to mark a difference."

I entertain the fantasy of attending my dissertation defense dressed completely in black leather. I imagine thigh-high boots, a leather and steel bra top, leather skirt, and perhaps a whip. No I'd better not turn defense into offense. I imagine the strength in my body as I would feel the clap of leather on my legs. It is only a fantasy. I am not so perverse as to follow through. I know enough to know it would not help my case. Although I also know that the best defense can be a quick striking offense. That thought makes me grin. And I wonder if I would be a stronger defendant if my defense were buffeted by the transgression of expected decorum?

The performance of self is multi-faceted. Shifting the context, so shifts the performance. Each context denotes new meanings. Sometimes the political potential is minimal, sometimes great. Sometimes the politics of a given situation are occluded from view, sometimes they are overt. To mistake self-performance as always political effaces the person and permits only a position. Living is messy. Performing a self is like carrying a heavy bucket full of water a long distance; it is awkward and not easy to contain. You do it knowing full well that the "water" will splash chaotically on the space between political aims and personal desires. Only some will make it to their anticipated destination. It is becoming increasingly difficult to mop up the mess in my wake. It is becoming increasingly clear that an abject body is not necessarily a powerless body.

A friend of mine, an assistant professor in another department at my university recounts to me how he often functions as the intermediary between strong women doctoral candidates who wear makeup and the chair of their committees, a feminist woman who, to use my friend's phrase, is more of an "old school feminist." He says that it happens frequently. The issues that divide the candidate from the chair originate with the candidates' performances of self. Aware of his pro-feminist stance and his unique ability to assuage the situation, these candidates apparently seek him out to help their cases. He tells me that he has informal conversations with the committee chair—conversations that are away from the candidate—in which they casually discuss the candidate's work. He puts the focus on the dissertation and emphasizes to his colleague how sound the candidate's arguments are. Not gratuitously, for he believes in the strengths of each of these candidate's arguments. He tells me that over time, the chair is won around and the problems dissipate.

I don't want to believe that this feminist chair is consciously standing in these candidates' way because of their self-performances. I do not want to believe that she is actively unwilling to let these women graduate because they do not match the right feminist profile. But, the obverse of that is equally unappealing: Can it be that the resistance she feels toward these candidates originates so deeply that she is unaware of what motivates it? "Gender is a performance with clearly punitive consequences" (Butler, "Performative," 273).

I walk down the halls of the department, red lips, painted eyes, a woman palpably aware that her brand of feminism is suspect to others. As I do so, I sometimes feel afraid to step. Potential obstacles line my path. Abjection and impropriety are perhaps the Charybdis and Scylla present in every context. The Academy is no exception. I try to navigate through these dangerous waters. I know there is no destination, only the perpetual journey. Standard expectations for appropriate self-performance for academic women are clearly charted on the map I'm using; I see them. Others before me have taken those routes. But that is not how I choose to go. The shores appear to be lined with learned feminists, feminists whose views on objectification and makeup and how makeup panders to the male ideal of beauty differ from my own. Is it their unadorned gazes that I feel scraping my sides as I brush past? I cannot tell if it is abject revulsion, confusion, or even pity in their eyes. Is it my overly sensitive imagination, or are they murmuring to themselves in my wake about the poor dear with inadequately raised consciousness? Or, are they tolerating me without tolerance? Or are they asking me to help them understand why I chose the course I have? Should I explain? Will they listen to me? Can I listen to them? Some never look my way. They do not notice, or don't care—I am grateful to acknowledge.

In the mornings at home, I sit before my mirror and get in touch with touch. I shape my lips. I pucker my little pillows and kiss a Kleenex to blot the excess. I recall that in occupied Paris during WWII, and also in Sarajevo during the Bosnian massacre, women went to their appointments dressed fashionably in hats, gloves, and full makeup as a way to announce their refusal to be subdued ("House of Dior"). I turn to the image in the mirror, spy my red-lined lips and recite Iris Marion Young: **"Such female imagination has liberating possibilities because it subverts, unsettles the order of respectable, functional rationality in a world where that rationality supports domination" ("Women Recovering Our Clothes," 186).** I walk the halls of my department wearing lipstick and my pillows become political. Am I performing resistance? I feel the suck of the whirlpool of impropriety and make friends with the monster of abjection.

I am now a body marked by the discourse that circulates about me. I can read. Aware of the arguments that denounced my "Spin the Ideological Bottle" performance, and aware that I sometimes offend others, I nevertheless agree to do a performance at a regional convention. Emboldened by the shift in my feminist perspective as I worked with strippers and annoyed by what I take to be intolerant voices in my academic departmental community toward the women I study, and by affiliation, toward me, I am more aware of how to navigate the obstacle course of academic abjectification. Still, I fear the journey.

"Lip Reading": Abject Conventions

Feeling awkward and fearful of how my performances are received, I nevertheless agree to do a performance at the convention. The topic is "performing womanly." I submit the idea for a performance that I want to do with a friend, also a bisexual, who is a male drag artist. The idea was to performatively speculate on how femininity circulates between our two different identity positions. We submit the title "Femme/Fey Tales" for the convention program. As the time draws near, my friend backs out. I need to come up with something solo, and fast.

Although I felt the abjectification of some audience members when I did "Spin the Ideological Bottle" and other subsequent performances, I decide not to put limits on my creative energies. I decide that I will not opt necessarily for something easily accepted or palatable, something beyond abjectification. I return to that icon of femininity: lipstick. I ponder the power of tubes of colored polymer. The script for "Lip Reading" emerges. The script is a combination of statistics about the cosmetic industry, the absurdity of cosmetic advertising, a narrative about my mother and her use of lipstick, a tale of the power of representation, replete with conflicted and conflicting feminist arguments, culminating with a parodic version of Hamlet's "To Be or Not to Be" soliloquy in which I deliberate on that profound existential question of whether to wear lipstick or not. It is a performance that will place me in the category of feminist Other to the audience I anticipate. It is a performance that could open the door to abjectification simply by being dismissible.

Arrival in the convention city: I am woefully underprepared. I vow to spend every moment I can in advance of the panel's scheduled time going over the performance. Two friends watch me do it a few times the night before until they are too sleepy to stay awake any longer. I soldier on until way after midnight. I pray to the performance gods that I may get this performance into my body and not make an ass out of myself. I am, to say the least, laced with performance anxiety. I feel sure I will lose my place and "dry" during the performance, in front of people whom I consider to be important. When I was a professional actress before I returned to school and decided to make higher education my professional home, I never had performance anxiety the way I do now. Some "home" I hear myself say ironically. The ante feels higher somehow. I anticipate an educated, critical, incisive, demanding audience—an audience upon whom my professional well-being depends. Ill-judged performances as well as ill-executed performances of self have a tendency to endure in the minds of convention audiences. The future is unknown and I may perhaps find myself applying for a job from one of these folks at some point. Also these audience members are well-versed in the feminist arguments that my performance may be seen to challenge.

There is one section of the performance that I cannot seem to get through. It is a list of forty-nine different names of lipstick colors. The list is organized according to shade of color and name association. It starts with names that connote activities—like "Kiss Me Red"—and moves to a whole slew of puns on the word mauve, for example, "Mauved," "Mauve On," and "Mauvelous." Later, I list several colors based on foods and fruits— everything from various types of coffee and wines to "Apricot Fantasy" and "Plum Brulée." I end with a series of lipsticks that are named after attitudes, for example, "Clever," "Angelic," and "Fawn Fatale." I have planned a gesture to go with every color. I have not had enough time to get the names and gestures to flow from me unhindered. In rehearsal I continually lose my place. In performance I will be even more tense. I preempt my fear by asking a friend to sit in the front row and prompt me should I need it. In my bones, I know I will.

At the panel: To make matters worse, I am the chair of this panel and so I must make some opening comments, an act that takes me away from focusing on the performance I will have to give. This is both a good and a bad thing. Fortunately, I get to go first. I am relieved at that, since I am a most terrible member of an audience for the other performers if I go late in the round; and, I usually perform worse.

I introduce the other performers and the respondent, and I inform the audience that my performance has changed from what was promised in the program. I look out to see who is there. I see three of the performance studies faculty members from my department, also several graduate students from my department as well as some I know from other universities. There are also several well-known performance studies scholars from other universities whom I do not know personally, but whom I have seen at previous panels or conventions. As I look at these people, I see no reason for them to like this performance. There is one person in the audience who performs her feminism similarly to me. I am grateful for her presence. In my anxiety I feel sure the rest will all sniff and turn away at the end. They have notepads in their laps and pens in their hands ready to jot down notes. Perhaps they will make lists of my offenses. I imagine they will scribble little notes of abjectification, little notes buffeted by and made powerful with sturdy feminist arguments that they will wield at the appropriate moment. I silently hope my expectations are misplaced, that I am too quick to assume their negative evaluations, that indeed, many will enjoy and be open to this critical performance.[1] I am sweating already and fear I will stumble over my words. I am hoping that the line I give my public speaking students is true: "You feel much more anxious than you look." No wonder my students never believe me.

I am dressed in conventional convention wear, clean crisp trousers in acceptable beige and a white freshly ironed blouse. I look the part. In clothes like these I can slip around the convention without standing out. I blend with the crowd. I wonder if the performance will make me stand out as someone to be avoided or as someone to be respected. Ambiguous clothes. I am uncomfortable in conventional clothes.

I have a metal television tray set up in the center of the performance space. On it are a small standing mirror, a box of Kleenex, and a small basket filled to the brim with tubes of lipstick. There is a stool behind the tray. I move the tray and stool down left a bit, turn and face the audience, ready to begin the performance. It will all be over soon. Why did I agree to do this? What was I thinking? The world will not be a better place for my having done this. There will be no way to blend back in once I perform this piece. Love the performance or hate it, each audience member will subsequently read me differently than they do now.

I begin: "By the mid-1980s, annual retail sales of cosmetics in the United States reached $16 billion. Impressive when compared to the motion picture industry's 4 banual, uh, billion annual box office ah, money, ah, receipts. Even more impressive when you consider that 65 percent of all cosmetics are bought on impulse." *I hold out the basket of lipsticks to the audience and cup a few in my other hand, letting those fall back in the basket.* "These came from my cosmetic case." *The audience laughs. They laughed! They appreciated the contradiction? I feel a small lightness breeze into my step. I do what I can to center myself. I know I must give the performance as fully as I can. Still, I feel outside myself as I worry about their judgments.*

"According to Revlon's current ad campaign, what we need is 'Revolutionary makeup for revolutionary women.'" *I pull out a retractable umbrella shaft on which I have replaced the umbrella with a white flag with a big set of red lips emblazoned across it. As I announce Revlon's catch phrase, I pop the button on the shaft and the flag shoots out even higher. The audience laughs again. Their approval again feeds my strength. It is silly what I'm doing. It is silly what advertisers imply. I take their laughter to mean that they acknowledge the contradictions between desire, cultural dictates, and ideological commitments that women may experience. As I wave this pathetic flag, I ask the audience:* "Just what color of red did Emma Goldman wear?" *A few laughs here and there. I wonder if the reference to communism embedded in the mention of the color red missed some of these audience members. Surely, they know who Emma Goldman was. Perhaps the joke is just too stupid.*

Then, having introduced the idea of colors and lipsticks, I proceed into that minefield of the list of colors. I begin slowly and I carefully do each gesture that accompanies the color. "Could it have been, Think Pink? Portfolio Pink? Forever Fuchsia, Red Scorcher, Serene Red, Kiss Me Red. Mauve Mystique, Make Mine Mauve, Mad About Mauve, Moonlit Mauve, Mauved, Mauve On, Mauvelous, A La Mauve, Orange Flip, Apricot Fantasy, Blasé Apricot" *I dry. I always dry here! I can't remember the next color. Fear about the politics of the piece give way to a more basic fear about performing badly. If they disagree with the ideas in the piece, I know they will be even more unaccepting if it is performed badly. There is a pause that seems like forever. I look at my friend in the front row. Subtly, carefully she says,* **"Crushed Cherry."** I resume: "Crushed Cherry, True Cherry, Cherriest, Berry Rich, Wild Berries, Rum and Raisin, ahhhhh" *I search. Uh. Found it.* "Plum Brulee, Burgundy, Wine Velvet, Divine Wine, Wine By Design, Wine . . . with Everything, Mocha Polka, Coffee Bean, Jive Java, Espresso, Maple Sugar, French Toast, Mousse Café, Chocolate" *oh, now I'm in the home stretch. I take a breath.* "Persuasion, Cool . . ." *Damn! A quick look to my friend. She mouths the next word.* "Precious, Feeling Fuchsia, Suitably Ruby, Just Peachy, Charmed, Smolder, Clever, Nutty, Angelic, Fawn Fatale." *I feel almost spent but am so happy that I am finished with that part. What's left I do not fear so much, for although the politics are more contested, I am comfortable with the words. They did laugh during this list of colors. I cling to the pathetic hope that maybe it came off better than I think. I shove away any thoughts that keep me focusing on their judgments. I clasp on to the momentum of the performance for that is where performative acumen resides; it is the place where I can lose the fear of evaluation and stride into the fullness of my performative being.*

I sit at the stool behind the TV tray. "My mother would look into her mirror, and in between telling us to `'hurry up or we'd be late,'` she'd color in the contours of her lips. . . ." *I pick up a tube of lipstick and begin to paint my mouth. I feel a flicker of embarrassment making this usually private matter so public.* ". . . Red. At a time when 60s fashion dictated little-girl pinks and white-glossy frosteds, my mother's mouth paid tribute to the days of *her* youth. . . ." *I am shaking and can barely put the lipstick on. I think I will end up with a clown mouth. I strain to bring the sensuousness of applying lipstick to the moment. My hands are traitors before me. The power of my nervousness overwhelms my will to do it well. I feel the failure of my efforts rankle throughout my body. My noncompliant hands feel foreign to me. The moment is denuded of the sensuousness I wanted to convey. I force myself to find the momentum and to re-center my energies.* ". . . And once fully applied, her mouth shaped with precision, and the lips trained into striking ellipses, a Kleenex blotted the excess . . ." *I tug out a Kleenex from the box and blot my mouth, just once.* ". . . and formed a scarlet letter to

Lana Turner, to Barbara Stanwyck, and to the divine Bette Davis. These stories of 'O'. . ." *I show the audience my lip print on the Kleenex. They giggle. I am hopeful that they catch that this lip print on the Kleenex is essentially a repeated image of the lips on the flag I waved earlier.* ". . . would then be carelessly cast . . ." *I let the lip embossed Kleenex float to the floor.* ". . . into the wastebin mounting up day by day like a bevy of rejected lovers." *I feel the audience is generally with me. They are indulging me. I am struck by an energy that comes to me from the joy in their laughter. The energy is pulsing between us. I stand and move center. I address them directly and earnestly. I move quickly and deliberately throughout this.*

"My mother's stillness at the mirror was a striking contrast to the ritual of frenzy and haste that sent my sister and me off to school and my mother to her job as a college English teacher. The ritual done, I would stand at the door restless for goodbye. Her bottle-blonde hair pulled tightly in a bun and stark horn-rimmed glasses in place to ward off the unsolicited advances of colleagues and to instill respect and fear in any student who might think her an easy touch. Only the lips, red and ripe, gave a glimpse of the woman inside the fortress. Then, like the opening moments of *The Rocky Horror Picture Show* as the fans bay ***'Lips, Lips, Lips, Let There Be Lips'*. . ." *I cower comically as if the lips approach.* ". . . the screen that fills my view darkens to reveal only my mother's lips puckering and descending toward my face, and obscuring my senses to anything but the envelopment of her kiss." *I punctuate the moment with a big smacking kiss. The absurdity of the action demands that they either go with me or dismiss me. If they dismiss me, I will feel the* **"rupture in mutuality" (Leder, *The Absent Body*, 97)** *with this performance as I have with others in the past. In the gap of that rupture is where I know their abjectification can take root.* ". . . Then, like the trail she blazed around the house leaving traces on tepid coffee cups, teaspoons, and napkins, my face too was marked by blood red blotches, as individual as fingerprints."

I pause. I face the audience and stand in one place. They are waiting for it. The energy of the moment is rising up in me. I can see several faces smiling at me. With chagrin: ". . .Truth is, I've always thought I'd rather be Bette Davis than Audrey Hepburn. As bold as Jezebel flouncing into the ball in red dress and matching lips, not the tepid and palatable Holly Golightly who masks her participation in the identical act under secret applications of pale pink or peach." *It is a confessional moment that asks for their indulgence. Do they get the implication of agency I am making by citing Bette? Do they grant me this position because I've asked so sweetly? If I'd demanded it in the manner that Bette would have would they have so easily shelved their resistance?*

I turn away, coy. And then with purpose. ". . .The bloody orifice. Is the painted mouth a public imitation of another private orifice that bleeds? The mark of a woman." *I pick up the pace again and dig in my heels as I move.* ". . . It bleeds over everything, cups, ice cream, cigarette ends and lovers. And depending on the lover . . ." *I pause and with reverence:* ". . . lips and lipsticks can combine to create new colors." *Another pause. Then quickly.* ". . . Later, inevitably it must be reapplied." *I race back to the basket of colors and choose a lipstick. I hold it up and uncap it. I turn the tube so the color peeks out the top. I tease them with my unabashed lust for this phallus in a tube.* ". . . The perfect commodity, complete with built-in obsolescence." *I pause. They wait for it. Will they embrace where I am about to go, or will it fall flat?*

"To paint, or not to paint, that is the question." *They laugh fully. I am steady in my stride. I force myself to cast off the worries I have about this parody being stupid and submit to a faith in the writing.*

"Whether 'tis nobler in the life to suffer
The slings and arrows of outraged feminists,
And th' hungry arms of a sea of sexists.
Or by opposing, egg them." *They laugh again! They seem willing to let themselves, those of them who are feminists, be made light fun of.*

"To paint, to have lips—
Once more, and with a paint to say we end
The heart-ache, and the thousand natural looks
That flesh is heir to; 'tis a consummation
Devoutly to be wished to paint the lips!
To have lips, perchance to gloss, ay there's the rub," *I search the basket for a tub of lip gloss. Finding it I hold it up and the audience laughs. I apply it lovingly. I feel an urge to laugh gurgle in my belly. I suppress it and move on.*

"For in that gloss of lips what dreams may come . . ." *A pause. Then I enact obvious distaste for the slippery feel of the gloss.*

"When we have bitten off this slippy oil." *I bite it off.*

"Must give us pause" *I search the basket for a suitable color.* "—there's the lipstick!" *I hold up the color with joy and begin to apply it.*

". . . That shakes calamity from such long life:
For who could bear the lips in absent hue?"

I stop, have a change of heart, tug out another Kleenex and wipe off the color. Sheepishly. I move into the denouement of the performance.

"Thus conscience does make cowards of us all,
and thus the native hue of resolution
Is sicklied o'er with the pale lick of tongue" *I lick my lips.*
"And enterprises of great cremes and frosteds
Must perforce be hidden in their boxes,
And lose the name of Woman."

Applause. I quickly move my props, relinquish the space and seat myself. I got through it. Did they like it? Is there abjectification in a feigned appreciation? I do not feel it so; but I am unsure, yet.

After my performance: I sit through the rest of the performances and the words of the respondent. She delivers prepared words on a theme about all our performances. I am lost in the mystery of it. Finally, at the break between panels several people catch me to smile at me and say that they enjoyed my performance. I feel reprieved. One comment lingers. A man whom I greatly admire says to me, "you have made me think that there is nothing to take for granted." I like this. I am charmed by this. I feel I have hit my mark. I breathe easier for the rest of the day.

Yes. Nothing is to be taken for granted. New meanings. New days. Always revolving. A shifting terrain. Track shoes are needed to keep up. Watching the signs as I go. I breathe. I breathe. I breathe and think, okay, no one is as afraid of what I'm saying as I am.

Does humor make it more palatable? Because I invite them to laugh can they just figuratively pat me on the head and say, "okay, darling, wear lipstick." But questions still linger in my head. If they pat me on the head are we just temporarily ignoring the wealth of feminist scholarship that argues profoundly about the objectification of women and the double bind in which cosmetic adornment enmeshes women? Have I unwittingly allowed that "out"? Or, have I opened the door, however narrowly, to an alternative variation of feminist academic?

Why do I need their permission to perform myself as I do? To be sure the power of performance can only be adequately measured by the relations between audience and performer; the power is symbiotically nurtured. The trick, if you will, in refusing abjection is to refuse to grant more authority to the audience than the performer grants to herself.

Easier said than done.

Is it easy to dismiss my performance and what I write here as just a tale about the trials and tribulations of a budding academic? Yes, perhaps, depending on where you stand in relation to the tale. However, the potential for punishments are real. I feel these worries gnaw at my confidence and wear on my body through the rigid self-consciousness in my walk and in how I speak to others. Will I not be invited to perform again at a convention? Will others decline to be on convention panels with me? Will I gain a reputation for the light and fluffy or the unnecessarily outrageous?

The performance still feels clunky, hard, and tentative. I don't feel at liberty with this performance. Yet.

Reading Abjection with and without Permission

I am the abject, the uncontrollable. I am the absurd. I am the meek. What power do I give you? What power do you take? The small rooms of conventions shape the discipline. Like rough stones lodged in the midst of a rushing stream we are worn and polished by the discourse of the discipline, over time. Yet, only the part that can be seen becomes smooth. The jagged underside, untouched by the rush of the water, remains, always threatening to turn over and reveal that abject underside. Some stones are more robust and recalcitrant than others. As the waters cascade around them, the rough edges cut through. But eventually even they will be smoothed. Are they more beautiful once polished? Or do the sharp edges hold a special beauty that is obliterated in the polishing? Can the sharp edges help us chisel our way toward understanding things we never were capable of before? I alternately resist and accept the luster that others would have me wear. It is not that I wish to cut or to hurt; but hold me gently yet fiercely and see what journey I invite you to join. Look closely. It requires eyes that are willing to see past the presumed ugliness of the jags. The jags are not flaws, necessarily; they may be places that invite an edge. They may be the cutting edges of the discipline. Edges, as with cut gemstones, allow light to pass through in interesting ways. Cutting edges takes purposefulness, care, and insight.

Eighteen months after the convention performance I am asked to perform at a benefit for the local HIV/AIDS charity. I pick up "Lip Reading" again. It is in need of revisiting if only so that I may challenge the strength of the text and finally learn to refuse any abjectification the performance seems to generate. I feel the need to do the performance again. With a month to prepare, entailing countless rehearsals, the performance becomes comfortable and ripe in my body.

New context. Not an academic context. The performance space is a rough alternative venue. The audience is composed of the charity's board members, locals, students, and some academics as well. The bill is filled with mostly students from my university's theatre department, many of whom have a lot less performance experience than I. I am also the oldest performer.

I am to perform both of the two nights of the benefit. Each night the audience arrives in a festive mood. They want to be entertained. They know what they like and what they don't, but they have put aside their disciplinary alliances. The possibilities for abjectification seem diminished from what they were at the convention. They are a more forgiving audience, a more indulgent audience, an audience more willing to engage my performance even while they may not agree with its politics.

I watch the other performers from a seat in the house. I feel centered. This time I do not mind going seventh on the bill. I am ready. In the months since I last performed this piece, I have become less willing to relinquish my power to the authority of the audience. In the two years since I performed "Spin the Ideological Bottle," I have grown more comfortable with being an uncomfortable and unexpected presence. I have grown more comfortable feeling that my unpolished jagged edges will threaten to reveal themselves. Since this performance is not being held at a professional academic meeting, I do not feel the audience holds any power over me in terms of my professional future, though some of my professors are in the audience. The twin threats that the audience may abjectify me and/or find the work transgressive of notions of propriety are less powerful here. Also, my convictions in the strength of the piece are emboldened by my having performed it before.

I am wearing a long flowing black gown that dips low in the back, a costume I would never have worn to the convention. The gown and the high scalloped-heel boots make me feel long, tall, sensuous, and strong. When I begin, I feel the words soar through me, the clear and positive result of weeks of good preparation. Especially on the second night of the performance, I feel exhilarated throughout the performance. The first night gave me more confidence in my abilities to perform the work and more confidence that this audience will enjoy it. I shake from nerves a bit when I put the lipstick on, but am able to break into an ad lib line about it that provokes some laughs. I get through all the names of the lipsticks easily, each of the gestures are done fully, completely, outrageously. The audience fills the hall with laughter. I have to hold the performance for laughs. I feel triumphant. The audience's obvious approval suggests that abjectification is absent here. They must take me or not. The other performers backstage have stopped their preparations to crowd around the stage entrance to watch me from the wings. I take my time, my glorious time. The audience's approval fuels my sureness of purpose.

After the first night, the benefit organizer—a close friend of mine who is a woman I love and who is also bisexual—suggests I kiss her when I get to the part about lesbian desire: "And depending on the lover, lips and lipstick can combine to create new colors." On the second night, I do. It turns into a yummy, provocative moment that hushes the audience and momentarily throws me. My friend's lips, even in the stark spotlight of performance, remind me how much I love the beauty and sensuousness of women. I am filled with the hope that making this moment public may make the power of that beauty evident. I am filled with the power that comes by making my sexuality visible. I balk at the thought that there will be those in the audience who will only see the shock of the kiss or take salacious personal pleasure in it. They anger me and make me more resolute in my desire to make lesbian desire more public. Although I know it to be a problematic strategy, I take pleasure in being in the face of heterosexism by being at that moment in her face. I kiss her a second time and in that instant I forget to say the next line about lipstick being the perfect commodity.

I launch into the *Hamlet* spoof and the audience is chortling and bellowing throughout. This audience feels more at ease to laugh out loud than did the convention audience. I feel the power of performance re-enter my body, the forgotten power I had before I left professional acting to return to the

Academy. I feel the mantle of shame and fear I've secretly worn fall away. I stand strong, the floor meeting my feet and energizing me. I move around the entire performance area. The audience is with me. As I make several swoops around the stage floor their eyes follow me as one. At the end the applause comes and seems ebullient.

The post-show reception is edifying. Several people I've never met before introduce themselves to me or ask others to introduce me to them. This is an audience filled with educated people. Expressions of enjoyment as well as discussions about political performance fill these discussions. These people speak to me with respect for my performative ability and with interest in the political message of the piece. The humor of the piece did not diminish the rhetorical point, it seems. Their collective message is appreciation for the power of the transgressive and the unexpected, and an appreciation for the power of the writing and my performance acumen.

Performing for a convention and performing at this benefit were utterly different experiences. They were different not just because I was more prepared. Conventions and audience expectations differed in each venue. I walk away from this performance with respect for these differences. I also walk away with a renewed conviction in the power and beauty of my voice, a voice that does not always sing in harmony with the majority. I may sing solo, or, in a small union of voices. Nevertheless, I am being heard.

I hear the other voices. They come to me in subtle ways. They visit me now and then. I feel them penetrate and shape me. Maybe they are only possibilities, just my dark imaginings.

"Well, so you have found your voice as an academic. Each of us has to develop that strength as we move into the field."

Yes. The performance of self is the negotiation of agency (HopKins, "The Performance Turn," 233). Yes, that negotiation is a tussle often; it is a tussle between myself and the real as well as imagined others.

"So, in order to negotiate your agency, you experienced abjectification. But the abjection you felt is what every young scholar goes through. Welcome to the discipline. Glad to see you've come of age."

Oh. You see this only as a tale about a rite of passage?

"Given that you speak so much from yourself, one might say that you leave yourself open to the critique that you're self-absorbed."

Yes. *This* is a personal tale. I could leave my feelings and personal perceptions out of it. It's true that a lot of scholarship is not predicated on an able use of the vertical pronoun.

"If not as a rite of passage, how would you like us to take this highly personal story? (smiling) And just to prod you a bit, tell me, why should I care about how you experienced these transformative and yes, abject moments?"

My hope is to bring those often obscured experiences out into the open. If as HopKins says, performance is a toss and turn in the negotiation of agency, then how I am tossed and how I turn as I struggle to find agency is the heart of performance. The heartbeat of performance. The blood and sinews of experience is the material of such an embodied practice. I could write with the traditional hand of a scholar. I could erase my experience from the pages of this work. If I did, I might find an easier path in the discipline. I would be better able to avoid the quick dismissal to my work that you cite.

"Why are you so defensive? There are ways to write from your experience that don't leave you open to the charge of being narcissistic."

. . . Okay. I can see how others, perhaps even you, find it so. Talking as baldly about the things I do makes others uncomfortable. I know. But it feels like I'm in a double bind. As narcissistic or jejune as others may find what I have to say, I also want my experience on the page. Among the things I have learned from feminism is to trust that the body and that experience has much to give us in understanding how we know.

"As I said,—and you know this too, I've seen you navigate this issue before in other work you've written—writing from experience doesn't have to be indulgent. It should speak in ways that are not narcissistic."

Yes. There are "two primary features" of personal narrative:

> (1) The story told points beyond the self, and (2) the story told reminds you that consequences happen on an individual level. In other words, politics only matter as they unravel in individual lives and individual lives [as told in personal narratives] only matter when they can make a political difference. (Pelias, *Writing Performance*, 283)

I believe that. I have striven to do just that here. Perhaps I don't manage to accomplish that for everyone who encounters my work. My hope, my leap of faith if you like, lies in my belief that my experience does resound beyond myself for I feel sure that I am not the first to feel what I have. I feel sure that a profound experience of risk in performance, both theatrical and everyday life, is something many of us go through in various contexts and at different junctures in our lives.

"Okay. I suppose all academics, and perhaps many professionals in other fields, feel as if we are frauds at points or, at least we worry that we might be found out to be such. It's the recurrent anxiety dream of most academics, I suspect.

[Laughter]

But how are you satisfying the second requirement you've cited?"

I guess I think that how we legitimize and constitute knowledge as a discipline, as individual academics, and just as individuals in any given culture—departmental, classroom, wherever—should be a matter of concern to us. It is a political act. How I am stifled and how I am given license for my expression are the felt consequences of those politics.

"How would you respond to me if I told you that I think what you're talking about here is more a matter of taste. I mean, some things are just tasteless and inappropriate."

You may be right. But increasingly I think that taste and ideology are so interconnected that they can no longer be separated. And sometimes I think we believe we're separating them when we really haven't. I still hope we can understand there are some differences between them. I still want to believe we might be able to find enough insight or reflexivity to separate them. I say this because I see those limitations in myself as well as in others. Yet I think we kid ourselves when we say we practice "separating the person from the person's ideas." I think *that* notion, although it is an oft cited dictum of professional tolerance, has outlived its actual use. That idea originated in an academic culture that privileged factuality at the expense of affect, a culture that privileged objectivity at the expense of experience. Academic culture has changed. Additionally, I think we now find it scary to admit that we really don't separate people from their ideas. Yet the ownership of ideas often incurs personal and professional penalties. It is precisely why I wrote about my experiences of academic intolerance. I hope you, and I hope others will feel the power those potential penalties can exert, or at least the power that the fear of those potential penalties have. My hope is that by inviting you to see from my perspective, the conceptual divide that prevents the legitimization of some knowledge and not others may be diminished. My hope is that our cluster of conceptual boxes can shift, can be turned, can be looked at from multiple angles, and just maybe they can be made profitably uncomfortable through provocative inquiry. I hope that we will explore the novelties that emerge and ask to be engaged rather than be so quick to quiet them. I think a fundamental openness, as difficult as that may be to maintain, is the impulse for inquiry—academic and otherwise. I say this in order to remind myself as well as to remind us all.

'Well, we are, and will consider again, what you say."

"We'll think about it and let you know."

"We are thinking about what you say. My hope is that you will come to a place where you will be able to acknowledge that we are."

Yes. Fair enough. I hope so too.

Epilogue: Bathing in Abjection and Coming Clean

I dive into the pool of mud. It is warm, thick, welcoming. When under the smooth, dense surface there is no light anywhere; it is absolutely opaque. As I plunge downward, I feel the wet, mildly grainy substance splurt in the spaces between my fingers and toes, fill the caverns under my arms, and pour through the gap between my legs. Over time I have learned to enjoy these sensations. It was difficult, even repellent, at first and I found it so hard to move. Now I am mostly comfortable here feeling my body massaged by the shifting weight and mass of it. Only occasionally do I feel I might be overwhelmed and swallowed by the density of the experience. Here now, I can barely touch the bottom, but soon my feet find it. My head bobs out from below; my hair is heavy with the weight of it. Each slat of wet, muddy, clinging hair slaps at my back as I turn my head. I move through the mud slowly, like a bug through molasses. The goopey sludge almost entirely supports my weight. I lean and fall, nearly held upright until the mud gently lowers me. I lean again and am held like a breath before it gives way.

There are others here with me. I didn't see them at first, but they have been here all along. We occasionally rub up against each other surprised by the slippery contact we inadvertently make. We smile and giggle at the discovery and soon glide away secure in the knowledge of each other's presence. We know this is more than self-indulgence; the meanings ripple away from us and evoke more than for ourselves alone

There are those who call from the shore. "Get out!" I hear them say. "It is dirty in there." But I turn and fall again, caressed by the mud. It sensuously envelops me. They hold out brushes made of well-tooled arguments to scrub away the mud. Pumice stones, soap, and sponges made of approval, permission, and control are the abrasions they would rub against me as I negotiate myself through this quagmire of abjection. One holds out a clean unfurled towel ready to cloak my mud-covered nakedness should I finally agree to step out. She tells me the towel is soft; it will fold around me, cover me, redeem me. Still I linger in the mud, embraced by it, buoyant, sloppy. I can hear some of them gasping at the filthy sight I make of myself. Many have already turned and are walking away in disgust. They cover their ears without looking back when I laugh merrily and tell them I am happy here. I guess I am teasing them, for I know they will not believe me. Some on the shore enjoin them to stay. They cry out that they need these others' help in order to save me. "Let them go; let them go," I reassure. I don't need saving. I tell them that the mud is good for my body. It is cleansing.

The curious are there too. They do not hold out hands to help me out; nor do they have theories or arguments with which to wipe away the disturbing image of my abject state. They watch with open mouths. I throw handfuls of mud at them and laugh as they scamper and get angry, trying desperately to keep their carefully starched white clothes unblemished. "You miss the point," I say as I turn away. There's no need to elaborate further to them.

Then, there is the small coterie, quite near to the sides of the pool, who kneel there. Some of them lean in and ask me "Why?" "Why do you do this?" It is a rhetorical question for them. They understand the answer, but are not sure the means justify the ends. Some of the others there are awash with the amazement of it. They do not want to join me there, but they understand in their bodies how mud is not only dirty. They see the possibility of new meanings. They see that they must look beyond the quick and common notion of filth to see the mud as something idiosyncratically liberating and empowering. A few of these individuals dive in to join me, some only briefly, others linger longer. As I see them experience the initial awkwardness and discomfort, I wonder if it was right to invite them in. I do not begrudge the space, for there is surely room enough; yet I know not everyone will experience what I do here. I hope they will.

Eventually, I step out of the pool and lie down on the shore. Offers to help me wash off are respectfully turned down. "It cannot be washed off entirely," I say. "I cannot wash away others' memories of what they've seen, and I do not wish to anyway. Every time I have immersed myself in the mud, it has been by my own doing. I embrace those experiences now." As I lie there, the sun begins to dry the mud on my body. It turns a lighter shade and begins to crack here and there. Inside the casing it makes around my body, I more readily feel the whole of my body. I sense the length of my arms and legs, the plane of my chest and belly, and the contours of my face. In touch with touch, in touch with myself, in touch with the space around me, I am in no hurry to move.

CHAPTER SIX

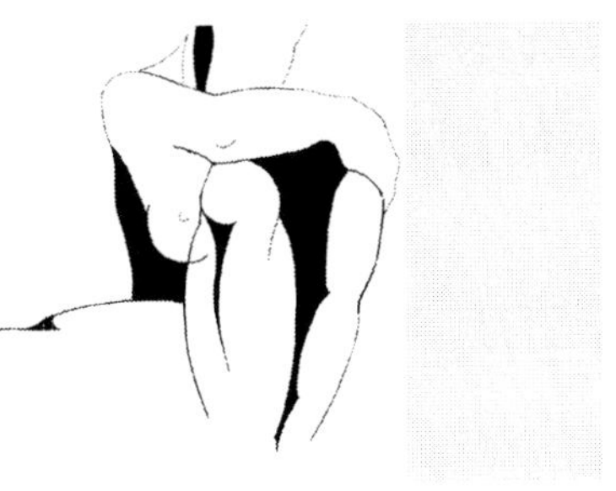

Thinking and Rethinking Tails, Tales, and Tellings

Is the real heresy what we do, what we desire, or whether we talk about it?

—CAROL QUEEN

Wisdom never provides answers, it just redefines the questions.

—DAVE DUNCAN

Works are not finished, they are abandoned.

—PAUL VALÉRY

On Being Stung by the Autoethnographic Tale

While preparing this book, as I was thinking and rethinking my abject body, my performances, and how to represent them on the page, I came across a photograph in a newspaper of a Malaysian man with four scorpions crawling over his face. One scorpion perches in the middle of the man's forehead, its two lobster-like claws curl over his eyes as he peers out to the camera. Another scorpion hangs perpendicular to and directly over his mouth with the eight little legs clinging to the man's moustache and beard; the sharp pointy pinchers encircle the man's chin. Another scorpion sits on the man's left cheek with its tail curled up, perhaps ready to strike. The last scorpion, the biggest of the lot, covers the man's right cheek and right side of his moustache. This scorpion's pinchers cling to the man's jaw.

The small caption beside the photo begins with the heading, "Odd selection of Roommates." The caption claims that this man, Ali Khan Shamsuddin, has been living in a container with 6,000 of these "venomous arachnids" for twenty-one days. The brief blurb goes on to say that despite having been bitten ninety-five times, Shamsuddin says he feels "healthy and fit." He was ending this stint the day the photo appeared. He had broken the record for most days in a container of scorpions.

I was struck by this photo; one might even say I was stung by it; its effect lingered for days. Even after repeated viewing, my desire to look could not be quelled. I wanted more than the photo and brief blurb could give me. I wanted to see the size of the container. I wanted to see his full body immersed in this scorpion sea. Though caught by the image, I also wanted to look away. I was simultaneously drawn to and repelled by the image. Still I continued to study the photo. I couldn't help but imagine the sensation of 6,000 pain-inflicting, poisonous, and carnivorous creatures crawling over my body. I couldn't imagine enduring this for one minute, let alone for twenty-one days.

I also wanted to know "why?" Why would anyone do this? Sure, I could easily dismiss him as a kook or an exhibitionist. Yet my lack of direct experience and the dissatisfaction I felt from the abbreviated exposure proffered by the photo and caption made me wonder whether or not other interpretations not immediately discernable from this small black and white photograph were possible. Were there cultural, spiritual, personal reasons for his behavior that I simply couldn't know of without further contextual knowledge?

The moment I begin to question Shamsuddin's motives my affective engagement with the image is stopped. Both in the initial moment when I want to dismiss him as a kook and in the moment when I begin to re-think why he would do such a thing, I no longer imaginatively "feel" what it might be like being immersed in a container of 6,000 scorpions. I am removed from the event and am, instead, engaged in cognitive contemplation. It is a clever escape, in a way. I don't exactly like feeling what it must have felt like to be plunged into a container of scorpions; the thought makes my skin crawl. Stepping back to intellectualize his motives brings relief from the shudder I feel as I gaze at the image.

Carolyn Ellis has commented that when she encounters autoethnographic writing, she "privilege[s] evocation over cognitive contemplation" ("Creating Criteria," 274). She notes that when she "think[s] *about* not *with* the story" a distanced reading is what is being brought forward (Ellis, "Creating Criteria," 274). Yet, Ellis also points out, and I agree, that cognitive contemplation has its place in understanding. By asking why Shamsuddin avails his body to the scorpions' stings, I am attempting to augment my felt understandings through cognitive processing. I try to make sense by vacillating between thinking *about* the image and feeling *with* the image. However, there's just too little information; thus, a satisfactory rationale for understanding Shamsuddin's behavior remains elusive. In all senses, I just keep finding it creepy.

An abject body is a creepy body, a body we want to reject because we are repelled by it. It is a body that we want to escape from through comfortable, perhaps familiar, cognitive rationales. It is also a body, perhaps because of its seeming inexplicability that we may be drawn to, although we may balk should it get too close. In various ways, with varying degrees of evocation, I have brought my abject body to the page. I have invited you on a journey of interpretive recursivity, a journey upon which you are asked to think about my body and to feel with it. I anticipate that you have been drawn in and repelled at various points along this journey. Where and why a reader might resist or not depends upon not only what is being evoked in the text, but upon what she or he brings to the page as a reader.

Recent changes in ethnographic writing prompted Norman Denzin to call for concomitant changes in reading practices. He urges an ethics of reading where the reader "works to avoid morally problematic ethical [reading] stances" (*Interpretive Ethnography,* 247). Fundamental to this ethics of reading is reader reflexivity, a consideration and reconsideration by the reader of where and why the reader refuses to grant the text and/or its author credibility. Ellis observes that when her first encounter with an autoethnographic text leaves her "insufficiently engaged," she considers how that reading may be due to "her own lacking" ("Creating Criteria," 274). She states:

> I will ask myself questions to inoculate against that. Is this a topic I know little about? I have built in biases about? I have not experienced? I have experienced differently? Okay, if so, why? I ask if my experience of the paper is a result of history or positioning different from the author's. Am I missing an opportunity to learn something about racial, class, ethnic, age, gender, political, or national difference? Am I missing an opportunity to experience vicariously relationships, feelings, thoughts, or acts connected to these categories? Is the author providing a view that complexifies how I look at the phenomenon? Or is this story, as I first suspected, simply not convincing enough? ("Creating Criteria," 274)

Interrogating the self in relation to the text is a tensive and tetchy process. Yet interpretive recursivity, the dynamic interplay between affective and intellectual understanding, and self-interrogation are fundamental to a new ethics of reading for autoethnographic texts. Scholarly texts do not usually demand that we read in this way. However, through the combining of literary and theory-driven scholarly voices, elements not typical to scholarship are present in autoethnographic texts and demand a different form of reader engagement. There is an element of exposure as that which obscures the author's professional observations from the author's personal self gives way. To write in this manner is to "write vulnerably," as Ruth Behar has aptly termed it (*The Vulnerable Observer,* 16). Exposure to the intimate, emotive, messy details of living revealed in autoethnographic texts also means that readers are prompted to respond vulnerably (Behar, *The Vulnerable Observer,* 16). Vulnerability occasions discomfort. It is much safer to retreat to cognitive rationales, much simpler to abjectify the other, much more comfortable to be the one who asserts a claim of knowledge than to subject one's resistances to critical self-interrogation.

"Does an emotional response lessen or enhance intellectual understanding?" Behar asks (*The Vulnerable Observer,* 16). While a felt response may not be strictly speaking "intellectual," by writing in ways meant to evoke the experience, I have taken for granted that a visceral or emotional encounter can enhance understanding for the reader.[1] But my assumption rests on a paradox. To represent the performances of abject identity, I had to conjure on the page that which makes them ripe for abjectification. You need to find my abject body creepy and want to reject me and what I say. In short, your understanding my abject performances is, at least in the first instance, potentially arrested through my engaging your desire to abjectify me. I have also had to solicit your desire to know more. I have had to win your willingness to continue on the journey. I have asked you to engage in the uncomfortable process of tacking between thinking about my abject performances and feeling with my abject body as well as questioning the resistances you find in my tales. Given this paradoxical interpretive dynamic, I cannot argue that it is emotional response per se that necessarily enhances understanding. For clearly, the emotion that summons abjectification is a forestalling of understanding. Rather, it is the dialogic negotiation between the writer and the reader as well as between the reader and her or himself that leads to understanding—an understanding that is both intellectually known as well as emotionally and viscerally felt. Bathing in scorpions or subjecting my body to dietary regimes, dancing naked in public, and adorning myself with the trappings of femininity may remain creepy somatic engagements for you, but unlike Shamsuddin's photo, I give you situated narratives to affectively engage and intellectually contemplate.

What then has this journey through abject embodiment revealed? In the remainder of this chapter I make observations about the interpretive interplay between this performer of an abject body and her audience, and how those dynamics potentially make meaning. I also discuss how I see abjection functioning across the performances I described. I further consider the subversive potential of each of these abject enactments.

Abjection in Performance: Telling the Tale

Abjection is both a state and an activity. It is something I do deliberately, something I perform. I render my body as abject and it is attributed as such by others. Abjection also is an activity that spectators may do in order to communicate their recalcitrance, rejecting and rebuking me. For clarification, I have given these two processes different names. I call my enactment *performing abjection* and the audience's process *abjectification*. The experience of abjection, then, is a complex interplay of overlapping communicative activities.

When performing abjection—the act of self-degradation as a performative strategy—my agency is brought into relief though my resolute defiance of the cultural script in which women in general are always already abjectified. I refuse my audience's abjectification by willfully embodying an abject body; it is a political act of defiance. Thus I possess a transgressive body, but in this refusal I also become subversive. Like David Graver's notion of the actor's body as commentator, the strategy of performing abjection places the performer's actions within an ongoing discourse of performance conventions and cultural practices and produces a corporeal presence of willful engagement ("The Actor's Bodies," 225–26).[2] How I, as a performer, "play" with expectations for female and feminist self-performance foregrounds my agency. I urge that the purpose of my performance be considered beyond its shock value, beyond the first dismissive flush prompted by visceral response. My performance demands consideration within the ongoing critical and cultural discourses about feminist performance and feminist performativity. Audiences are implicated in my act of supposed and actual self-abnegation. As spectators view my intentional act of transgression or even self-defilement, their agency is likewise brought into relief through the palpability of their affective response. When audience members render my body abject, the rejection I feel may take the form of a psychic, physical, critical, or political act. There are punishments for performing an abject body that may be enacted on the interpersonal, social, or cultural level.

I discovered that the place of my abject body is one circumscribed by fear and threats to my personal and/or professional well-being. It is a tense, touchy, and contested place: My abject body is both a body scrambling to retain power slipping away under the mantle of abjectification, and a body emphatically clasping power to my breast, a body that turns abjection into energy, and reacts to that fear either by cowering or by seizing power and indicting those who decry me. My abject body is a body that experiences my being with a hyperpalpability. If, as Leder argues, the body appears in times of error, and, as I argue, it also appears during times of pleasure, my abject body is—despite efforts to dismiss it—a body that refuses to go away (*The Absent Body*). It is a re-membered body. I have discovered that the place of my abject body is a position of resistance, a place where I can refuse abjection by denouncing the quick or shallow reasoning of those who would denounce me. When I refuse abjection, I do so through an *articulate refusal*, a refusal based upon *alterity*, and an *acceptance of the ambiguity* my abject status constitutes. My body makes me ever-mindful of my actions and the interpretations I may deliberately or inadvertently court.

Ideological constructs circumscribe the abject body. In my performance of weight loss, I locate my experience within a sea of scholarly voices. There I discover how the double inscription of cultural dictates and the countercultural feminist arguments against performing femininity delimit my performance. I seek a place between these two realms of ideological power where I can more comfortably articulate and negotiate my agency, even while I realize as I lose weight that I am both complicit with and critical of the cultural dictates. Moreover, I am critical of a monolithic feminist framework that assumes weight loss for women is only and always complicit with cultural dictates that oppress women. I continue to engage in weight loss despite the abjectification I receive when I am seen to be complying with the dominant cultural expectation that I have a slim body and despite my knowledge and tacit approval of the feminist critique. I position myself in this abject state, preferring to do so than to eschew the activity of losing weight. Despite the abjection I experience, I nevertheless feel more in touch with the world around me and stronger as a result when my body is not buffeted by the rounded dullness of being fat. I somatically understand my transgression, and having both felt and understood the norms I have transgressed, I seek to critique them by articulating my refusal of abjection.

I learn that the process of the weigh-in confounded my experiential understandings and instead urged me toward a product orientation of my body size. I learn as a result that both the dominant understandings of women's embodiment and the feminist critique of weight loss fail to appreciate the processual nature of embodiment. By moving to this process-oriented thinking, I challenge a monolithic acceptance of the feminist critique concerning women's debilitating self-surveillance. I introduce an alternative possibility, that performing my change in body size entails a kind of "gnostic tactility" (Sheets-Johnstone, *The Roots of Thinking*, 335), a knowing through the body by staying attuned to the changes in my body. It is not self-surveillance, but bodily attunement, awareness, a somatic witnessing.

Weight loss is a process of perpetual negotiation that makes my embodied performance of self present to me. The refusal of abjection through articulation calls into question the truth and tenacity of those norms and those interpretations that would constrain my performance as only an abject one. The space I occupy when I refuse abjection is not a static space, intractably marked as abject, but a shifting terrain in which I negotiate a valid and valuable feminist performance. Both the cultural standards for female embodiment and the feminist cultural critique are discourses that objectify the fact of my body by failing to recognize the processual nature of the act of embodiment. Refusing the cultural and feminist abjectification through an articulate resistance contributes to a subversion of those competing ideological constraints.

In my performance as a stripper for a night I bared my body in the strip club and sought to render the bare truth of that experience in an avowedly personal, narrative voice. I discovered how sedimented those overlapping ideological constructs are within my body. I felt my body to be inferior to what the dominant cultural expectations urge women to possess. I also felt the debasement that the feminist arguments that funded my feminist development enculturated me to expect. I feared the gaze of the people in the club—the actual people in the club *and* those I imagined might be present—and I feared the implicit reproachful academic gaze and the potential for professional reprisals I could suffer for having transgressed academic and social decorum and for making that transgression visible.

Performing a striptease renders me abject according to the feminist cultural critique, yet the fear I experienced crippled my performance and made me even more abject since I became incapable of performing stripper femininity in any way other than as a decidedly clumsy, weak, and ineffectual woman. At one point I managed to use a strategy of resistance against the stultifying and objectifying gaze of the men at the back stage. In that momentary act of resistance, I deliberately performed my abjection, making myself an ugly, aggressive, and grinding body, insisting that these men look despite their obvious desire not to. Mine is a fleeting victory, however, for overwhelmingly I find I cannot remove my sedimented understanding of the ideological constructs circumscribing my body and constraining my activities.

To find a position where my abjection can be refused, I must shift my ideological lens and find an alternative vision. The refusal of abjection is a refusal predicated upon alterity. Amanda's otherness, her decidedly different experience of stripping, is placed alongside my own. Whereas I feel myself to be doubly inscribed with abjection, Amanda refuses that positioning altogether. Whereas my personhood is delimited by the experience, Amanda remains a powerful agent in her own right. I then place Amanda's experience alongside the feminism vocalized by the pro-sex or sex-positive sex workers. That view altered how I understood sex work and made me question the original perspective I had wherein I considered that sex work is always dehumanizing. The sex-positive feminist view altered the way I viewed and interviewed the subjects of my research. This conceptual shift permits me to see that sex work for some women is edifying and, furthermore, it gives the subjects of my research a space wherein they can refute the victimage implicated by the feminist cultural critique.

The experience of abjection I receive as a result of my academic interests tracks along a time span beginning with my performance of "Spin the Ideological Bottle" through two differing performances of "Lip Reading." Attending self-consciously to the sensory somatic experience of doing these performances, I employ a poetical voice in order to evoke them. The strategies I use to perform abjection differ in each of those performances, yet they result in my finding myself immersed in a culture of abjectification. In "Spin the Ideological Bottle," I render my body abjectly, first, by enacting a striptease and, second, by consuming the bottle of Coke in a manner reminiscent of pornographic films' iconic "money shot." My intention in performing abjection during this performance was to convey an avowedly and widely accepted feminist message, the message that women are systematically debased by the cultural objectification of women and by the attendant absenting of women's part in cultural memory.

In "Lip Reading," I perform abjection by challenging the feminist arguments against feminine adornment by announcing my conflicted but ultimately celebratory wearing of lipstick. Aware that mainstream feminist thought is pervasively present in Academe, I perform "Lip Reading" at an academic convention knowing my message will be antithetical, if not heretical, to the feminist positions held by the majority of my audience. I therefore anticipate the possibility of their abjectification. When I perform the same text at a nonacademic venue, the performance conventions diminish the possibility of abjectification. Before my professional colleagues and peers, I perform with an implicit understanding that I will be subject to academic scrutiny, that my performance is a comment upon academic arguments about feminine embodiment that widely circulate in the academic community. The audience members at the performance venue appear to me to be more interested in being entertained and they therefore appear to give in to the performance's carnivalesque qualities. My interpretation of their response enables me to feel more free to heighten those qualities in my performance and to more fully express the meanings in the text. In that performance, I am not so much performing abjection as I am performing celebration and iconoclasm.

As the creator and performer of texts that celebrate and embody ideas and behaviors outside mainstream feminism, these abject performances invite academic abjectification. I discover that the abjectification I experience is not contained within the aesthetic frame; rather the interpretations made of my performances exceed the theatrical playing spaces and fund interpretations of my everyday performance of self, which constitutes my social identity. What unfolds is a process of interpretive and performative resolve. *Resolve without resolution.* I discover and confront the resoluteness of individuals who are unwilling to engage my performance beyond their initial discomfort and/or conceptual frames of understanding; I occasionally counter their positions by refusing their abjectification of me through resolute defiance of their (mis)readings. Thus, while some individuals refuse to think beyond their initial assumptions of my abject body, I refuse to accept their logic. Competing texts of real and/or my imagined expectations of audience abjectification are thereby written and read across my body by self and others. In the aftermath of "Spin the Ideological Body," I ultimately move toward an acceptance of my abject and ambiguous status. I accept that altering the negative interpretations will more than likely be impossible. Understanding how my abject body calls attention to ideological and social norms in an effort to critique and possibly subvert them may be outside some people's conceptual categories. Perhaps too they are simply threatened and defensive. Perhaps too, I am too sensitive to their critique. Throughout the process I become more willing to accept the ambiguity of my position. I learn how refusing abjectification and opening up toward an acceptance of ambiguity foregrounds my agency. I call for those individuals who are willing to think twice about my performances to do so, and I call for myself to re-think where I am failing to understand the interpretations being made of me; I call for us to collectively think beyond our initial assumptions and interpretations. I ask myself to consider, then consider again, how I help create the conditions for audience abjectification, and I ask my audience to reconsider what meanings are in play when I perform abjection. I also recognize that there are those who are willing to think twice and to imaginatively traverse the experiential differences that divide us in an effort to understand. Moreover, I recognize that while those same individuals may not approve of my tactics, they may be willing to expand their conceptions of what it means to perform feminist identity; thus, as they move to accommodate my alternative conception for feminist embodiment, their original understandings may have been subverted by my performance.

Refusing abjection through *articulation*, *alterity*, and *ambiguity* are three strategies I use to subvert static conceptions for performing woman, and for performing feminist identity. By employing these strategies, I urge an expansion and/or a perpetually mutable negotiation of that identity. These strategies emphasize that the performance of femininity is saturated with agency, the desire to be a purposeful being in the world.

Feminism(s) and Femininity: A Tale Told by Many Tellers

One of my purposes has been to further the immanent feminist critical dialogue and to encourage all feminists to better respond to the wide variety of women's experience. To make my case, I have critically examined various feminist arguments. Of course, interpretations are necessarily the product of partial perspectives. I have pointed to the ways that individuals have stopped or potentially stop their interpretations of my abjection-making performances and how they dismiss me. I have suggested that they may do so out of an affective response to what I do. Or perhaps they do so because of some interest or ideological perspective that encourages them to see in a particular way. I have also suggested that while feminist arguments do enable particular views on the world, they may forestall appropriate understanding of some situations. Making interpretations about a particular experience while guided by a general argument is always tricky. Let me urge a cautious application of our feminism.

My concerns echo those made in a published conversation between Jane Gallop, Marianne Hirsch, and Nancy K. Miller. They consider the subject of how feminist scholars have tended to "trash" other feminist scholars and their scholarship in various public forums. Not only does such trashing affect individual women's professional lives (and also, no doubt, their personal lives), it has the additional effect of promoting problematic interpretations of these scholars' work, interpretations that affect how upcoming generations of feminists understand the work that has come before them. Jane Gallop argues that an environment of no-conflict is simply unrealistic (Gallop, Hirsch, and Miller, "Criticizing Feminist Criticism," 367). It would also be antithetical to a critical movement that requires immanent critique in order to develop and sustain feminisms. Yet if what we are doing as feminists becomes characterized by conflict, as has increasingly been the case, we must accept that fewer and fewer women will identify as feminists and enter our critical dialogue. Gallop ends the conversation by suggesting that what we need is "to distinguish between a criticism that actually attends to something and a criticism that's really dismissive. . . . What we need is an ethics of criticism" (Gallop, Hirsch, and Miller, "Criticizing Feminist Criticism," 368).

In my exploration of abjection and subversion, I have questioned my own motives, trying to move beyond dismissive critique and to open the door to an ethics of interpretation. While acts of femininity may continue to be problematic performances, I believe that how we fathom the nuances of meaning in those performances is more important than arriving at conclusive interpretations. We must take a considered look and then look again. There is no stable, all-inclusive feminism or one singular accounting for acts of femininity. Like feminism and femininity, the interpretations I have made here are not immutably defined.

The Sting Is in the Tale

As my head pops up from what has at times felt like a sea of scorpions, I can say I am healthy and fit. It has not always been comfortable. It has always been questionable, questionable to me and to my audience.

I knew I might get bit. I knew I might occasionally be hurt. I can feel the poison enter me. Still I have let the creepy crawly legs slither and slide and scramble up my body. They cling to me in awkward, even unmentionable places. They nestle in my soft and fleshy parts. Their claws and tails threaten me.

I have occasionally regretted my choice to place myself in this predicament.

I have occasionally found solace there.

I and my antagonists make odd bedfellows. Sometimes I scold them. Other times I ignore them. Occasionally we renegotiate our relationship and secure some modicum of detente between us. Over time, some of us have even become cautious friends. Still I know if I carry on, the potential for injury remains. We coexist in a revolving process of irritation and toleration.

Some of them, I discover, are not my adversaries at all, for I soon learn that they are not scorpions; I have only imagined that they were.

Still others are only figments of my imagination; I only think I feel them crawling about me ready to sting when there wasn't anything threatening me at all.

I cannot entirely blame those who bite me. It is I who put myself in harm's way. As often as not, they are as irritated by this situation as I am. When I disturb them, they curl up, their tails ready to strike. Others appear not to care why I am there; they just wish I would go away. Some are not troubled by my presence at all. Perhaps it is I who is more troubled by them than they are by me.

Some demand to know "Why?" I ponder the question: Why do I do this? I find myself defining my reasons in the negative: It is not simply that I wish to gain some intangible glory by having lived to tell the tale. It is not that I am attempting to break some record, nor am I simply trying to make myself stand out and to shock. I think we all do things that make us uncomfortable, that subject ourselves to others' scrutiny, and that are potentially damaging. What I have done is perhaps more obvious, and more viscerally repellent to others. The reasons that I give may never satisfy those who question me; they may never fully satisfy me either. Words fail.

I rub my fingers along the scars and wounds my adversaries leave upon my body. Some marks are my own doing. I touch these scars and wounds; they sting and I wince. I feel the lesions and I embrace them as manifest evidence of my sentient life. There, my history is written upon me. There, a tale is waiting to be told, a tale that lies beyond the marks, beyond the sting, a story to tell but one that can never be completely told, a tale without a tail.

Notes

Chapter One

1. In addition to autoethnography, my work here is methodologically informed by phenomenology. In her essay "'I Like to Watch,'" Lenore Langsdorf (1994) proposes a five-phase, recursive model for critical hermeneutic phenomenological inquiry. The phases are "participation/observation," "reflection," "assertion," "variation," and "communication/participation." Suffice it to say that employing these recursive phases begins with the researcher's experience, urges a reflexive description and consideration of that experience, leads to a series of assertions and then their reconsideration in which alternative assertions are proposed, and ends with the communication of findings. In short, the model demands that the researcher thinks at least twice about any assertions she or he may make in the process of inquiry. In exploring the performances I engage in this book, I variously employ Langsdorf's model. The phases of the model are much more explicitly marked in the structure of the chapter on weight loss where I write with a more traditional scholarly voice. As I proceed through the book, moving from performance to performance and shifting from a narrative voice to a more poetical voice, the phases of the model become less and less explicit in the structure of those chapters. My point in addressing these issues here is simply to note that the model in its explicit and more implicit form guides the flow of inquiry across the chapters.

2. Three factors guided my selection of the scholars and arguments I include here. First, I chose scholars whose work has been influential in my feminist development and

therefore have been important as my analysis emerged. In particular, works by Sandra Lee Bartky and Susan Bordo were chosen because they have influenced me greatly. Second, these scholars are well respected and have therefore been influential in the ongoing development of feminist thought. Third, their work often provides the clearest example of what I take to be fundamental arguments about the politics of feminine representation.

3. Amelia Jones in her essay "Unnatural Acts: Interpreting Body Art," working separately but concurrently with my enterprise here, comes to a similar position on how transgressive acts engage audiences and the interpretations they make. Also see my essay, "Performing the Abject Body: A Feminist Refusal of Disempowerment," *Theatre Annual* 55 (2002): 48–60.

4. Elinor Fuchs, "Staging the Obscene Body," *TDR* 33 (1989): 33–58.

5. Catherine Schuler, "Spectator Response and Comprehension: The Problem with Karen Finley's *Constant State of Desire*," *TDR* 34 (1990): 131–45.

6. Jill Dolan, "The Dynamics of Desire: Sexuality in Pornography and Performance," *Theatre Journal* 39 (1987): 156–74.

7. Joanna Frueh, *Erotic Faculties* (Berkeley: University of California Press, 1996).

8. Shannon Bell, *Reading, Writing, and Rewriting the Prostitute Body* (Bloomington: Indiana University Press, 1994).

9. Peggy Phelan, *Unmarked: The Politics of Performance* (New York: Routledge, 1993).

10. Rebecca Schneider, *The Explicit Body in Performance* (London: Routledge, 1997).

11. This list is representative rather than exhaustive.

Chapter Two

1. I propose an account of the stages overweight women may go through in my essay "Social Drama in the Spectacle of Femininity: The Performance of Weight Loss in the Weight Watchers' Program," *Women's Studies in Communication* 19 (1996): 291–312. Crisis is one stage.

2. For an insightful analysis of the sociological implications of patriarchy and women's bodies see Bryan S. Turner, *The Body and Society: Explorations in Social Theory* (London: Routledge, 1993), 115–36.

3. In Millman's book the organization is referred to as the National Association to Aid Fat Americans. In a telephone conversation in March 2001 with Maryanne Bodolay, executive administrator of NAAFA, she confirmed that the name was changed around 1988. For more on the organization see Gina Kolata, "The Fat-Enabling Culture: Society Made Me Eat it!" *New York Times,* 1 December 1996, natl. ed.: 4, 4; also NAAFA's website at www.naafa.org. Moreover, I should like to note that NAAFA is quite clear on why they use the word "fat" in their name and in reference to their members. On their website they state, "Why do we use the word 'fat' so freely? 'Fat' is not a four-letter word. It is an adjective, like short, tall, thin, or blonde. While society has given it a derogatory meaning, we find that identifying ourselves as 'fat' is an important step in casting off the shame we have been taught to feel about our bodies." Their aim is "size acceptance" by society and by the fat individual himself or herself. By implication, using the term "overweight,"

as I admittedly do in this book, suggests a standard to which the individual in question does not adhere. Their point is well taken. Yet I continue to use overweight as it is the more generally used term and helps call attention to those standards.

4. Quoted in Anthony Synnott, *The Body Social: Symbolism, Self, and Society* (London: Routledge, 1993), 77, from Janusz Kaczorowski, "The Good, the Average and the Ugly: Socioeconomic Dimensions of Physical Attractiveness," MA Thesis, McGill University, Montreal, Canada, 1989.

5. I've taken this phrase from the title of Kim Chernin's book on eating disorders, *The Obsession: Reflections on the Tyranny of Slenderness* (1981; New York: HarperPerennial, 1994).

6. The connection between capitalism and the subjugation and disciplining of bodies surely was explored prior to Foucault. Indeed, Bryan Turner argues that Max Weber's notion of the "rationalization" of bodies anticipates Foucault (*The Body and Society*, 2–3; 164–65). Moreover, though he notes the similarities between the two theorists, Turner also identifies their differences. Significantly, Weber, particularly in *The Protestant Ethic and the Spirit of Capitalism*, locates the "rationalization" of bodies in religion, specifically Protestantism. Foucault situates the control of bodies within politics (cf. Synnott, *The Body Social*, 260). Considering this connection, then, it may not be surprising that the cultural anthropologist Robert Murphy makes the following claim:

> the pursuit of the slim, well-muscled body is not only an aesthetic matter, but also a moral imperative. . . . Fasting and self-inflicted physical punishments are the modern-day equivalents of medieval flagelantism. They are religious rituals, part of the immortality project of secularized middle class that no longer believes in redemption of the soul and has turned instead to redemption of the body. (*The Body Silent*, 114)

Arguably, Karl Marx's analysis of labor and capital explores how bodies are subjugated and thus, also anticipates Foucault's contribution.

7. The internal quote in the final sentence is attributed to Alison Jaggar, *Feminist Politics and Human Nature* (Totowa, NJ: Rowman & Allanheld, 1983), 122.

8. See Bartky, "Toward a Phenomenology of Feminist Consciousness," 11–21 for a clear discussion of the process of attaining a "fully developed feminist consciousness" (12). Admittedly, since its publication and others, feminist analysis has significantly moved on. Yet I believe the importance of political awareness, whether or not the psychologically inflected term "consciousness" is used, continues as part of all the feminisms. I chose to elucidate this concept with this early "second-wave" example for the clarity with which it articulates the idea.

9. It perhaps bears noting the implicit heterosexual bias in this quote. Arguably, a lesbian femme and, I would argue, a bisexual femme, whose sexual identities are enacted overtly, may challenge the assumption of their supposed compliance with patriarchy.

10. The term "cultural dope" was coined by Howard Garfinkel in "Studies of the Routine Grounds of Everyday Activities," *Studies in Ethnomethodology* (Cambridge: Polity, 1967), 68. Bordo attributes the phrase to Anthony Giddens on page 303–04, note 34. The phrase in both cases nevertheless denotes the mistaken notion that people behave

according to the whim of socialization and that they are therefore incapable of critical awareness of these social forces. Yet equally mistaken is the idea that people have the agency to transcend culture and free themselves from socialization. Thus, human agency is enacted with an awareness of social forces and in the tensions between one's will and the social restraints.

11. Admittedly, an overweight woman might escape feminist censure if her decision to lose weight was prompted by health reasons rather than a concern for appearance. Since obesity may lead to a variety of health risks, appearance is not the sole reason for endeavoring to lose weight.

12. I explore this strategy, performing female disempowerment in order to further a feminist agenda, in more detail in chapter 4. Worthy of note is the fact that Steinem suffered personal attacks by both feminists and others for participating as a Bunny and for making the critique. In a 1983 postscript to the article (originally written in 1963), she states that among other disagreeable and threatening things, she received "obscene and threatening" phone calls and suffered the "loss of serious journalistic assignments because [she] had now become a Bunny—and it didn't matter why" ("I Was a Playboy Bunny," 68). Also, *Playboy* repeatedly continues to publish her employee photograph as a Bunny. The caption under the photo in a 1983 issue boasted, with perhaps more bravado than truth, that her article "'boosted Bunny recruiting'" ("I Was a Playboy Bunny," 69).

13. In 1990, she established the Cosmetic Surgery Network (CSN) whose aim, according to her website, "is to demystify cosmetic surgery and empower patients with unbiased information." For a fee, people considering cosmetic surgery can consult with the CSN and also purchase her book and video. The information the organization dispenses is based upon Jackson's experience and advice from a host of cosmetic surgeons, as well as information obtained from others who have gone under the knife. Her first book was self-published under the title *Cindy Jackson's Image and Cosmetic Surgery Secrets.* Her video is entitled *The Making of Cindy Jackson.* Her most recent book is an autobiography entitled *Living Doll.*

14. As if to explicitly affirm the connection between physical attractiveness and success, Gordon Patzer, the author of *The Physical Attractiveness Phenomena* whom I cited earlier, is quoted in one of the links on Jackson's website in apparent support of the practical and scientific knowledge offered by Jackson (Jackson, Home Page).

15. The phrase is Scott's, *Domination and the Arts of Resistance,* 203–06.

16. Although Jackson was not born to wealth, *20/20* reported the total cost of her surgeries up to the date of that broadcast to be in excess of $100,000 ("Becoming Barbie").

17. In his text, Scott never provides an example exactly akin to how I am arguing that Jackson is subversive. His examples are typically about how language is used in the presence of an oppressor and what is said in the oppressor's absence. Although Jackson asserts that without a more equitable world it is okay to enjoy the benefits of that oppressive system, and although she embodies the cultural standards, I argue that her actions attempt to subvert the system in that the extremity of her actions are articulations against the system.

18. Originally Orlan planned to have seven operations. Yet in both Peg Zeglin Brand's interview with Orlan and on Orlan's home page, Orlan states that she has had nine operations. Orlan also states this number at a conference held at the Institute of Contemporary Art in London. See, The Body as Site, *Towards the Aesthetics of the Future: Seduced and Abandoned Conference.* Audiotape. Linda Dement, Susan Alexis Collins, Kathleen Rogers, Orlan. Institute of Contemporary Art, March 13, 1994. No. 1009.

19. My exposure to this panel discussion is by way of an audio recording I obtained from the Institute of Contemporary Art in London.

20. I am using the English translation of Orlan's words by an unnamed translator provided on the tape. Additionally, Orlan claims that she does not feel pain during the operations (Body). However, this is a claim that some have argued is more strategic than true. See Philip Auslander, "Orlan's Theatre of Operations," *Theatre Forum: International Theatre Journal* 7 (1995): 31. Orlan is given an epidural block and uses local anesthetic during the performance/operations (Rose, "Is It Art?" 86). Typically, these surgeries are done with general anesthetic.

21. This quote is from the video played during the panel discussion. Orlan's voice was translated on an English soundtrack. The video, we are told, was played at the Sydney Biennale and is entitled "The Text."

22. Statement made by Sarah Wilson on the audiotape, Orlan Panel Discussion. A similar sentiment was articulated by Laurent Delaye at the same panel. However, Philip Auslander notes that the implants Orlan had put in her forehead to give her the forehead of the Mona Lisa gave her a "distinctly unnatural" appearance and brought her work closer to an act of "intentional uglification" ("Orlan's Theatre of Operations," 28). Furthermore, he comments that during her visit to Atlanta in 1994, "her face was described repeatedly (and rather rudely) as evoking that of a space alien on Star Trek" ("Orlan's Theatre of Operations," 28). Orlan herself notes that her "work is all about my own image, which is supposed to represent today's standards of beauty as well as some 'counter-standards,' because these two bumps are like a counter-standard of beauty today" (Brand, "Bound to Beauty," 295).

23. "Image" is used here in the sense of a representation in a work of art rather than in the sense of self-image or image for self-presentation.

24. It's worth noting that Jackson invites the focus on her bodily transformation even while she claims its purpose has been to effect other presumably more important changes in her social and professional lifestyle. On her website a photographic image of her preoperative self and an image of her current embodiment continually oscillate placing a striking and unavoidable focus on the fact of her physical transformation (Jackson, Home Page).

25. "Expressive" here connotes the capacity for signifying enactments rather than as might be construed, a capacity to reveal interiority.

26. Moreover, I should like to note that Jackson's Cosmetic Surgery Network, although it surely financially benefits Jackson, is an organization intended to empower other individuals seeking cosmetic surgery.

27. As is implied by the title of her article "Is It Art?: Orlan and the Transgressive Act," Barbara Rose focuses on the contested place Orlan's work occupies within art criticism.

In defense of the artistic worth of Orlan's work, Rose makes the following claim: "In the end, the two essential criteria for distinguishing art from nonart, intentionality and transformation, are present in all [Orlan's] efforts" (87).

28. The "first wave" of American feminism is generally understood to be late-nineteenth- and early-twentieth-century activism that led to women's suffrage. Aside from gaining the vote, this "wave" helped expand the "view of women as persons able to exist as individuals outside the family" (Nicholson, *Gender and History,* 56). The "second wave," beginning in the early 1960s, continued the expansion of women's influence in the public sphere. The central second-wave effort was to eliminate the obstacles preventing women's equality in the public sphere through advocacy and enacting legal changes (Nicholson, *Gender and History,* 22). The "third wave" evolved out of the second wave sometime during the early 1980s. The scholarship and activism of this wave is distinguished by a challenge to the largely white, liberal, and middle-class concerns of the second wave and a turn toward a concern for multiplicity and difference. Furthermore, third-wave feminism generally calls for a reappraisal of the entire political and social structure in light of the various concerns held by women of different races, classes, ethnicities, and sexual orientations. I should also note that there are those who would claim we are currently in a "post-feminist" era. This is a claim I resolutely disavow first because as of this writing women have yet to attain equality—including the most visible and easily indexical injustice of wage parity—with their male counterparts, a fact that contributes to the need for continued feminist theorizing and feminist activism. Furthermore, to declare a post-feminist era when women of color were just managing to have their concerns voiced and heard in the third wave seems to me to concede to an apparent and insidious backlash against women in general and women of color in particular, a move that yet again silences their and therefore all women's interests.

Chapter Three

1. Lesa Lockford, "'What's a Nice Scholar Like You Doing with a Topic Like This'? or Interpretive Communities Make Sense," Performing the Transgressive Body panel, Speech Communication Association Convention, Rivercenter Marriott, San Antonio, November, 19, 1995.

2. The 1994 annual meeting of the Speech Communication Association. The organization has since been renamed the National Communication Association.

3. The "not me/not not me" experience of performing is described by Richard Schechner in "Restoration of Behavior," *Between Theater and Anthropology* (Philadelphia: University of Pennsylvania Press, 1985), 110–12. The phrase, as may well be evident, denotes that reflexive experience in performance when one performs a role and in so doing simultaneously feels oneself to be both the role (not oneself) and oneself (not not oneself) as well.

4. This point is similar to the point made by Sandra Lee Bartky that I cite in chapter 2.

5. Since I began this project there has been an increasing number of books published that bring the voices of sex workers into print. Some notable examples of books that have been published both before and during my work with sex workers are Laurie Bell, ed., *Good Girls/Bad Girls: Feminists and Sex Trade Workers Face to Face* (Seattle: Seal, 1987); Wendy Chapkis and Jill Posener, *Live Sex Acts: Women Performing Erotic Labor* (New York: Routledge,1997); Frédérique Delacoste and Priscilla Alexander, eds., *Sex Work* (Pittsburgh: Cleis, 1987); Kamala Kempadoo and Jo Doezema, eds., *Global Sex Workers: Rights, Resistance, and Redefinition* (New York: Routledge, 1998); Jill Nagle, ed., *Whores and Other Feminists* (New York: Routledge, 1997); Matt Bernstein Sycamore, ed., *Tricks and Treats: Sex Workers Write about Their Clients* (New York: Haworth, 2000). See also Katherine Liepe-Levinson, *Strip Show: Performances of Gender and Desire* (London: Routledge, 2002), for a good examination of strip clubs through the performative lens. A comprehensive account of the neglected history of whores can be found in Nickie Roberts, *Whores in History: Prostitution in Western Society* (London: HarperCollins, 1993).

6. Some of these organizations are COYOTE (Call Off Your Old Tired Ethics), the NTFP (National Task Force on Prostitution), the U.S. Prostitutes Collective, and WHISPER (Women Hurt In Systems of Prostitution Engaged in Revolt).

7. Gayle Rubin calls it a "sex-radical" perspective.

8. Many of the narratives told to me by the women I interviewed appear in my essay "An Ethnographic Ghost Story: Adapting 'What's a Nice Commodity Like You Doing in a Spectacle Like This?'" *Text and Performance Quarterly* 20 (2000): 402–15.

9. The women I spoke with sometimes voiced anger at the control the club owners exercise at their expense rather than, as one might expect, at the punters. Some women in my study claimed that they had more autonomy and experienced less-oppressive work environments in clubs owned and operated by women. This point is also made by Debi Sundahl, "Stripper," in *Sex Work: Writings by Women in the Sex Industry*, eds. Frédérique Delacoste and Priscilla Alexander (Pittsburgh: Cleis, 1987), 175–80. See also, Erika Langley's *The Lusty Lady: Photographs and Texts* (New York: Scalo, 1997).

10. Ronai's experience and my own differ in that Ronai had previous experience as a dancer before taking on the subject as a scholarly pursuit.

11. For example, during the English occupation of Scotland there was the English Pale. In Ireland the section occupied by the English was simply called The Pale. In both cases, English rule was maintained within these so-called pales. Since they were established by the English, the English regarded life within these pales as places of civility and rule. To be beyond the pale came to be known as being outside civility and, more colloquially, the expression connotes being outside the bounds of decency.

12. "Agnes" was a nineteen year old who presented herself as a female, displayed secondary female sexual characteristics, such as developed breasts, and sought sex-reassignment surgery at UCLA in 1958. She was granted the surgery only after a series of medical, psychological, and sociological examinations determined that her sex/gender confusion was due to an organic abnormality rather than her deliberate intervention. Later, after she was given a "man-made vagina," it was discovered that she had taken female hormones from the age

of twelve. Thus, she was "passing" as a female in her everyday life and passing for the doctors during the examinations as a "normal" and "natural" female who just happened to have the wrong genitalia (cf. Garfinkel, "Passing"; Appendix).

13. See Garfinkel, "Passing," 134–35, for a description of the resistances Agnes experienced.

14. The implicit hierarchy of bodies and social status is discussed in chapter 2 with regard to how embodiment affects financial reward. See Berscheid and Walster, "Beauty and the Best"; and Patzer, *The Physical Attractiveness Phenomena.*

15. That said, I must also note that during my fieldwork I did observe some dancers who were my age or older, whose bodies I took to be similar to mine or fleshier, who exuded confidence and seemed to enjoy themselves, and who appeared to make a good living in the club. Again, Amanda's words that confidence is all return to haunt me. Yet while I cannot believe that all it takes is confidence, her suggestion challenges me to understand that refusing abjection at least *begins* with confidence. Additionally, it must be said that the contemporary standard for the "ideal" feminine shape is not every customer's ideal. Dancing ability and ability to "hustle" the customers well, not only body shape, affect the dancer's status in the club. In effect, how she negotiates her agency affects her success in the club.

16. This is a term coined by Carol Queen, "Introduction," in *Real, Live, Nude, Girl: Chronicles of Sex-Positive Culture* (Pittsburgh: Cleis, 1997), xii.

17. Compare Rubin, "Thinking Sex," 281.

18. The notion of honoring desire is from Queen, "Pornography and the Sensitive New Age Guy," in *Real, Live, Nude, Girl: Chronicles of Sex-Positive Culture,* 145.

19. While I use both Gayle Rubin's and Carol Queen's work throughout this section, it is perhaps important to note that Rubin terms her view a "sex-radical" theory rather than "sex-positive" as Queen does. The difference between the two positions is minimal with one notable difference. Rubin would perhaps be more willing to include cross-generational desire than Queen. The point is important in that I believe Queen would be less willing to argue that desire between a legal adult and a person who is under the legal "age of consent" could ever be consensual.

20. Queen references the name of the infamous San Francisco red light district in her discussion of sex and art and the politics of artistic legitimacy. See Queen, "Porno-Formance: Some Notes on Sex as Art," in *Real, Live, Nude, Girl: Chronicles of Sex-Positive Culture,* 58. I am appropriating the reference here with regard to the politics of scholastic legitimacy.

Chapter Five

1. Subsequent to this conference presentation I manifestly learned that these fears are not misplaced. During a presentation I gave at an international conference in which I discussed my ethnographic experiences with exotic dancers and at a point where I raised questions from a pro-sex feminist position, a group of five women, whom I knew to be mainstream feminists, stood up and with deliberate disruption, very noisily walked out.

Chapter Six

1. Perhaps because alternative forms of scholarship such as autoethnography garner knowledge in ways beyond the "intellectual" that the form's scholarly legitimacy is sometimes an issue. For example, following the publication of a special issue of "Alternatives in Writing about Performance" in the January 1997 issue of *Text and Performance Quarterly*, a vociferous debate raged between January and March of that year on the Communication Theory and Research Network (CRTNET) online bulletin board. At issue was not only the legitimacy of the scholarly form in general but also the relative merits of the specific authors and their work contained in that journal issue. The debate not only impugned the essays, but also the authors themselves as scholars. Furthermore, following this online debate, the journal's survival was called into question as continued support by the National Communication Association, the organization that publishes the journal, was subjected to review. Within that online debate those opposed to the form were typically scholars who do not write autoethnography. However, I should also like to note that even writers who participate in this form of writing have sometimes published searing reviews of other authors' autoethnographic works. Also see the final chapter of Ruth Behar's *The Vulnerable Observer: Anthropology that Breaks Your Heart* (Boston: Beacon Press, 1996), 161–77, for an eloquent discussion of the academic torture that the publication of Renato Rosaldo's "Grief and the Headhunter's Rage" received. In his essay, Rosaldo in part passionately explores the grief and rage he experienced when his wife unexpectedly died during their fieldwork in the Philippines. For some, then, autoethnography is abject scholarship.

2. Graver primarily focuses his notion of the actor's body as commentator on how an actor adds her or his comment to the history and development of a particular role, as in the case of a new interpretation of Hamlet, or to how a particular performer comments upon theatrical conventions and expectations. I believe there is room to extend his conception to include cultural practices. How a performer plays with audience expectations for, say, politeness and propriety render the performer's body as commentator likewise present. Moreover, despite efforts to sort them, distinctions between cultural conventions and theatrical conventions are to my mind frequently necessarily blurred.

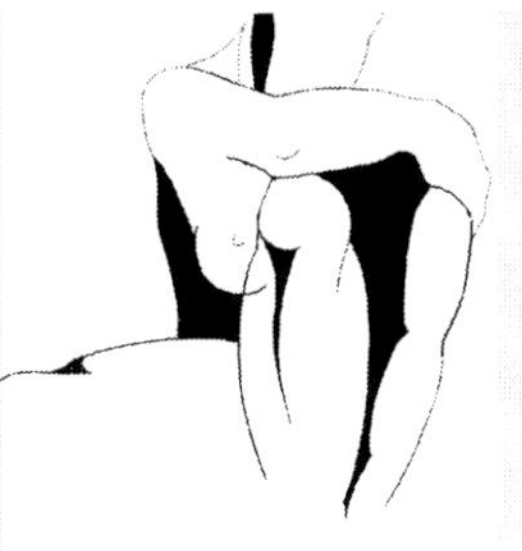

References

Alexander, Priscilla. "Introduction: Why this Book?" In *Sex Work: Writings by Women in the Sex Industry*, edited by Frédérique Delacoste and Priscilla Alexander, 14–18. Pittsburgh: Cleis, 1987.

Auslander, Philip. "Orlan's Theatre of Operations." *Theatre Forum: International Theatre Journal*, 7 (1995): 25–31.

Bachelard, Gaston. *The Poetics of Space*. Translated by Maria Jolas. New York: Orion Press, 1964.

Barthes, Roland. *Image, Music, Text*. Translated by Stephen Heath. New York: Farrar, Straus & Giroux, 1977.

Bartky, Sandra Lee. "Feminine Masochism and the Politics of Personal Transformation." In *Femininity and Domination: Studies in the Phenomenology of Oppression*, 45–62. New York: Routledge, 1990a.

———. "Foucault, Femininity, and the Modernization of Patriarchal Power." In *Femininity and Domination: Studies in the Phenomenology of Oppression*, 63–82. New York: Routledge, 1990b.

———. "Introduction." In *Femininity and Domination: Studies in the Phenomenology of Oppression*, 1–10. New York: Routledge, 1990c.

———. "Narcissism, Femininity, and Alienation." In *Femininity and Domination: Studies in the Phenomenology of Oppression*, 33–44. New York: Routledge, 1990d.

———. "On Psychological Oppression." In *Femininity and Domination: Studies in the Phenomenology of Oppression*, 22–31. New York: Routledge, 1990e.

———. "Toward a Phenomenology of Feminist Consciousness." In *Femininity and Domination: Studies in the Phenomenology of Oppression,* 11–21. New York: Routledge, 1990f.

Bayrd, Edwin. *The Thin Game: Dietary Scams and Dietary Sense.* New York: Avon Books, 1978.

"Becoming Barbie—Plastic Surgery and Beauty." *20/20.* [Video]. ABC. KABC, Los Angeles. June 28, 1996.

Behar, Ruth. *The Vulnerable Observer: Anthropology that Breaks Your Heart.* Boston: Beacon Press, 1996.

Bell, Laurie, ed. *Good Girls/Bad Girls: Feminists and Sex Trade Workers Face to Face.* Seattle: Seal, 1987.

Bell, Shannon. *Reading, Writing, and Rewriting the Prostitute Body.* Bloomington: Indiana University Press, 1994.

Berger, John. *Ways of Seeing.* New York: Penguin, 1972.

Berscheid, E., and E. Walster. "Beauty and the Best." *Psychology Today,* (March 1972): 42+.

Bierce, Ambrose. *The Devil's Dictionary.* New York: Dover, 1958.

Bochner, Arthur P. "Criteria against Ourselves." *Qualitative Inquiry,* 6 (2000): 266–72.

Bochner, Arthur P., and Carolyn Ellis. "Introduction: Talking over Ethnography." In *Composing Ethnography: Alternative Forms of Qualitative Writing,* edited by Carolyn Ellis and Arthur P. Bochner, 13–45. Walnut Creek: AltaMira Press, 1996.

Bodolay, Maryanne. Telephone Interview. March 16, 2001.

The Body as Site. *Towards the Aesthetics of the Future: Seduced and Abandoned Conference.* [Audiotape]. Linda Dement, Susan Alexis Collins, Kathleen Rogers, Orlan. Institute of Contemporary Art, March 13, 1994. No. 1009.

Bordo, Susan. "Beauty (Re)Discovers the Male Body." In *Beauty Matters,* edited by Peg Zeglin Brand, 112–54. Bloomington: Indiana University Press, 2000.

———. "Hunger as Ideology." In *Unbearable Weight: Feminism, Western Culture, and the Body,* 99–134. Berkeley: University of California Press, 1993a.

———. "Introduction." In *Unbearable Weight: Feminism, Western Culture, and the Body,* 1–42. Berkeley: University of California Press, 1993b.

———. *Unbearable Weight: Feminism, Western Culture, and the Body.* Berkeley: University of California Press, 1993c.

———. "Whose Body Is This? Feminism, Medicine, and the Conceptualization of Eating Disorders." In *Unbearable Weight: Feminism, Western Culture, and the Body,* 45–69. Berkeley: University of California Press, 1993d.

Brand, Peg Zeglin. "Bound to Beauty: An Interview with Orlan." In *Beauty Matters,* edited by Peg Zeglin Brand, 289–313. Bloomington: Indiana University Press, 2000.

Brownmiller, Susan. *Femininity.* New York: Fawcett Columbine, 1984.

Butler, Judith. *Gender Trouble: Feminism and the Subversion of Identity.* New York: Routledge, 1990a.

———. "Performative Acts and Gender Constitution: An Essay in Phenomenology and Feminist Theory." In *Performing Feminisms*, edited by Sue-Ellen Case, 270–82. Baltimore: Johns Hopkins University Press, 1990b.

Carlson, Marvin. *Performance: A Critical Introduction*. London: Routledge, 1996.

Chapkis, Wendy, and Jill Posener. *Live Sex Acts: Women Performing Erotic Labor*. New York: Routledge, 1997.

Chernin, Kim. *The Obsession: Reflections on the Tyranny of Slenderness*. New York: HarperPerennial, 1994.

The Compact Edition of the Oxford English Dictionary. "Pale." Oxford: Oxford University Press, 1981 (originally published 1971).

Conquergood, Dwight. "Rethinking Ethnography: Towards a Critical Cultural Politics." *Communication Monographs*, 58 (1991): 179–94.

———. "Performing as a Moral Act: Ethical Dimensions of the Ethnography of Performance." *Literature in Performance*, 5 (1985): 1–13.

Conran, Shirley. *Superwoman: For Every Woman Who Hates Housework*. New York: Crown, 1978.

Coward, Rosalind. *Female Desire: Women's Sexuality Today*. London: Paladin, 1987.

de Beauvoir, Simone. *The Second Sex*. Translated by H. M. Parshley. Harmondsworth: Penguin, 1983 (originally published 1949).

Delacoste, Frédérique, and Priscilla Alexander, eds. *Sex Work: Writings by Women in the Sex Industry*. Pittsburgh: Cleis, 1987.

Denzin, Norman K. *Interpretive Ethnography: Ethnographic Practices for the 21st Century*. Thousand Oaks: Sage, 1997.

Dolan, Jill. "Desire Cloaked in a Trenchcoat." *Presence and Desire: Essays on Gender, Sexuality, Performance*, 121–34. Ann Arbor: University of Michigan Press, 1993.

———. "The Dynamics of Desire: Sexuality in Pornography and Performance." *Theatre Journal*, 39 (1987): 156–74.

Duncan, Dave. Personal communication. May 4, 2004.

Eagleton, Terry. *Ideology: An Introduction*. London: Verso, 1991.

Ellis, Carolyn. "Creating Criteria: An Ethnographic Short Story." *Qualitative Inquiry*, 6 (2000): 273–77.

English, Jane. "Introduction." In *Feminism and Philosophy*, edited by Mary Vetterling-Braggin, Frederick A. Elliston, and Jane English, 1–21. Totowa: Littlefield, Adams and Co., 1977.

Featherstone, Mike. "The Body in Consumer Culture." In *The Body: Social Process and Cultural Theory*, edited by Mike Featherstone, Mick Hepworth, and Bryan S. Turner, 170–96. London: Sage, 1991.

Forte, Jeanie. "Women's Performance Art: Feminism and Postmodernism." *Theatre Journal*, 40 (1988): 217–35.

Foucault, Michel. *Discipline and Punish: The Birth of the Prison*. Translated by Alan Sheridan. New York: Vintage, 1979.

Frueh, Joanna. *Erotic Faculties*. Berkeley: University of California Press, 1996.

Fuchs, Elinor. "Staging the Obscene Body." *TDR,* 33 (1989): 33–58.

Gadamer, Hans-Georg. *Truth and Method.* New York: Continuum, 1975 (originally published 1960).

Gallop, Jane, Marianne Hirsch, and Nancy K. Miller. "Criticizing Feminist Criticism." In *Conflicts in Feminism,* edited by Marianne Hirsch and Evelyn Fox Keller, 349–69. New York: Routledge, 1990.

Garfinkel, Harold. Appendix to Chapter Five. 1967. In *Studies in Ethnomethodology,* 285–88. Cambridge: Polity, 1984a.

———. "Passing and the Managed Achievement of Sex Status in an 'Intersexed' Person Part One." In *Studies in Ethnomethodology,* 116–85. 1967. Cambridge: Polity, 1984b.

———. "Studies of the Routine Grounds of Everyday Activities." In *Studies in Ethnomethodology,* 35–75. Cambridge: Polity, 1984c (originally published 1967).

Geertz, Clifford. *Local Knowledge.* New York: Basic Books, 1983.

Gendlin, Eugene T. "Thinking Beyond Patterns: Body, Language, and Situations." In *The Presence of Feeling in Thought,* edited by B. den Ouden and M. Moen, 27–189. New York: Peter Lang, 1991.

Goffman, Erving. *Stigma: Notes on the Management of Spoiled Identity.* Englewood Cliffs: Prentice-Hall, 1963.

Goodall, H. L. Jr. *Writing the New Ethnography.* Walnut Creek: AltaMira Press, 2000.

Graver, David. "The Actor's Bodies." *Text and Performance Quarterly,* 17 (1997): 221–35.

Greer, Germaine. *The Female Eunuch.* London: Paladin, 1989 (originally published 1970).

Hakim-Dyce, Aisha. "Reality Check." In *Listen Up: Voices from the Next Feminist Generation,* edited by Barbara Findlen, 230–38. Seattle: Seal, 1995.

Hekman, Susan J. *Gender and Knowledge: Elements of a Postmodern Feminism.* Boston: Northeastern University Press, 1990.

Hirsch, Marianne, and Evelyn Fox Keller, eds. *Conflicts in Feminism.* New York: Routledge, 1990.

hooks, bell. *Remembered Rapture: The Writer at Work.* New York: Henry Holt, 1999.

Hopcke, Robert H. *Men's Dreams, Men's Healing.* Boston: Shambhala, 1990.

HopKins, Mary Frances. "The Performance Turn—and Toss." *The Quarterly Journal of Speech,* 81 (1995): 228–36.

"House of Dior." Narr. Susan Stamberg. *All Things Considered.* National Public Radio. WSIU, Carbondale. February 7, 1997.

Israel, Betsy. "The Original Bad Girl." *Mirabella,* July–August (1997): 128–31.

———. *Grown-Up Fast: A True Story of Teenage Life in Suburban America.* New York: Poseidon Press, 1988.

Jackson, Cindy. *Living Doll.* London: Trafalgar Square, 2002.

———. Home Page. Last accessed June 4, 2001. Available at: http://cindyjackson.co.uk/Cindynav.html.

Jaggar, Alison. *Feminist Politics and Human Nature.* Totowa, N.J.: Rowman & Allanheld, 1983.

Jones, Amelia. "Unnatural Acts: Interpreting Body Art." In *Decomposition: Post-Disciplinary Performance,* edited by Sue-Ellen Case and Susan Leigh Foster, 10–17. Bloomington: Indiana University Press, 2000.

Kaczorowski, Janusz. "The Good, the Average and the Ugly: Socioeconomic Dimensions of Physical Attractiveness." MA Thesis, McGill University, Montreal, Canada, 1989.

Kappeler, Susanne. *The Pornography of Representation.* Minneapolis: University of Minnesota Press, 1986.

Kempadoo, Kamala, and Jo Doezema, eds. *Global Sex Workers: Rights, Resistance, and Redefinition.* New York: Routledge, 1998.

Kolata, Gina. "The Fat-Enabling Culture: Society Made Me Eat It!" *New York Times,* 30 December 1996, natl. ed: 4.4.

Kristeva, Julia. *Powers of Horror: An Essay on Abjection.* Translated by Leon S. Roudiez. New York: Columbia University Press, 1982.

Kuhn, Thomas S. *The Structure of Scientific Revolutions.* 2nd ed. Chicago: University of Chicago Press, 1970.

Langley, Erika. *The Lusty Lady: Photographs and Texts.* New York: Scalo, 1997.

Langsdorf, Lenore. "'I Like to Watch': Analyzing a Participation-and-Denial Phenomenon." *Human Studies,* 17 (1994): 81–108.

Leder, Drew. *The Absent Body.* Chicago: University of Chicago Press, 1990.

Lehrman, Karen. *The Lipstick Proviso: Women, Sex and Power in the Real World.* New York: Doubleday, 1997.

Liepe-Levinson, Katherine. *Strip Show: Performances of Gender and Desire.* London: Routledge, 2002.

Lockford, Lesa. "Performing the Abject Body: A Feminist Refusal of Disempowerment." *Theatre Annual,* 55 (2002): 48–60.

———. "An Ethnographic Ghost Story: Adapting 'What's a Nice Commodity Like You Doing in a Spectacle Like This?'" *Text and Performance Quarterly,* 20 (2000): 402–15.

———. "Social Drama and the Spectacle of Femininity: The Performance of Weight Loss in the Weight Watchers' Program." *Women's Studies in Communication,* 19 (1996): 291–312.

———. "'What's a Nice Scholar Like You Doing with a Topic Like This?' or Interpretive Communities Make Sense." Speech Communication Association Convention. Rivercenter Marriott, San Antonio, November 19, 1995.

Lorde, Audre. "Uses of the Erotic." In *Weaving the Visions: Patterns in Feminist Spirituality,* edited by Judith Plaskow and Carol P. Christ, 208–13. San Francisco: Harper, 1989.

Lugones, Maria C., and Elizabeth V. Spelman. "Have We Got a Theory for You! Feminist Theory, Cultural Imperialism and the Demand for 'The Woman's Voice.'" *Women's Studies International Forum,* 6 (1983): 573–81.

Maslow, Abraham H. *Toward a Psychology of Being.* 2nd ed. New York: Van Norstrand Reinhold, 1968.

Merleau-Ponty, Maurice. *Phenomenology of Perception.* Translated by Colin Smith. London: Routledge, 1994.

Millman, Marcia. *Such a Pretty Face: Being Fat in America.* New York: Berkeley, 1982.

Mulvey, Laura. "Visual Pleasure and Narrative Cinema." *Screen,* 16, no. 3 (1975): 6–18.

Murphy, Robert. *The Body Silent.* New York: Norton, 1990.

Nagle, Jill. "First Ladies of Feminist Porn: A Conversation with Candida Royale and Debi Sundahl." *Whores and Other Feminists,* edited by Jill Nagle, 156–66. New York: Routledge, 1997a.

———. "Introduction." In *Whores and Other Feminists,* edited by Jill Nagle, 1–15. New York: Routledge, 1997b.

———, ed. *Whores and Other Feminists.* New York: Routledge, 1997c.

National Association to Advance Fat Acceptance (NAAFA). Home Page. Last accessed March 15, 2001. Available at: http://www.naafa.org.

Nicholson, Linda J. *Gender and History: The Limits of Social Theory in the Age of the Family.* New York: Columbia University Press, 1986.

Nietzsche, Friedrich. *Beyond Good and Evil.* Translated by Helen Zimmerman. Buffalo: Prometheus, 1989.

"Odd Selection of Roommates." *Daily News,* July 26, 1997, 2.

Orbach, Susie. *Fat Is a Feminist Issue.* London: Paddington, 1978.

Orlan. Home Page. Last accessed June 5, 2001. Available at: http://www.cicv.fr/creation_artistique/online/orlan/index.html.

Orlan Panel Discussion. *Performance, Theatre, and Music: Totally Wired Conference.* Audiotape. Orlan, Dr. Sarah Wilson, Rachel Armstrong, Laurent Delaye, Gray Wilson. Institute of Contemporary Art, London, April 16, 1996. No. 1539.

Patai, Daphne, and Noretta Koertge. *Professing Feminism: Cautionary Tales from the Strange World of Women's Studies.* New York: Basic Books, 1994.

Patzer, Gordon L. *The Physical Attractiveness Phenomena.* New York: Plenum, 1985.

Pelias, Ronald J. *Writing Performance: Poeticizing the Researcher's Body.* Carbondale: Southern Illinois University Press, 1999.

Phelan, Peggy. *Unmarked: The Politics of Performance.* New York: Routledge, 1993.

Pollner, Melvin. "Left of Ethnomethodology: The Rise and Decline of Radical Reflexivity." *American Sociological Review,* 56 (1991): 370–80.

Queen, Carol. "Bisexual Lesbians among the Leather Lesbians." In *Real, Live, Nude, Girl: Chronicles of Sex-Positive Culture,* 23–29. Pittsburgh: Cleis, 1997a.

———. "Dykes and Whores: Girls Gone Bad." In *Real, Live, Nude, Girl: Chronicles of Sex-Positive Culture,* 177–88. Pittsburgh: Cleis, 1997b.

———. "Everything that Moves." In *Real, Live, Nude, Girl: Chronicles of Sex-Positive Culture,* 39–47. Pittsburgh: Cleis, 1997c.

———. "Fucking with Madonna." In *Real, Live, Nude, Girl: Chronicles of Sex-Positive Culture,* 106–18. Pittsburgh: Cleis, 1997d.

———. "Introduction." In *Real, Live, Nude, Girl: Chronicles of Sex-Positive Culture,* ix–xviii. Pittsburgh: Cleis, 1997e.

———. "Porno-Formance: Some Notes on Sex as Art." In *Real, Live, Nude, Girl: Chronicles of Sex-Positive Culture,* 58–61. Pittsburgh: Cleis, 1997f.

———. "Pornography and the Sensitive New Age Guy." In *Real, Live, Nude, Girl: Chronicles of Sex-Positive Culture,* 134–48. Pittsburgh: Cleis, 1997g.

———. "The Queer in Me." In *Real, Live, Nude, Girl: Chronicles of Sex-Positive Culture,* 10–15. Pittsburgh: Cleis, 1997h.

Roberts, Nickie. *Whores in History: Prostitution in Western Society.* London: HarperCollins, 1993.

Ronai, Carol Rambo, and Carolyn Ellis. "Turn-Ons for Money: Interactional Strategies of the Table Dancer." *Journal of Contemporary Ethnography,* 18 (1989): 271–98.

Rosaldo, Renato. "Introduction: Grief and a Headhunter's Rage." In *Culture and Truth: The Remaking of Social Analysis,* 1–21. Boston: Beacon Press, 1989.

Rose, Barbara. "Is It Art? Orlan and the Transgressive Act." *Art in America* (February 1993): 82+.

Rubin, Gayle. "Thinking Sex: Notes for a Radical Theory of the Politics of Sexuality." In *Pleasure and Danger: Exploring Female Sexuality,* edited by Carole S. Vance, 267–319. Boston: Routledge and Kegan Paul, 1984.

Schechner, Richard. "Restoration of Behavior," *Between Theater and Anthropology,* 35–116. Philadelphia: University of Pennsylvania Press, 1985.

Schneider, Rebecca. *The Explicit Body in Performance.* London: Routledge, 1997.

Schuler, Catherine. "Spectator Response and Comprehension: The Problem with Karen Finley's *Constant State of Desire.*" *TDR,* 34 (1990): 131–45.

Scott, James C. *Domination and the Arts of Resistance: Hidden Transcripts.* New Haven: Yale University Press, 1990.

Sheets-Johnstone, Maxine. *The Roots of Thinking.* Philadelphia: Temple University Press, 1990.

Shweder, Richard A. "Divergent Rationalities." In *Metatheory in Social Science: Pluralisms and Subjectivities,* edited by Donald W. Fiske and Richard A. Shweder, 163–96. Chicago: University of Chicago Press, 1986.

Spitzack, Carole. *Confessing Excess: Women and the Politics of Body Reduction.* Albany: SUNY Press, 1993.

Steinem, Gloria. "I Was a Playboy Bunny." In *Outrageous Acts and Everyday Rebellions,* 29–69. London: Flamingo, 1984.

Stoltenberg, John. *Refusing to Be a Man: Essays on Sex and Justice.* New York: Meridian, 1990.

Sundahl, Debi. "Stripper." In *Sex Work: Writings by Women in the Sex Industry,* edited by Frédérique Delacoste and Priscilla Alexander, 175–80. Pittsburgh: Cleis, 1987.

Sycamore, Matt Bernstein, ed. *Tricks and Treats: Sex Workers Write about Their Clients.* New York: Haworth, 2000.

Synnott, Anthony. *The Body Social: Symbolism, Self, and Society.* London: Routledge, 1993.

Taylor, John. *Laugh, and Be Fat.* London: Whitehall, 1612.

Tillmann-Healy, Lisa M. "A Secret Life in a Culture of Thinness: Reflections on Body, Food, and Bulimia." In *Composing Ethnography: Alternative Forms of Qualitative Writing,* edited by Carolyn Ellis and Arthur P. Bochner, 76–108. Walnut Creek: AltaMira, 1996.

Turner, Bryan S. *The Body and Society: Explorations in Social Theory.* London: Basil Blackwell, 1984.

United States Congress. House. Subcommittee on Regulation, Business Opportunities, and Energy. *Hearings on the "Deception and Fraud in the Diet Industry" Part II.* 101st Cong., 2nd sess. Washington, D.C.: GPO, 1990.

Williams, Linda. "Fetishism and Hard Core: Marx, Freud, and the 'Money Shot.'" In *Hard Core: Power, Pleasure, and the "Frenzy of the Visible,"* 93–119. Berkeley: University of California Press, 1989.

Wittgenstein, Ludwig. *Philosophical Investigations II.* Translated by G.E.M. Anscombe. 3rd ed. New York: Macmillan 1958 (originally published 1953).

Wolf, Naomi. *The Beauty Myth: How Images of Beauty Are Used against Women.* New York: Doubleday, 1992 (originally published 1991).

Young, Iris Marion. "Pregnant Embodiment: Subjectivity and Alienation." In *Throwing Like a Girl and Other Essays in Feminist Philosophy and Social Theory,* 160–74. Bloomington: Indiana University Press, 1990a.

———. "Women Recovering Our Clothes." In *Throwing Like a Girl and Other Essays in Feminist Philosophy and Social Theory,* 177–88. Bloomington: Indiana University Press, 1990b.

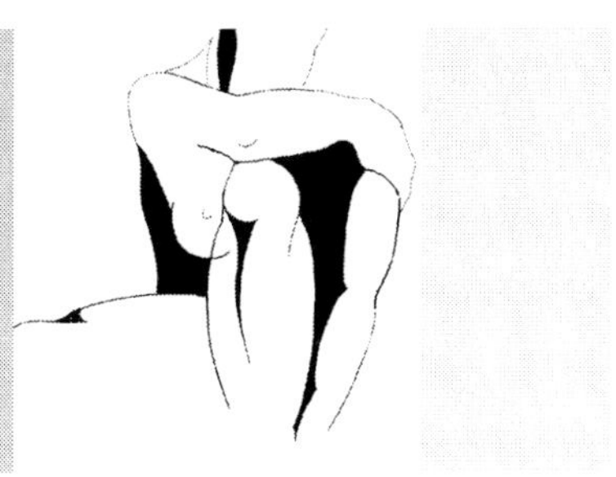

About the Author

Lesa Lockford teaches courses in theatre and performance studies at Bowling Green State University in Ohio. Currently, her scholarly interests are performance methods and composition, gender and sexuality, alternative forms of scholarly representation, and qualitative methods of inquiry. Journals in which her work has appeared include *Text and Performance Quarterly*, *Qualitative Inquiry*, *Theatre Annual*, and *Women's Studies in Communication.* She has performed her original creative texts and texts by others at regional and national academic conferences. Before returning to the Academy to pursue graduate studies, she trained and worked as a professional actor in the United Kingdom.